Meaning and Context

LISBON PHILOSOPHICAL STUDIES
uses of language in interdisciplinary fields

A Publication from the Institute of Philosophy of Language at the New University of Lisbon

edited by
António Marques (General Editor)
Nuno Venturinha (Executive Editor)

Editorial Board:
Gabriele De Angelis, Humberto Brito, João Fonseca, Franck Lihoreau, António Marques, Maria Filomena Molder, Diogo Pires Aurélio, Erich Rast, João Sàágua, Nuno Venturinha

Advisory Board:
Jean-Pierre Cometti (Université de Provence), Lynn Dobson (University of Edinburgh), Ernest Lepore (Rutgers University), Renato Lessa (IUPE-Rio de Janeiro), Andrew Lugg (University of Ottawa), Stefan Majetschak (Universität Kassel), Jesús Padilla Gálvez (Universidad de Castilla-La Mancha), Joachim Schulte (Universität Zürich)

Supported by

FCT Fundação para a Ciência e a Tecnologia
MINISTÉRIO DA CIÊNCIA, TECNOLOGIA E ENSINO SUPERIOR   Portugal

PETER LANG
Bern · Berlin · Bruxelles · Frankfurt am Main · New York · Oxford · Wien

Luca Baptista & Erich Rast (eds)

Meaning and Context

PETER LANG
Bern · Berlin · Bruxelles · Frankfurt am Main · New York · Oxford · Wien

Bibliographic information published by Die Deutsche Nationalbibliothek
Die Deutsche Nationalbibliothek lists this publication in the Deutsche Nationalbibliografie;
detailed bibliographic data is available on the Internet at ‹http://dnb.d-nb.de›.

British Library Cataloguing-in-Publication Data: A catalogue record for this book is available
from *The British Library*, Great Britain

Library of Congress Cataloging-in-Publication Data

Meaning and context / Luca Baptista & Erich Rast (eds.).
p. cm. – (Lisbon philosophical studies. Uses of language in interdisciplinary fields ; v. 2)
Includes bibliographical references and index.
ISBN 978-3-0343-0574-7
1. Pragmatics. 2. Semantics. I. Baptista, Luca, 1963- II. Rast, Erich H.
B831.5.M43 2010
401'.45–dc22
        2010050170

ISSN 1663-7674
ISBN 978-3-0343-0574-7

© Peter Lang AG, International Academic Publishers, Bern 2010
Hochfeldstrasse 32, CH-3012 Bern, Switzerland
info@peterlang.com, www.peterlang.com, www.peterlang.net

All rights reserved.
All parts of this publication are protected by copyright.
Any utilisation outside the strict limits of the copyright law, without the permission of
the publisher, is forbidden and liable to prosecution.
This applies in particular to reproductions, translations, microfilming, and storage and
processing in electronic retrieval systems.

Printed in Switzerland

Contents

1 Luca Baptista & Erich Rast
   Introduction 1

2 Manuel García-Carpintero
   Norms of Presupposition 17

3 Emma Borg
   Minimalism and the Content of the Lexicon 51

4 Anne Bezuidenhout
   Contextualism and Information Structure: Towards a Science of Pragmatics 79

5 Agustín Vicente & Fernando Martínez-Manrique
   Lexical Concepts: From Contextualism to Concept Decompositionalism 111

6 Isidora Stojanovic
   Referring With Proper Names: Towards a Pragmatic Account 139

7 Kepa Korta & John Perry
   Intentions to Refer 161

8 Brian Ball
   What Is Semantic Content? 187

9 Sandy Berkovski
   Some Remarks on Mthat 213

10 Teresa Marques
   Truth and the Ambiguity of Negation 235

11 Ana Falcato
   The Contextualist Fight Against Minimalism 255

12 Salvatore Pistoia-Reda
   *Some Notes on Game Theory and the Pragmatics of
   Alternatives* 269

13 Andrei Moldovan
   *Can Uses of Language in Thought Provide Linguistic
   Evidence?* 283

Author Index 307

Preface

This volume of the series *Lisbon Philosophical Studies* is partly based on the conference 'Context and Levels of Locutionary Content' which was hosted by the Philosophy of Language Institute (IFL) and took place at the Universidade Nova de Lisboa in December 2009. Some of the articles in this volume are based on talks given at that conference. More contributors have been invited in order to make sure that a broad range of positions concerning linguistic context-dependence could be covered.

We would like to thank all conference participants, all contributors, and numerous other people that have been involved in the creation of this volume for their support and efforts. Particular thanks go to Caroline Schopfer of Peter Lang AG for her kind and professional assistance in all matters related to the publishing process. We would also like to thank the editors of the series António Marques and Nuno Venturinha for their advice and patience during the preparation of this book. Finally, we would like to express our gratitude to the Portuguese *Fundação para a Ciência e a Tecnologia* for financial support in the form of project-related funding and two research grants, a *Ciência 2007* fellowship and research grant SFRH/BPD/34914/2007, under which work on this volume was conducted.

The Volume Editors
Lisbon, 28. October 2010

— 1 —

Luca Baptista & Erich Rast

Introduction

Neither contemporary truth-conditional semanticists nor any of their predecessors such as Frege, Russell, and Quine seriously doubt that natural language is systematically context-dependent. As Comrie (1985) lays out, practically all languages of the world grammatically realize tenses and merely differ in the variety of tenses they realize and their interplay with grammatical mood and the corresponding modalities on the semantic side. Likewise, indexical expressions like 'I', 'tomorrow', 'here' and demonstratives like 'this' and 'that', or 'over there' are pervasive in natural languages and obviously context-dependent. Indexicals are already mentioned in Frege (1892), and under the label 'egocentric particulars' indexicals and demonstratives play a crucial role in Russell's theory of knowledge by acquaintance. Reichenbach's (1947) account of indexicals based on occurrences of linguistic signs (tokens) and a similar approach by Burks (1949) also deserve to be mentioned.[1]

Nowadays, the prevalent way to specify the semantic contribution of an indexical, including tenses, to the truth-conditional meaning of an utterance as a whole is based on Kaplan's (1989) 'Logic of Demonstratives', which he introduced in a series of talks in the early 70s. In Kaplan's approach, the linguistic meaning (character) of a

---

[1] Perry's (2001a, 2001b) influential theory of reflexive-referential content of utterances is based on these earlier token-based approaches.

sentence in a context yields an intension (content), which in turn, depending on the circumstances of evaluation, has an extension. Formally, contexts are in this approach regarded as n-tuples consisting of the missing ingredients needed for the saturation of indexicals: the speaker for uses of 'I', the addressee(s) for uses of 'you', the time of utterance for 'now' and more complex temporal indexicals like 'tomorrow' or 'Thursday in two weeks', and the world of the utterance for a use of 'actually'.[2] In Kaplan's original view, tenses and modal expressions such as 'it is necessary that' were analyzed as modal operators of basic tense logic and normal modal logic, which implicitly quantify over the circumstances of evaluation but do not affect the context parameter. Thus, evaluation proceeds in two steps. First, indexicals are saturated: the missing ingredients are provided by the context parameter. In a second step, tenses and modal expressions operate on the resulting intension and evaluate it with respect to different circumstances of evaluation.

Since Kaplan's approach has been very influential, it is worth taking a look at an example of how it works.[3] Let the linguistic meaning of 'I' be represented by a function $[\![I]\!]$ from contexts to a function from circumstances of evaluation to an element in a domain D such that $[\![I]\!](c)(i)$ is the agent of the context c no matter what the circumstances of evaluation i are. By the same token the linguistic meaning of 'you' could be represented by a function just as the one for 'I' except that $[\![you]\!](c)(i)$ yields the addressee of c. Suppose that the linguistic meaning of 'know' is a function from contexts to a function that given some circumstances of evaluation i yields the set of all ordered pairs $\langle x, y \rangle$ such that x and y are in the domain D and x knows y at the time of i in the world of i. It would go beyond the scope of an introduction to specify a formal language or use a

---

2 See Rast (2007: 155-6, 133-4) for a discussion of this meaning of 'actually'; it is hardly the way the expression is understood in everyday conversations.

3 The following example does not work in exactly the same way as Kaplan's 'Logic of Demonstratives' and no formal language is defined, but it should suffice to illustrate the approach in general. See Kaplan (1989) and Rast (2007: ch. 5-7) for more information and García-Carpintero (2006) for an overview of semantic two-dimensionalism and other forms of two-dimensionalism.

Introduction

full fledged categorial grammar here, so let us for the purpose of this example just assume that $[\![\alpha\ know\ \beta]\!](c)(i)$ is true if and only if $\langle [\![\alpha]\!](c)(i), [\![\beta]\!](c)(i) \rangle \in [\![know]\!](c)(i)$. The sentence 'I know you' is then true in a context c with respect to circumstances of evaluation i if and only if $\langle [\![I]\!](c)(i), [\![you]\!](c)(i) \rangle$ is in $[\![know]\!](c)(i)$, i.e. if and only if the pair ⟨the speaker of c, the addressee of c⟩ is an element of the binary relation $\{\langle x,y \rangle : x,y \in D$ and x knows y at the time of i in the world of $i\}$.

What is crucial about this way of introducing context-dependence is that a modal expression in such an approach only shifts the circumstances of evaluation. For example, in our example $[\![it\ is\ possible\ that\ \Phi]\!](c)(i)$ would turn out true if and only if there are circumstances of evaluation i' that are accessible (via the world component) from i by a suitable modal accessibility relation[4] such that $[\![\Phi]\!](c)(i')$ is true; but since 'I' and 'you' only depend on the context c, only 'know' would semantically depend on this operator. In other words, 'it is possible that I know you' turns out true with respect to c, i if and only if the pair consisting of the speaker of c and the addressee of c is an element of the set $\{\langle x,y \rangle : x,y \in D$ and x knows y at the time of i' in the world of $i'\}$. This means that in contrast to 'know' the indexicals 'I' and 'you' are interpreted as rigid expressions whose extension does not depend on the time or world of the circumstances of evaluation.

Kaplan's approach was very successful; it allowed theorists to maintain the traditional distinction between semantics and pragmatics and in the meantime integrate indexicals and demonstratives in an – at least prima facie – adequate way into traditional truth-conditional semantics. It also allows for a number of appealing distinctions. Contextually stable and unstable expressions can be distinguished, the rigidity of indexicals can be explained to some extent, and truth in every proper context can be distinguished from logical validity by also taking into account 'improper' contexts that for example do not contain a speaker. However, at least from Kaplan's writings it

---

4 This relation could, for example, be an equivalence relation to yield the familiar modal logic S5, but for the current purpose the choice does not matter.

is clear that he never intended his 'Logic of Demonstratives' to be an approach to linguistic context-dependence in general, and it has become increasingly clear during the past three decades that linguistic context-dependence is generally more pervasive and complicated than the one that is elicited by overt indexicals and demonstratives.

Recanati (2004) marks the starting point of a recent debate about linguistic context-dependence. In his view, a vast number of phenomena of context-dependence can in principle not be explained adequately on the basis of a traditional semantics-pragmatics distinction as the one underlying the Kaplanian account. In the traditional view, lexical meanings of expressions are combined to form larger meanings in a rule-governed way by the syntactic and semantic components of a grammar without the interference of any pragmatic factors. This traditional view has been extended by Perry (1998, 2005) and many others whose position can be considered moderately contextualist. For example, Perry suggested that hidden indexicals, i.e. unarticulated constituents that semantically behave like indexical expressions, may account for contextual variabilities of sentences that do not contain overt indexicals such as an utterance of 'It is raining'. Against such fairly traditional and moderately contextualist positions, which acknowledge a few forms of nonindexical context-dependence such as an implicit dependence on a place or implicit quantifier domain restrictions but attempt to analyze this context-dependence essentially in the same way as that of indexicals, Recanati (2004) has argued that free enrichment and other pragmatic modulation processes must already take place at early stages during the composition of 'semantic' content and that these processes are so ubiquitous that in the end it doesn't make much sense to consider purely semantic composition of lexical meanings without taking into account additional pragmatic factors already during composition of complex meanings or interpretations from the meanings or interpretations of their parts. Ultimately, Recanati argues, instead of truth-conditional semantics we should do truth-conditional pragmatics.

To give a typical example, while Recanati doesn't deny that 'I've had breakfast' has a literal meaning according to which the speaker of the utterance had breakfast at least once in his life, for instance

40 years ago, this literal meaning in his opinion is not the first step in computing the prevalent reading that the speaker had breakfast in the morning of the day of the utterance. Rather, speakers of a language are able to arrive at the prevalent interpretation directly without resorting to literal meaning. The literal meaning might not be psychologically realized and often plays no substantial role for the computation of the actual meaning of an utterance. The saturation of indexicals, when it is modeled in a descendant of traditional, Kaplanian two-dimensional semantics, on the other hand, is based on the very idea that first the linguistic meanings of expressions are combined without the influence of pragmatic factors, and then missing ingredients are taken into account to yield the actual semantic content of the utterance. While this works well for genuine indexicals whose context-dependence is at least partly linguistically mandated and overt this model fails in Recanati's opinion for other cases of apparent linguistic context-dependence like that of 'enough', 'ready', 'having breakfast', or 'tall'.

In the wake of Recanati's frontal assault on the neat traditional semantics/pragmatics distinction – which, perhaps, has never really existed outside of introductory linguistics courses – a vast number of different philosophical positions about linguistic context-dependence has evolved. Rather than trying to give an exhaustive characterization of all of them let us only mention rough categories or 'labels' under which the main positions may be put. On the one hand, semantic minimalists such as Borg (2004, 2007, this volume, forthcoming) and Cappelen & Lepore (2005) maintain that linguistic expressions have a clear-cut minimal meaning.[5] That the actual understanding of a sentence often deviates from its literal meaning in their view has to be explained by the pragmatic component. Minimalists do not deny that utterances seem to elicit a form of context-dependence that goes beyond the mere saturation of tenses and overt indexicals. These additional context-dependences do, however, only concern speech

---

[5] Borg's (2004) early contribution to the debate appeared in the same year as Recanati (2004) and is not a reaction to it. However, in the authors' opinion it is fair to say that Borg's minimalist position was mainly gaining momentum later when Cappelen & Lepore (2005) was already being received.

act content; from the point of view of a semantic minimalist it is a mistake to conclude from examples of the contextual variability of speech act content that the semantic content of the corresponding sentence is contextually variable.

Contextualists have given various replies to this position and semantic contextualism comes in varying degrees. A relatively modest form of contextualism has been proposed by Stanley and Szabó (2000) and Stanley (2004; 2005) and dubbed indexicalism. In their view, it must be possible to trace back a genuine semantic context-dependence to the logical form of the sentence which is being analyzed. They suggest a criterion, the Binding Criterion, for determining whether a sentence elicits a genuine semantic context-dependence, and they analyze phenomena such as quantifier domain restrictions in terms of variables that might either be bound by antecedent expressions or, when there is no antecedent, their value has to be provided by the context like the value of any other open variable in the logical form. Only when a linguistic example can be found that clearly illustrates that a respective context variable can be bound can we speak of a case of genuine semantic context-dependence whereas otherwise the respective phenomenon must be explained at the pragmatic level of linguistic theorizing, for example by resorting to Gricean maxims or speaker meaning.

Bach (2005) argues for another relatively modest form of contextualism, which depending on the viewpoint might also be regarded a form of semantic minimalism. In Bach's opinion every sentence has a literal meaning. However in contrast to other minimalists Bach claims that this meaning is not necessarily truth-evaluable; many sentences only express 'propositional radicals' which by themselves are neither true nor false, and Bach is willing to accept the consequences of this view. For example, he suggests that persons might have attitudes towards a semantically incomplete content, i.e. some content that is not a truth-bearer on its own. Hearers interpret utterances on the basis of semantically incomplete literal content and additional contextual factors. However, finding out how they do this is the task of pragmatics, not semantics.

According to Recanati's (2004) radical contextualism, on the other hand, literal meaning really ought not be of major concern to the semanticist; it is ultimately an 'idle wheel' for linguistic theorizing. If the alleged 'literal meaning' of an utterance is often not even intuitively available to competent speakers in generic contexts when they are asked – for example, competent speakers do not intuitively judge 'I've had breakfast' to mean that the speaker had breakfast once in his life – and metaphors, non-literal speech, and free enrichment are ubiquitous, should we then really care about literal content? As laid out above, Recanati's answer is essentially 'No'. For similar reasons, and additionally motivated by work of the later Wittgenstein, Travis's (2008) occasionalism goes one step further and abolishes literal meaning altogether. According to Travis's point of view, sentences simply do not have a meaning independently of their use. The actual use of a sentence constitutes what it means as a whole and what its parts mean (meaning holism), and since uses may differ from occasion to occasion the meaning of an utterance may differ from occasion to occasion, too.

Recently, there has also been a trend to re-evaluate and extend Kaplan's original framework.[6] For example, Predelli (2005) argues that a two-dimensional account can adequately represent the truth-conditions of purportedly ambiguous sentences like 'The leaves are green' (on the inside/outside). Relativists like Lasersohn (2005, 2008) and MacFarlane (2005, 2007, 2008) have suggested a further departure from Kaplan's original framework. They locate certain sources of contextual variability in the circumstances of evaluation instead of the context parameter.[7] With this 'relativist move' Lasersohn manages to describe what he considers cases of faultless disagreement about the meaning of utterances involving predicates of personal taste. For example, in Lasersohn's opinion two people might disagree about the same semantic content of 'Roller coasters are fun' and both be right, because they evaluate the content from different perspectives – where

---

6 An overview can be found in García-Carpintero (2008).
7 See Stojanovic & Predelli (2008) for a comparison of that position to Kaplan's.

different 'judges' in the circumstances of evaluation resolve the purported context-dependence of the predicate of personal taste 'fun'.[8] MacFarlane, on the other hand, uses relativist two-dimensionalism in order to explain the context-sensitivity of knowledge ascriptions (MacFarlane 2005) and implement the irreality of the future view in a double-index modal logic as an alternative to supervaluationism (MacFarlane 2008).

All these approaches concern, in one way or another, the relation between the meaning of items stored in a shared lexicon (if there is one) and those of sentences as a whole and utterances of those sentences made by a particular speaker. They raise questions like: What factors influence the composition of word meanings into the meanings of more complex expressions? Can the traditional semantics/pragmatics distinction be maintained? Where does semantics end and pragmatics start? The contributions to this volume all deal with these questions from different perspectives and at different levels of detail.

In his contribution, Manuel García-Carpintero argues for a pragmatic account of presuppositions. Presupposing is viewed as a linguistically ancillary speech act that is governed by regulative rules concerning a common-knowledge norm in communicative situations. Based on a lengthy critical discussion of Stalnaker's positions on this subject, he claims that a speaker can correctly presuppose a proposition just in case the proposition is common ground in a given group (with common ground defined in terms of common knowledge). The phenomenon of sentence presupposition is explained in terms of the use of a sentence conveying that the speaker presupposes a certain proposition. García-Carpintero compares his view with Williamson's well-known normative account of assertion (according to which one must assert a proposition only if one knows it). It is his contention that his communicative approach to presupposition puts strain to Williamson's account of assertion (as well as others related to it), since the latter would miss the communicative dimension of asserting and could be seen, then, as more appropriate for the act of judging.

---

8 See Stojanovic (2007) and Iacona (2008) for a critique of this position.

Introduction

Lexical meaning is one of the battlegrounds where the ongoing debate between minimalism and contextualism takes place. Emma Borg defends minimalism against criticisms coming from an 'internalist' position on meaning, according to which minimalism, insofar as it sees word meanings as atomic concepts, can't account for intralinguistic aspects that should be explained by a semantic theory – such as possible and impossible readings for sentences, patterns of syntactic distribution, 'impossible words', synonymy, analyticity and polysemy. Specifically, she takes issue with the view that a characterization of word meanings as structured entities (concept decompositionalism) is the only way to explain these phenomena. Borg presents a view of lexical meaning, called 'Organisational Lexical Semantics' (OLS), purporting to show that an atomistic and referentialist view of word meanings is in fact able to offer explanations to at least some of those cases. According to OLS, word meaning is atomic and referential, and it is lexical organisation that allows the minimalist to explain the intralinguistic semantic phenomena. Lexical organisation involves assigning properties to word-meaning pairs, which can then be grouped according to their categories. But crucially, these properties are not part of the words' meanings; rather, they indicate what kind of expression a given word is and, for instance, what are the permissible combinations it can get into.

Coming from the opposite extreme, Agustín Vicente and Fernando Martínez-Manrique attack atomistic views of meaning and advocate decompositionalism. Adopting a mentalistic account of meaning, they offer a framework that is purported to explain both the stability of meanings across contexts and the phenomenon of polysemy. Vicente and Martínez-Manrique envision lexical meanings as consisting of structured complexes of representational contents. These complexes are constituted by a core to which variable components can be combined. The core would account for stability, while the variable parts would be involved in polysemy. Vicente and Martínez-Manrique see their position as rejecting what they take to be the excesses of both minimalism and radical contextualism. They argue for semantic indeterminacy, but are critical of the atomistic leanings of most contextualists, such as happens in relevance theory (following Fodor, who is one of Vicente and Martínez-Manrique's main targets in their article). Specifically regarding RT's notion of 'ad hoc concepts', it is their contention that they would be much better explained as concept compositions than as modulations of atomic concepts.

In her contribution, Anne Bezuidenhout takes aim at those critics of contextualism who claim that it cannot offer a scientific (or at least theoretically tractable) explanation of pragmatic modulation. Based on empirical evidence from psycholinguistics, she claims that the process of modulation is constrained (against those who see it as a kind of 'magic') and the constraints are established, among other things, by discourse coherence relations – which are the focus of her article. These are relations that hold between contents of sequences of utterances, relating one to the other, and can be expressed explicitly (e.g., by so-called discourse connectives) or implicitly (being inferred from background information regarding the kind of discourse in a given situation). In each case, multiple constraints may be involved. Bezuidenhout offers evidence in support of the view that discourse coherence relations are operative in cases of disambiguation, pronoun resolution and free enrichment. She forcefully argues for the systematicity of pragmatic modulation, trying to show that it can be the object of scientific study.

Isidora Stojanovic presents here a pragmatic view of the meaning and reference of proper names. According to this view, names are pragmatic devices used to enable the addressee to identify to whom the speaker is referring to. They are similar, then, to pointing gestures. Stojanovic argues for the primacy of the act of referring over the referring devices people may use in any given circumstance (and which may, but also may not, involve linguistic expressions used to refer). She draws on her previous work on indexicals, used to illustrate her view that the only semantic content of an expression is its lexically encoded content; what is referred to by an expression is not part of the semantics, even though it is relevant for truth-value assignments. This doesn't mean that reference is irrelevant: direct identification of referents conveys information about them, information that is crucial for communication. Regarding the pragmatic view of names, Stojanovic does not intend to make a case for adopting it (against, say, traditional direct-reference and descriptivist perspectives), but to show that it is an option worth considering.

The article by Kepa Korta and John Perry is one of the first publications where they present their new pragmatic theory of singular reference, based on referential plans and referential intentions. The acts of referring are the focus of their theory, which involves reflexive intentions of a Gricean type (intentions to achieve effects by their very recognition) and a complex structure of planning. In order to flesh out this structure, Korta and Perry introduce two key concepts: 'roles' and 'cognitive fixes'. The role played by an object is a relational property that helps organizing information about it (of course, a single object can play various roles). The cognitive fix is a way of thinking (broadly construed) about an object, and regards the pragmatic and/or epistemic roles the object may play for an individual in a given situation. The act of referring, then, involves the speaker's intention to make a certain object play a role in the addressee's life. The speaker exploits the fact that he has a cognitive fix on a given object so that the addressee recognizes this, recognizes the intentions behind the plan, and (if all is successful) adopts the cognitive fix herself. According to Korta and Perry, their theory is part of a paradigm shift in the accounts of singular reference in philosophy of language, from names and descriptions to indexicals. Since singular reference involves what they call role-management, something they take to be at stake in indexicals and demonstratives, these are seen as the best models for their new approach.

One question that looms large in the debates about semantic content regards its very nature. Brian Ball asks the question, 'What is semantic content?', as well as four other related questions, and uses the different answers that might be given to them as a guide to a taxonomy of the different approaches on offer. His taxonomy is composed of five perspectives: nihilism, which he associates with Paul Pietroski, denies that content (in the sense of 'word-world' relations) is the proper domain of semantics. All the other four claim that there is semantic content, disagreeing on the other questions. Free enrichment theories deny that all content is syntactically constrained; minimalism argues for syntactically constrained, truth-evaluable, propositional content;

propositional radicalism claims that some content is no more than a 'proposition radical' (needing contextual completion or saturation for becoming a proposition); indexical contextualism resorts to lots of covert syntactic indices in order to explain context-sensitivity; finally, relativism claims that the evaluation of semantic content demands more parameters than the classical circumstances of evaluation (such as words and times). In the course of his argument, Ball advocates the view that semantic content is a property of sentences, not utterances, and concludes that minimalism, indexical contextualism and relativism are the only live options concerning this issue.

Sandy Berkovsky undertakes a critical appraisal of Josef Stern's theory of metaphor, which relies on Stalnaker's account of context and Kaplan's semantic theory of indexicals. The article discusses the operator 'M-that', introduced by Stern as a counterpart, for metaphors, of Kaplan's rigidifying operator 'D-that'. Berkovsky claims that the attempt to combine Stalnaker's and Kaplan's perspectives is a source of serious problems for Stern's view. Recall that Kaplan's main motivation is to offer a systematic account of indexicals that does justice to their context-sensitive nature. A context is defined as a set of parameters fit for semantic theorizing. But since on the Stalnakerian view contexts include speakers' presuppositions, which are not amenable to the same kind of systematic analysis, this poses a threat to Stern's project. According to Berkovsky, this is so because speakers' presuppositions fit in a contextualist framework that is at odds with the idea of universal semantic rules and/or procedures. This would lead Stern's position, in practice, to be indistinguishable from a contextualist approach, hence undermining his project of a systematic theory of metaphors.

The alleged semantic ambiguity of negation is the issue tackled by Teresa Marques in her contribution. Claims of ambiguity are motivated by problems with the principle of bivalence, posed by paradoxes (especially the Liar), presupposition failure and borderline cases of vagueness. Marques explores these problems and the solutions that resort to ambiguity, finding the latter wanting. The main target of her article is the putative distinction between an external and an internal sense of negation. Marques's argument is based on the claim, supported by empirical evidence as well as by philosophical theorizing, that negation is not lexically ambiguous. She uses the well-known test devised by Kripke in order to assess ambiguity: for instance, if negation were ambiguous in English, there should be at least one natural language other than English in which there would be two expressions for the two different meanings. The application of the test to the case of negation is backed by evidence from Larry Horn and other authors concerning negation operators in natural languages, as well as the relation between these operators and presuppositions. Another problem for the ambiguity thesis is the fact, pointed out by some of its supporters, that in the case of paradoxes it can't cope with a strengthened version of the Liar. Marques's conclusion is that the ambiguity thesis is just a technical maneuver that is not supported by independent justification.

The debate between minimalism and contextualism is the focus of Ana Falcato's article. Siding with the contextualists, and more specifically with Charles Travis's occasionalism, she criticizes Borg's and Cappelen & Lepore's minimalist proposals, arguing that they offer a very poor account of content, which misses the massive contextual contributions needed for achieving truth-evaluability (or propositionality). Following Travis, Falcato argues that there is no such thing as the state of affairs described by all possible utterances of a sentence, and also that a particular understanding must always be specified before we can check if the utterance of a sentence has a truth-evaluable content. The notion of 'minimal proposition', as long as it involves the idea of talking about things and states of affairs without specific understandings, should then be dispensed with.

The affinities between Grice's account of communication and game theory have been noted for quite a while now, and Salvatore Pistoia-Reda gives us an updated account of the attempts to join them in a fruitful theoretical framework, focusing on the topic of scalar implicatures. Grice's account of communication emphasizes the rationality of participants in the communicative process, and the game-theoretic approach fits nicely with the idea of reasoned choice among alternatives, especially regarding the generation of implicatures. To model scalar implicatures, Pistoia-Reda discusses the notion of complexity in Horn scales, opting for structural complexity, whose principles function as filters, operating before the (rational) conversational process. The alternatives filtered out are not available to that process, and this might help explaining why scalar implicatures (which are generalized implicatures) zero in on defaults that are only defeated given contextual information to that effect.

Andrei Moldovan addresses the issue of the use of language in thought, critically appraising the arguments presented by Jeff Speaks on this matter. Speaks claims that what happens both in the communicative use of language and in the use of language in thought cannot be explained by the Gricean conversational principles. Basically, the argument goes, there is no generation of implicatures in thought, since there is no way the thinker himself could be the intended audience. Gricean principles are operative only in those 'asymmetric' cases in which a phenomenon is present in conversation but not in the use of language in thought. Moldovan develops an analysis of putative cases of such uses, and centers on what he calls 'thinking out loud'. These would be the relevant cases for Speaks's approach. However, by appealing to Grice's theory of non-natural meaning, Moldovan shows that in these cases the solitary vocalization cannot play a causal role in the entertaining of thoughts: meaning something by an utterance involves intentions, and the intentions must be formed before the utterance; hence, someone who 'thinks out loud' entertains the thought independently of uttering the corresponding sentence.

The variety of views and topics discussed in the contributions to this volume makes it clear that the issue of contextual contributions to meaning will keep being a live one in philosophy of language. The appeal to results from other disciplines, especially linguistics and psychology, enriches a debate that may itself contribute in significant ways to the more empirically oriented approaches. This book is meant as a contribution to this ongoing enterprise.*

---

* The editors would like to thank FCT (Fundação para a Ciência e Tecnologia) for funding the project 'Context and Communication' (PTDC/FIL/68643/2006), which made possible the conference 'Context and Levels of Locutionary Content' (IFL, December 3-4, 2009). Luca Baptista also thanks FCT for the research grant *SFRH/BPD/34914/2007* and Erich Rast would like to express his gratitude to FCT for the funding of his work under the *Ciência 2007* program.

References

Bach, K. (2005). Context ex machina. In Szabó, Z. G. (Ed.). *Semantics versus pragmatics,* (pp. 16-44). Oxford: Oxford University Press.

Borg, E. (2004). *Minimal semantics.* Oxford: Oxford University Press.

—— (2007). Minimalism versus contextualism in semantics. In Preyer, G. & Peter, G. (Eds.). *Context sensitivity and semantic minimalism: Essays on semantics and pragmatics,* (pp. 546-71). Oxford: Oxford University Press.

—— (forthcoming). Semantic minimalism. In Cummins, L. (Ed.). *The pragmatics encyclopedia.* London: Routledge.

Burks, A. (1949). Icon, index and symbol. *Philosophy and Phenomenological Research, 9*(4), 673-689.

Cappelen, H. & Lepore, E. (2005). *Insensitive semantics.* Oxford: Blackwell.

Comrie, B. (1985). *Tense.* Cambridge: Cambridge University Press.

Frege, G. (1892). Über Sinn und Bedeutung. *Zeitschrift für Philosophie und philosophische Kritik, 100,* 25-50.

García-Carpintero, M. & Kölbel, M. (Eds.) (2008). *Relative truth.* Oxford: Oxford University Press.

Iacona, A. (2008). Faultless or disagreement. In García-Carpintero, M. & Kölbel, M. (Eds.). *Relative truth,* (pp. 287-295). Oxford: Oxford University Press.

Kaplan, D. (1989). Demonstratives: An essay on the semantics, logic, metaphysics, and epistemology of demonstratives and other indexicals. In Almog, J., Perry, J. & Wettstein, W. (Eds.). *Themes from Kaplan,* (pp. 481-564). Oxford: Oxford University Press.

Lasersohn, P. (2005). Context dependence, disagreement, and predicates of personal taste. *Linguistics and Philosophy, 28*(6), 643-686.

—— (2008). Quantification and perspective in relativist semantics. *Philosophical Perspectives, 22*(1), 305-337.

MacFarlane, J. (2005). The assessment sensitivity of knowledge attributions. In Gendler, T. S. & Hawthorne, J. (Eds.). *Oxford Studies in Epistemology, Vol. 1,* (pp. 197-233). Oxford: Oxford University Press.

—— (2007). Nonindexical contextualism. *Synthese, 166*(2), 231-50.

—— (2008). Truth in the garden of forking paths. In García-Carpintero, M. & Kölbel, M. (Eds.). *Relative truth*, (pp. 81-102). Oxford: Oxford University Press.

Perry, J. (1998). Indexicals, contexts and unarticulated constituents. In *Proceedings of the 1995 CSLI Amsterdam Logic, Language and Computation Conference*.

—— (2001). Indexicals and demonstratives. In Hale, B. & Wright, C. (Eds.). *A companion to the philosophy of language*, (pp. 586-612). Oxford: Blackwell.

—— (2001). *Reference and reflexivity*. Stanford: CSLI Publications.

—— (2005). Using indexicals. In Devitt, M. (Ed.). *The Blackwell guide to the philosophy of language*, (pp. 314-334). Oxford: Blackwell.

Predelli, S. (2005). *Contexts: Meaning, truth, and the use of language*. Oxford: Oxford University Press.

Rast, E. H. (2007). *Reference and indexicality*. Berlin: Logos Verlag.

Recanati, F. (2004). *Literal meaning*. Cambridge: Cambridge University Press.

Reichenbach, H. (1947). *Elements of symbolic logic*. New York: Macmillan.

Stanley, J. (2004). On the linguistic basis for contextualism. *Philosophical Studies, 119*(1-2), 119-146.

—— (2005). Semantics in context. In Preyer, G. & Peter, G. (Eds.). *Contextualism in philosophy: Knowledge, meaning, and truth*, (pp. 221-253). Oxford: Oxford University Press.

Stanley, J. & Szabó, Z. G. (2000). On quantifier domain restriction. *Mind & Language, 15*(2 & 3), 219-261.

Stojanovic, I. (2007). Talking about taste: Disagreement, implicit arguments, and relative truth. *Linguistics and Philosophy, 30*(6), 691-706. Stojanovic, I. & Predelli, S. (2008). Semantic relativism and the logic of indexicals. In García-Carpintero, M. & Kölbel, M. (Eds.). *Relative truth*, (pp. 63-80). Oxford: Oxford University Press.

Travis, C. (2008). *Occasion-sensitivity*. Oxford: Oxford University Press.

— 2 —

Manuel García-Carpintero

Norms of Presupposition

1 Introduction

Some natural language expressions are conventional indicators of illocutionary types: thus, the interrogative mood conventionally indicates a question, and appending the appositive clause 'I promise' to a declarative sentence S – S, I promise – is a conventional indicator of a promise. Davidson (1979) argues against the existence of conventional indicators of force, but, as far as I understand it, his argument depends on the false premise that all executions of an action-type that, as a matter of convention, 'counts as' another – i.e., constitutes another action-type – in fact count as it, with whatever normative consequences this might have. As Davidson points out, alleged conventional indicators of forces do not meet this requirement. If someone on the stage appends 'I promise' to his utterance of a declarative sentence, he does not thereby make a promise, nor commits himself to anything; if he utters a sentence in the interrogative, imperative or declarative moods he does not thereby put forward (respectively) a question, a directive or an assertion. But the same applies if someone goes on the stage through the conventional trappings that, under ordinary circumstances, count as the constitution of a marriage or a contract. Quite in general, only under certain circumstances does the execution of an action-type constitute another, even when this relation is secured by convention.

According to Searle (1969), referential expressions such as proper names, indexicals and demonstratives (and perhaps definite and even indefinite descriptions, at least in some uses) share an expressive feature that is a conventional indicator of an ancillary speech act, referring – 'ancillary' in that it is an auxiliary for the performance of another speech act. In this article, I want to argue for two interrelated claims. Firstly, I will support an assumption many researchers make, while others dispute: that some expressions traditionally considered presupposition-triggers, such as clefts or definite descriptions, are conventional indicators of another ancillary speech act, presupposing. Secondly, I will argue for a normative account of this speech-act, on which it is constituted by a common knowledge norm, and I will discuss the implications of this claim for Williamson's well-known normative account of assertion, on which it is constituted by a knowledge norm. Let me elaborate a little on the nature of these two claims in the remainder of this introductory section.

I find it useful to classify theories of speech acts along two dimensions. First, they can be normative or descriptive, depending on whether or not they posit norms or rules as constitutive of such acts. Secondly, they can be individual or communicative, depending on whether or not they characterize the acts in terms of relations between speaker and hearer, or rather appeal only to mental states of the speaker not involving those relations. For my present purposes, I do not need to go into a more articulate characterization of those conditions; I will limit myself to providing illustrative examples. Let us compare first a paradigm Gricean account of the speech act of assertion, such as the one to be found in Bach & Harnish (1979), with Williamson's account, for they differ along the two dimensions I am interested in emphasizing. Williamson (1996/2000) claims that the following norm or rule (the knowledge rule) is constitutive of assertion, and individuates it:

(KR) One must ((assert p) only if one knows p).

In the course of the debate that Williamson's proposal has generated, other writers have accepted the view that assertion is defined by constitutive rules, but have proposed alternative norms; thus, Weiner (2005) proposes a truth rule, (TR), and Lackey (2007) a reasonableness rule, (RBR):

(TR) One must ((assert p) only if p).

(RBR) One must ((assert p) only if it is reasonable for one to believe p).

In is important to note that the obligation (KR) imposes is not all things considered, but prima facie or pro tanto; in any particular case, it can be overruled by stronger obligations imposed by other norms. For present purposes, we can think of it as having a sui generis source, specific to speech acts.[1] Given this, we can tighten them up. Perhaps the reason why Williamson gives only a necessary condition for correctness, and not a sufficient one, lies in the fact that he thought that knowing a proposition does not suffice for making an assertion of it correct. And this is true, of course, with respect to all things considered correctness; however, as far as I can tell, no bad consequences follow from accepting that there is nothing wrong with asserting anything that one knows, in the speech-act specific sense of correctness – even if, all things considered, there may well be many reasons for such incorrectness. Thus, we can tighten the analysis; in the case of (KR), the proposal would be this:

(KR') For one to assert p is correct if and only if one knows p.

Thus, on Williamson's view assertion is the unique representational act such that, if one makes it, one is thereby committed to knowing the represented proposition (on the others, to its truth, or to its being reasonable for one to believe it); i.e., the propositional act such that, if one performs it without knowing the intended proposition, one is doing something wrong.

As Hindriks (2007) notes, although it is indeed a feature of our assertoric practices that we criticize performances that violate those

---
[1] A more thorough analysis might reveal that these norms ultimately have a more general source, in ethics, say, or (as in fact I think) in rationality.

rules, these facts about our practices of appraising assertions are by themselves insufficient to justify normative accounts. For we also evaluate assertions relative to (invoking Rawls's (1955) well-known distinction) merely regulative norms, norms that regulate, relative to certain purposes, acts in themselves constitutively non-normative – for instance, as witty, polite or well-phrased. Hindriks shows that norms for assertion could be merely regulative of a constitutively non-normative practice, definable in the psychological Gricean account that Bach & Harnish proposed, GA below ('R-intending' there is to be explicated in terms of Gricean communicative intentions). The regulative norms in question would then be derived from an ultimately moral sincerity rule such as (SR):

> (GA) To assert p is to utter a sentence that means p thereby R-intending the hearer to take the utterance as a reason to think that the speaker believes p.
>
> (SR) In situations of normal trust, one ought to be sincere.

Bach & Harnish's Gricean account (GA) – perhaps the most popular account of assertion until Williamson's article brought back into the limelight normative accounts previously favored by such writers as Austin, Dummett and Searle – is a descriptive account, not a normative one like the three mentioned: unlike them, by itself it does not mention norms, but only certain psychological states. Of course, normative consequences would follow, derivative from further rules such as (SR), or perhaps from the fact that the mental states in question are themselves constitutively normative, but this does not suffice for an account to count as normative. By itself, (GA) is descriptive, not normative.

Consider now the other dimension of variability. Williamson's (KR) account, as much as (TR) and (RBR), are individual in that they only mention obligations or commitments of the speaker, obligations or commitments not in regard to anybody else. (GA) is communicative instead, in that it appeals to the presence in the speaker of a specific sort of intention, whose content demands its own recognition by someone else. Promises, as they are usually understood, are the paradigm case of a normative and communicative act; they constitutively impose obligations on their performers, and they are constitutively addressed to an audience – whose 'uptake' is required, on most accounts, for them to have taken place.

My ultimate goal is to argue for a normative-cum-communicative account of the main speech acts, in particular assertion. I believe that norms such as (KR), (TR) and (RBR) are at best good candidates to characterize the individual act of judging, but not the communicative act of asserting. Here, however, I will only develop a small piece of a more complex argumentative line intended to support that view. In the next section I will provide an initial intuitive characterization of presuppositions, which, against skeptical claims to the contrary, suggests that we have here a robust kind, in need of elucidation. In the third, I will present the most popular account of them, the Stalnakerian account. In the fourth section, I will show how the well-known practice of informative presupposition puts heavy strain on such an account, and I will suggest that the problem is a particular case of well-known difficulty for descriptive accounts of speech acts, which Stalnaker's is for the case of presupposition. In the final section I will show how a normative account along the lines of the one sketched a few paragraphs back deals with that problem, and how it deals with what is known as the Triggering Problem for presuppositions; finally, I will discuss the consequences of the proposal for the adequacy of individual accounts of assertion such as Williamson's.

2 Presupposition

Our semantic competence underwrites the validity of inferences such as the following, for both (1) and (2):

(1)   John infected the PC.

(2)   It was John who infected the PC.

   ∴ Someone infected the PC.

However, there is a difference between the syntactic constructions in (1) and (2); unlike the less marked way of expressing what we perceive as the same content in (1), the cleft construction in (2) also validates the same inference when placed under different embeddings, such as negation (3), conditionals (4), modals (5), and still others; presuppositions are said to be thereby 'projected', i.e., inherited by the embedding constructions:

(3)   It was not John who infected the PC.

(4)   If it was John who infected the PC, the Mac is also infected.

(5)   It may have been John who infected the PC.

∴ Someone infected the PC.

Other presuppositional constructions exhibit this behavior; for a second serviceable illustration consider the case of definite descriptions:

(6)   The Sants station newsstand sells The Guardian.

(7)   The Sants station newsstand does not sell The Guardian.

(8)   If the Sants station newsstand sells The Guardian, we will buy it there.

(9)   The Sants station newsstand may sell The Guardian.

∴ There is exactly one Sants station newsstand.

This projecting behavior invites the traditional characterization of presuppositions as conditions for the truth and the falsity of the sentences/propositions including them. But, as the discussion in the past decades has shown, this cannot be right. In the first place, Strawson pointed out cases of what Yablo (2006) calls 'non-catastrophic presupposition failure'. For instance, if as a matter of fact there are two newsstands in Sants station, but both of them sell The Guardian, many people feel that (6) is nonetheless true; on the other hand, if there is no newsstand there, many people feel that (10) is false, not just neither true nor false:

(10) I waited for you for two hours at the Sants station newsstand.

Secondly, presuppositions are not projected in some cases, and hence they cannot be in those cases conditions for the truth and falsity of the whole claim:

(11) If someone infected the PC, it was John who did it.

(12) Someone infected the PC, and it was John who did it.

Finally, conventional implicatures, which intuitively differ from presuppositions, share the projection behavior with presuppositions in the embeddings we have considered, and thus should similarly count as conditions for the truth and falsity of the claim; following Potts (2007), I use non-restrictive wh-clauses as illustrative examples:

(13) John, who infected the PC, teaches in Oxford.

(14) It is not the case that John, who infected the PC, teaches in Oxford.

(15) If John, who infected the PC, teaches in Oxford, he will attend the conference.

(16) It may be the case that John, who infected the PC, teaches in Oxford.

∴ John infected the PC.

Geurts (1999: 6-8) uses the projection behavior illustrated by (3)-(5) and (11)-(12) as an intuitive test to characterize presuppositions; even though he acknowledges that the test is defeasible, I think the fact that conventional implicatures also pass it shows that it is not even a good intuitive characterization, aside from its defeasibility.[2] Von Fintel (2004: 271) proposes an alternative 'Hey, wait a minute!' test; consider the following dialogues, with '#' being an indication of impropriety or infelicity:

---
2 Beaver (2001: 19-20), Chierchia & McConnell-Ginet (1990: 283) and Kadmon (2001: 13) make a similar point.

(17) It was not John who infected the PC.

(18) # Hey, wait a minute, I had no idea that John did not infect the PC.

(19) Hey, wait a minute, I had no idea that someone infected the PC.

(20) It is not the case that John, who infected the PC, teaches in Oxford.

(21) # Hey, wait a minute, I had no idea that John does not teach in Oxford.

(22) # Hey, wait a minute, I had no idea that John did not infect the PC.

Intuitively, this is why von Fintel's test provides a better initial characterization of presuppositions. As opposed both to asserted contents and conventional implicatures, presuppositions are presented as information already in possession of the conversational participants. Asserted content is presented as new information for the audience, and the same applies to conventionally implicated contents, even if the latter are somehow backgrounded relative to the main assertion. This is why targeting the asserted or conventionally implicated content with the 'Hey, wait a minute!' objection does not feel right, whereas objecting in that way to the presupposed content does. In other words, presuppositions are presented as part of the 'common ground', while asserted and conventionally implicated contents are presented as new information.

Of course, von Fintel's is only a good test providing an initial intuitively plausible characterization of the phenomenon, useful for us to isolate what we want to discuss. However, I think it at least shows that the skepticism expressed by writers such as Böer & Lycan (1976) and Levinson (1983) – who argue for a form of the eliminativist view about presuppositions we will describe below, in part on the basis of the alleged miscellaneous character of the phenomenon – is prima facie unreasonable. The intuitions unveiled by the 'Hey, wait a minute!' test are robust, and robustly related to grammatical constructions like those we have used for illustration, as the reader might establish by considering variations on them (or others in the list given by Levinson (1983: 181-5), taking heed of the distinction between conventional implicatures and presuppositions, there ignored). The robustness of the intuitions suggests at least prima facie that we are confronted with a sufficiently 'natural' kind, amenable to a precise characterization. What we are after is a philosophically adequate definition, which, if it is good, should elaborate on the preceding intuitive explanation for why von Fintel's characterization succeeds where the others previously considered fail. This is what we will try to accomplish in the next pages; we will start by presenting Stalnaker's influential proposal.

3 The Stalnakerian Picture

In a series of articles staring in the early 1970s, Stalnaker (1973, 1974, 2002) has provided an influential account of the phenomenon of presupposition. The account has been slightly modified along the way; here I will just present what I take to be the core aspects.[3] Stalnaker's account is in the spirit of Grice's account of phenomena such as conversational implicature in particular and meaning in general: it purports to account for those phenomena as a specific form of rational behavior involving communicative intentions, averting irreducibly social notions such as conventions or (socially construed) norms; Bach & Harnish's account of assertion (GA) above is an example of such Gricean accounts.

Stalnaker takes as the basis for his analysis a notion of speaker presupposition, which he then uses (reluctantly, as we are about to see) to provide a notion of sentence presupposition. Speaker presupposition is explained in terms of common beliefs about what is accepted by the conversational partners; and common belief follows the pattern of Lewis's notion of common knowledge: p is common belief in G just in case (almost) everybody in G believes p, believes

---

3 Simons (2003) provides a helpful sympathetic discussion of the evolving details.

that (almost) everybody in G believes p, and so on. Acceptance is in its turn defined by Stalnaker (2002: 716) as a category of mental states 'which includes belief, but also some attitudes (presumption, assumption, acceptance for the purposes of argument or enquiry) that contrast with belief and with each other. To accept a proposition is to treat it as true for some reason.' The need to invoke acceptance in the definition derives from many cases in which, intuitively and according to our initial characterization above, p is presupposed while not commonly believed. Thus, consider Donnellan's example: the secret conspirator asks the usurper's minions, 'Is the king in his countinghouse?' Here the speaker does not believe that the intended referent is king, nor perhaps that there is a king, and hence does not believe that these propositions are commonly believed in the context, but nonetheless it is presupposed that the referent is king and that there is exactly one king.[4] Nonetheless, acceptance cannot be invoked all the way down; the account is given in terms of common belief about what is commonly accepted, because only the more specific category of belief and not acceptance has the needed explanatory links with behavior.

This is thus the final account. We first define a proposition p to be in the common ground in a group G – $CG_G(p)$ – and then we define speaker presupposition:

(CG_G) $CG_G(p)$ in G if and only if it is common belief in G that everybody accepts p.

(SpP) Speaker S presupposes p (relative to G) if and only if S believes that $CGS(p)$.

Stalnaker (1973: 451; 1974: 50) then defines a notion of sentence presupposition in terms of this:

---

4 I believe this is an intuitively correct characterization of what is presupposed in this case, which I take to be a referential use of the description; in general, as I argue in García-Carpintero (2000), all cases of reference involve 'identification' presuppositions.

(SnP) Sentence S presupposes p if and only if the use of S would for some reason be inappropriate unless the speaker presupposed p.

Stalnaker (1978) complements this analysis of presuppositions with an equally deservedly influential analysis of assertion, on which an assertion is a proposal to update the common ground, which, if accepted, is 'added' to it (i.e., it then becomes common belief that every participant accepts it); and he combined the two accounts to suggest intuitively plausible explanations of some aspects of the projecting behavior we presented in the previous section. This (together with the related independent work of Lauri Karttunen) was the origin of the new important tradition of Dynamic Semantics, developed for instance in Heim (1983), Beaver (2001) or von Fintel (2004). This tradition has the resources to provide the account requested at the end of the previous section. Unlike the traditional account of presuppositions as conditions for the truth and falsity of claims, it can explain the selective projection behavior we have seen to be characteristic of presuppositions, and it can distinguish them from conventional implicatures, accounting also for the adequacy of von Fintel's test; last but not least, when properly elaborated it also has the resources to explain the phenomenon of non-catastrophic presupposition failure (cf. von Fintel 2004). Geurts (1999: 17), however, is right in pointing out the important conceptual differences between the DS tradition and Stalnaker's viewpoint, which in fact go to the heart of the main issues I want to discuss here. Renouncing Stalnaker's Gricean reductive aims, in this tradition presuppositions are taken to be, both with respect to their triggering and projecting behavior, a constitutive feature of the semantics of natural language expressions.[5]

---

[5] While Geurts distances himself from Dynamic Semantics on account of their betrayal of Stalnaker's truly pragmatic stance, like Stalnaker he helps himself to a notion of expression-presupposition, defined to be sure in terms of the pragmatic notion of speaker presupposition: 'In the previous section we defined presuppositions as inferences that are triggered by certain expressions, and that exhibit projection behaviour. For Stalnaker, a presupposition is an assumption which a speaker takes for granted. These two definitions may seem to contradict

Let us be a bit more clear and explicit about the differences between Stalnaker's 'pragmatic' view and the 'semantic' one I want to defend here. As Stalnaker (1974: 61) notes, there are two contrasting ways of understanding the semantic/pragmatics divide. In one of them, semantics deals with the truth-condition of sentences, and the truth-conditional import of expressions. It is in this sense that presuppositions understood as conditions for the truth and falsity of sentences are said to be a semantic phenomenon. An important strand of Stalnaker's early defense of a pragmatic account, as he notes, is to oppose such a 'semantic' conception; for reasons I have summarized in the previous section, I think that this opposition was well made. However, as I have argued in detail elsewhere,[6] this way of tracing the semantic/pragmatic divide is not theoretically useful, because it displaces from the purview of semantics facts that should be studied together with those it keeps there: among others, semantically driven context-dependence, semantics for conventional indicators of speech acts such as the interrogative and imperative mood, and, indeed, the presuppositional facts we are discussing if the view to be promoted here is correct.

On a different understanding of the divide, linguistics in general purports to theoretically characterize the constitutive facts about natural languages (in an indirect way of putting this, the linguistic competence of speakers), and semantics is the part thereof dealing with constitutive meaning facts. This is, I think, the conception of the divide that Grice had in mind when he tried to account for the

---

each other, but the contradiction is only an apparent one. For we can plausibly say that a given form of words requires that the speaker presuppose something or other.' (Geurts 1999: 14, my emphasis). This definition is less nuanced in its appeal to normative notions than Stalnaker's; moreover, unlike Stalnaker, Geurts also appeals to unexplained normative notions in characterizing speaker presupposition: 'a speaker who presupposes something incurs a commitment... regardless whether he really believes what he presupposes' (Geurts 1999: 11). Geurts never explains where those requirements and commitments come from, given the pragmatic stance he vows to adopt. It is at the very least fair to think that his understanding of the pragmatic stance is closer to the one to be adopted here than to Stalnaker's own.

6 Cf. García-Carpintero (2001, 2004, 2006).

apparent asymmetric, non-truth-conditional behavior of conjunction or referential uses of descriptions as generalized conversational implicatures, i.e., as 'pragmatic' features. After noting the two different interpretations of the divide, Stalnaker (1974) points out that he is mainly arguing for a pragmatic account of presuppositions only on the first understanding, but notes also that his arguments have repercussions for the other: while he is open to the possibility that in some cases 'one may just have to write presupposition constraints into the dictionary entry for a particular word' (Stalnaker 1974: 61), he conjectures 'that one can explain many presupposition constraints in terms of general conversational rules without building anything about presuppositions into the meanings of particular words or constructions' (*ibid*).

In fact, although as we have seen Stalnaker introduced a notion of sentence presupposition (SnP) in his early writings, and continues to assume it in recent writing, he repeatedly expresses qualms about it, because of the unexplained appeal to the normative notion of inappropriateness, and even more because it suggests, he (2002: 712-3) says, the existence of a 'mysterious relation X' between sentences and propositions worthy of analysis, while 'we don't need the mysterious relation X to describe the phenomena, and it does not make any contribution to explaining them'. We may say that Gricean generalized conversational implicature accounts of referential uses of descriptions or manifest non-truth-conditional asymmetries in conjunctions are not simply reductionist, but in fact eliminativist vis-à-vis semantic accounts of those phenomena, on the second understanding of the semantics/pragmatics divide: although it is acknowledged that definite descriptions and conjunctions are in fact commonly used in those ways, the claim is that a semantic theory should not encompass them. The Stalnakerian view of presuppositions, in contrast with the DS view, is ultimately similarly eliminativist vis-à-vis this understanding of the divide; this was clear from the beginning, even if the emphasis is stronger in more recent work:

> [O]ne might define a notion of sentence presupposition in terms of speaker presupposition, but [...] the attempt to do so

would be a distraction, and would not yield any theoretically useful notion. (Stalnaker 2010: 150)

In what remains of the article I will critically examine these contentions. While I will essentially agree with Stalnaker that presupposition is a pragmatic, not semantic phenomenon in the first interpretation, ultimately having to do with the propositional attitudes of speakers, I will find reasons to question his Gricean eliminativist stance, and hence to reject that it is a pragmatic phenomenon also in the second interpretation.

4 The Problem of Accommodating Accommodation

As Stalnaker (1973: 449; 1974: 51-2) noted in his early writings, it is frequent for speakers to communicate information by uttering sentences that carry presuppositions with such contents. These are real life examples from Abbott (2008):

(23) The leaders of the militant homophile movement in America generally have been young people. It was they who fought back during a violent police raid on a Greenwich Village bar in 1969, an incident from which many gays date the birth of the modern crusade for homosexual rights.

(24) If you're going into the bedroom, would you mind bringing back the big bag of potato chips that I left on the bed?

Speakers who utter sentences (23) and (24) do not typically assume their presuppositions – that some people fought back during a violent police raid on a Greenwich Village bar in 1969, and that there is exactly one big bag of potato chips that the speaker left on the bed, respectively – to be in the common ground. To utter sentences with those presuppositions is just an expedient resource for them to inform their audiences of such contents, plus the assertion, woven together in a terse package. That the contents are nonetheless presupposed is shown by the 'Hey, wait a minute!' test – even though, understandably, a 'Hey, wait a minute!' objection in these cases feels, even if technically adequate, a bit 'autistic', exactly as failing to grasp an obvious conversational implicature feels.

The examples above help us to appreciate the extent of the phenomenon, but it is better to have a simpler case for the ensuing discussion.[7] We are to assume that the speaker utters (25) in the knowledge that his audience knows nothing about his family:

(25) I cannot come to the meeting – I have to pick up my sister at the airport.

Here again, the 'Hey, wait a minute!' test evinces the presence of the presupposition that the speaker has a sister, even if, as before, precisely to the extent that speakers are entitled to assume that the presupposition will be accommodated without further ado by ordinary audiences, it would feel strange if somebody objected to it with the 'Hey, wait a minute!' complaint. (Compare the situation if the speaker had made the utterance with 'my secret lover' substituting 'my sister'.) These are cases where speakers exploit what Lewis (1979) called the 'Rule of Accommodation for Presuppositions', which he characterized thus:

(RA) If at time t something is said that requires presupposition p to be acceptable, and if p is not presupposed just before t, then – ceteris paribus and within certain limits – presupposition p comes into existence at t.

Cases in which a 'Hey, wait a minute!' complaint is actually made (which the 'my secret lover' variant may illustrate) manifest the need for the hedge. Now, the initial problem for Stalnaker's account that cases of accommodation pose is as follows: (i) as the 'Hey, wait a minute!' test corroborates, and he (1973: 449; 1974: 51-2) wants to

---

[7] Stalnaker (1974: 52, fn. 2) attributes the ensuing example to Jerry Saddock.

acknowledge, a presupposition is present;[8] however, (at first sight) (ii) the speaker does not presuppose it, on Stalnaker's characterization, because he does not believe that his audience accepts it; while (iii) the fact that cases like these are commonplace suggests that there is nothing inappropriate in their use, and certainly nothing feels inappropriate in them.

Although he has been aware of the issue all along, only in recent work has Stalnaker confronted it squarely, arguing that in fact these cases are not at odds with his account, because only at first sight is (ii) correct; in fact, when the matter is properly examined, it turns out that the speaker is presupposing the relevant content. I will critically discuss the adequacy of his arguments in some detail, because of its intrinsic interest and also because writers sympathetic to his pragmatic account of presupposition and antagonistic to the semantic one I am defending, such as Simons (2003: 267-8) and Schlenker (ms),[9] appear to endorse it without qualification.[10]

---

8 Kadmon (2001: 219-21) chooses to describe these as cases of presupposition 'disappearance', on the basis of her characterization of presuppositions as propositions 'intuitively felt to be taken for granted'. But I think this is a bad choice; von Fintel's test is a much better intuitive indication of the presence of presuppositions.

9 Simons (2003: 267-9), who shares Stalnaker's eliminativist leanings, shows that more complex sentences may pose difficulties for Stalnaker's 'idealized time' after utterance but before acceptance or rejection strategy. In more recent work (Simons ms.), in which she deepens her eliminativist viewpoint, she nonetheless questions that the strategy might suffice to account for informative presuppositions, with considerations related to the ones to be developed below.

10 In his insightful discussion of accommodation (to which I am much indebted), von Fintel (2008) makes heavy use of Stalnaker's point about the proper time at which presuppositions should be satisfied by the common ground. However, his view of presuppositions differs from Stalnaker's precisely on the matter we are discussing: 'Stalnaker holds out some hope that pragmatic presuppositions do not need to be traced back to hardwired encoding in the sentence meaning of natural language sentences. The vision is that they might rather be derivable from presupposition-free sentence meanings together with simple pragmatic principles [...] Other people have tried to sketch similar stories. I am very skeptical that any such story can succeed' (von Fintel 2008: 138). My own account of accommodation in the next section is very close to von Fintel's.

Stalnaker (2002: 708-9) points out that utterances themselves are manifest events, which become part of the common ground; and, given that speakers take advantage of this, speakers' presuppositions should only be satisfied at a '(perhaps somewhat idealized) point after the utterance event has taken place, but before it has been accepted or rejected'. In a previous article, Stalnaker motivates this with a convincing example:

> The point of a speech act – an assertion, for example – is to change the context, and since the way the speech act is supposed to change the context depends on its content, interpretation must be done in the prior context – the context as it is before the assertion is accepted, and its content added to what is presupposed. But the prior context cannot be the context as it was before the speaker began to speak. Suppose Phoebe says 'I saw an interesting movie last night'. To determine the content of her remark, one needs to know who is speaking, and so Phoebe, if she is speaking appropriately, must be presuming that the information that she is speaking is available to her audience – that is shared information. But she need not presume that this information was available before she began to speak. The prior context that is relevant to the interpretation of a speech act is the context as it is changed by the fact that the speech act was made, but prior to the acceptance or rejection of the speech act. (Stalnaker 1998: 101)[11]

The claim then is that the speaker presupposition was there after all, not before the speaker made his utterance, but at that 'idealized time' at which it should be; and so (ii) was, after all, wrong. Now, although the point Stalnaker makes about the time when presuppositions should be present is undoubtedly correct, I do not think it lets him off the hook; for bringing to bear cases like Phoebe's use of 'I' in order to deal with informative presuppositions crucially begs the question at stake. I will now develop this contention with some care.

---

11 The point was in fact made earlier by Stalnaker (1978: 86): 'the context on which assertion has its essential effect is not defined by what is presupposed before the speaker begins to speak, but will include any information which the speaker assumes his audience can infer from the performance of the speech act'.

Remember the dialectics; what we are trying to establish is whether informative presuppositions are compatible with the Gricean eliminativist stance that Stalnaker professes. It is clear that this is what he (2002: 713-4) wants to vindicate: 'Suppose we assume that the semantics tells us exactly this about the sentence "I have to pick up my sister at the airport": it is true if and only if the speaker has a sister whom he or she has to pick up at the airport, and false otherwise. So we are supposing that the semantics tells us nothing either about relation X, or about what speakers must take to be common ground. Are there facts about the use of the sentence that cannot be explained by this semantic hypothesis, together with general conversational rules?' He goes on to explain why the answer to his rhetorical question is, as rhetorically expected, 'no'. I will come back to his considerations presently. But let us see before why the facts of informative presupposition establish that, on the contrary, the answer should be 'yes', disappointing the rhetorically expressed expectations.

The problem with the Phoebe example is that, in the context of the present dialectics, Stalnaker should instead have considered an utterance of, say, 'there is exactly an agent of this very utterance, and she/he saw an interesting movie last night'. Would an ideal interpretation of this utterance require two different interpretative 'moments', an earlier one at which a speaker presupposition identifying an individual as the agent of the speech is checked – and perhaps graciously accommodated if not present – and a later one at which acceptance or rejection of the claim that that individual saw an interesting movie is decided? I do not see why, and Stalnaker has not told us so far. There does not appear to be any reason for it; and, by parity of reasoning, the same applies to the case in dispute of (25) on Stalnaker's assumptions about what the semantics tells us.

In other words, Stalnaker's opponent will contend that 'I' is as much a conventional presupposition trigger as 'my sister' is; which is why the existence of the two idealized interpretative moments can be accepted outright. What is in dispute is whether the existence of such an ideal moment can be assumed given Stalnaker's Gricean eliminativist assumptions. The idealization that Stalnaker proposes, like other idealizations in science, is not at all suspect by itself. But it has to be accounted for; for idealization in science is something like a proposal for imagining a fictitious situation that highlights the main features of an explanation. The explanation is the main point, and must be there for the idealization to have a clear content. Simply assuming that the ideal moment in question exists even on Stalnaker's assumptions blatantly begs the question at stake: for it simply assumes with no independent justification at all that, even without conventional indicators, the presuppositional requirement (as opposed to an additional aspect of the asserted content) is somehow triggered.

Given that it is not under dispute that utterances carry presuppositions which are not linguistically triggered, to hammer home the point I am making I will now examine how the presence of the two interpretative moments that Stalnaker posits might be accounted for also in such a case. Presuppositions without a conventional basis might be triggered either by the literal content, given the context, by a process analogous to the one described by Grice for conversational implicatures, and, more in general, by Searle and others for indirect speech acts; or they might be less specifically dependent on the literal content and more on purely extra-linguistic aspects of context. Consider first an example of the latter sort: the day after the 2010 World Cup final, a foreign colleague e-mails me: 'I'm sure the party lasted long into the night'. Here he is presupposing that Spain won the Cup, that I am happy about it, that I am interested in football, and so on and so forth. Precisely to the extent that we have an acceptable explanation of how these presuppositions are (non-linguistically) triggered in the situation, we can accept that an ideal interpretation process of the utterance includes a moment, after the utterance but previous to acceptance or rejection of his guess, at which his presuppositions should be contemplated.

More interesting for our present concerns are cases of non-linguistic presupposition of the former sort – presuppositions conveyed through general Gricean conversational mechanisms. Since the classic discussions of these matters in the 1970's, several writers have pointed out that some presupposition triggers are 'softer' than others, in that they allow for the 'disappearance' of the presupposition in linguistic or even extra-linguistic contexts other than the 'filtering' ones illustrated with (11) and (12) in section 2 above. Simons (2001) provides several examples including (26), which we might contrast with (27).

(26) I have no idea whether Jane ever smoked, but she hasn't stopped smoking.

(27) # I have no idea whether someone infected the PC, but it was John who infected the PC.

If the presuppositions of change-of-state verbs such as 'stop' resulted from Gricean conversational processes, then (26) would be a case of discourse-based cancellation, the process that Grice showed conversational implicatures are subject to; and other examples in Simons (2001) would illustrate the possibility of their purely contextual cancellation – while (27), and analogous examples for definite descriptions, would show that the presupposition triggers I used in the second section appear to be more straightforwardly semantically encoded. Similarly, factives usually presuppose their embedded propositions, and examples like (28) – uttered in a context in which Jane's whereabouts are not known – might suggest that such presuppositions are similarly cancellable:

(28) If Henry discovers that Jane is in New York, he will be upset.

Consistent with this evidence, Stalnaker (1974: 55) attempts a derivation from Gricean maxims of the usual presupposition of the factive 'know' – which Simons (2006: 366) further develops – and then (Stalnaker 1974: 56-8) suggests the account in terms of Gricean implicature cancellation of the intuitive disappearance of the similar presupposition of 'discover'.[12]

---

12 I am not sure that this explanation works; I am bringing it up just for the sake of having a convenient illustration to make my main point against Stalnaker's account of informative presuppositions. As Abusch (2010: 50) points out, the fact that 'A knows that S' and 'A is right that S' appear to have the same assertive content (something to the effect that A believes that S, S is true, and A's belief is

Both in this case and in the above case of non-linguistic presupposition, to the extent that we have a convincing Gricean explanation of the triggering of the presupposition, we can accept for them the existence of the two 'moments' in idealized interpretation; but only to the extent that we do have such explanation. As I said before, the idealization is not in question. Let us suppose that, even assuming that the semantics tells us that 'A knows that S' just means, say, 'A beliefs that S, S is true, and A's belief is justified-in-a-Gettier-immune-way', we can see why the 'S is true' part would be usually contextually presupposed. Under the assumption, we are entitled to claim that, in idealized interpretation, at a first moment 'the context on which assertion will have its essential effect' should be seen to entail the proposition that S is true, and only at a later moment would it be decided whether the proposition that A believes S in a properly justified way is accepted or rejected. This is because we have an acceptable explanation for the presence of the requirement concerning the first interpretative moment. The 'World Cup' example provides an alternative (albeit related) explanation, which equally justifies that propositions such as that Spain won the Cup should be satisfied by 'the context on which assertion will have its essential effect', previous to deciding whether or not it can have that essential effect.

In contrast to these two cases, for Stalnaker to posit as a primitive fact that idealized interpretation in the 'my sister' case requires the two moments, even on his contention that 'the semantics tells us nothing either about relation X, or about what speakers must take to be common ground', simply assumes without justification that some such explanation exists (alternative to the one provided by the

---

justified-in-a-Gettier-immune-way) but contrasting presuppositions (that S is true in the case of 'know', and that A believes S in the case of 'is right') tells against Stalnaker's and Simon's pragmatic explanations of their triggering. There are alternative explanations of the apparent disappearance of the presuppositions which I think are compatible with their semantic triggering, for instance in terms of the – badly termed, as von Fintel (2008: 155-7) says – 'local accommodation', change of contextual assumptions, or perhaps in the way suggested by Abusch (2010). Cf. the nuanced discussion by Chierchia & McConnell-Ginet (1990: 310-7).

conventionalists),[13] and it thus begs the question at stake. On the contrary, for all we can say and Stalnaker has established, an ideal interpretation of an utterance of 'I have a sister whom I have to pick up at the airport' does not require that at the intermediate moment 'prior to the acceptance or rejection of the speech act' it should be established that 'the context on which assertion will have its essential effect' entails that the speaker has a sister. And the same applies to 'there is exactly an agent of this very utterance, and she/he saw an interesting movie last night' (which, as I said, should be the example discussed by Stalnaker, as opposed to his Phoebe example, not to prejudice the issue) vis-à-vis the proposition that there is a single agent of the utterance: for all we can say, in this case this would just be part of the assertoric content, the essential effect that the assertion is intended to have.

In reply to Abbott (2008: 529-30), who makes points close to the ones I have been presenting in the previous few paragraphs, Stalnaker keeps, I think, simply begging the question. In the article we have been quoting from, Stalnaker (2002: 714) insists that 'if the simple semantic hypothesis [about the absence of the mysterious relation X] were right, one would expect these facts [those concerning presuppositions we are discussing] to be just as they are'; and he goes on to explain why:

> If we assume, as is obviously reasonable, that it is common belief, prior to Alice's statement, that she knows whether or not she has a sister, and common belief that she is being honest, then the fact that she says something that entails that she had a sister is enough to account for it becoming shared information

---

[13] Throughout this article I am using clefts and definite descriptions as good candidates for conventional presuppositional triggers, given the existing attempts for Gricean conversational explanations in the case of factives, change-of-state verbs, etc. (about which I have anyway expressed doubts in the previous footnote). Levinson (1983: 220-2) summarizes joint work with Jay Atlas providing an eliminativist account for clefts. With other writers (Beaver 2001: 29-30; Simons 2006: 367), I doubt that such an account (putting aside its plausibility) is truly eliminativist, because it relies on 'Gricean' inferences sensitive to a specific logical form they ascribe to clefts. To me, this just sounds like an alternative semantic account.

that she does, even if the statement itself is rejected. (Stalnaker 2002: 714)

In this passage, as Abbott suggests, Stalnaker appears to be subscribing to a suggestion by Saddock about how to characterize presupposition in the face of informative uses, which he had reported in his earlier work (1974: 52, n. 2) and correctly rejected. The suggestion was to characterize presuppositions as propositions that speakers assume their audiences have no reasons to doubt. Stalnaker (1974) was right to reject this, because 'it would do away with the distinction between presupposing and asserting'. If, for instance, in one of those situations in which one is led to 'make conversation', one says 'Nice weather', one knows very well that the audience has no reason to doubt what one says, but one is nonetheless asserting it, not presupposing it. But Stalnaker's (2002) proposal just quoted may appear to be essentially Saddock's, and so, Abbott (2008: 59) points out, it similarly 'runs the risk of doing away with the distinction between presupposition and assertion altogether'. Now, this is Stalnaker's reply:

> But the general account does provide some guidance for distinguishing the consequences of assertion from those of presupposition accommodation. One relevant fact ... is that, in cases of accommodation, the information that is added to the context continues to be accepted even if the assertion itself is rejected. Even if you reject my claim that I have to pick up my sister, you continue to accept, as common ground, that I have a sister. (Stalnaker 2008: 541)

Here I think that Stalnaker once more begs the question. He allows himself to distinguish the information that the speaker has a sister from 'the assertion', in that 'it is added to the context' even if the latter is rejected. This is equivalent to the appeal to the existence of two separate 'moments' in idealized interpretation. But the problem is that we have not been given any reason to distinguish two parts in 'I have a sister whom I have to pick up at the airport', only one of which is 'the assertion', corresponding to the distinction we are trying to trace between the presupposition and the assertion in 'I have to pick up my sister at the airport'. The only distinction for which Stalnaker provides motivation is the one between a less and a more controversial part; but, as he himself correctly pointed out before, in his reply to Saddock, this is not the distinction we are after.

5 A Normative Account of Presupposing

I will present now the normative account I announced in the first section, and will then motivate it and provide some justification for it. We first modify the previous definition of common ground in a group G, going back to Lewis's original account, and then we redefine speaker and sentence presupposition:

(CG'$_G$) CG'$_G$(p) in G if and only if p is common knowledge in G.

(SpP') For one to presuppose p (relative to G) is correct if and only if CG'$_G$(p).

(SnP') Sentence S presupposes p if and only if the use of S conveys for some reason that the speaker presupposes p.

This proposal is truly in the spirit of Stalnaker's original discussion, even if it goes against his more recent eliminativist leanings. Presupposing is a pragmatic notion involving attitudes of speakers, in fact the notion of a (linguistically ancillary) speech act, although it is explicitly defined in normative terms and not in the psychological ones that Stalnaker prefers. It can be triggered in different ways, even when standardly associated with sentence-types – allowing for conventional triggering in such cases, but not requiring it.

The main justification for this proposal lies in that it offers explanations for the phenomena we have examined in the previous sections, which other accounts miss. Given my ultimate aims, it will be useful to present this justification in parallel to Williamson's justification for his normative account of assertion, introduced in the first section.

As a first motivation for his account, Williamson (1996/2000: 252) mentions intuitive conversational patterns: we challenge assertions politely by asking 'How do you know?' or, more aggressively, 'Do you know that?' Austin (1962) pointed out these patterns:

> [I]t is important to notice also that statements too are liable to infelicity of this kind in other ways also parallel to contracts, promises, warnings, &c. Just as we often say, for example, 'You cannot order me', in the sense 'You have not the right to order me', which is equivalent to saying that you are not in the appropriate position to do so: so often there are things you cannot state – have no right to state – are in no position to state. You cannot now state how many people there are in the next room; if you say 'There are fifty people in the next room', I can only regard you as guessing or conjecturing. (Austin 1962: 138)

Now, we can observe this same pattern in the case of presuppositions, addressing in this case not just whether the speaker knew the presupposed proposition, but whether or not it is common knowledge. In fact, we can see that it is this that von Fintel's 'Hey, wait a minute!' objection is questioning; in saying 'I had no idea . . . ' (alternatively, 'I did not know . . . ') one questions that the proposition is in the common ground, in the sense characterized in (CG'$_G$).[14]

As I said above, Hindriks (2007) notes that these facts about our evaluative practices are by themselves insufficient to justify normative accounts. For we also evaluate acts relative to merely regulative norms, norms that regulate, relative to certain purposes, acts in themselves constitutively non-normative – for instance, as witty, polite or

---

14 Perhaps the reader has experienced annoyance at the practice of disparaging one's views by presupposing the criticism, thus pretending that we agree on the disparaging: 'How was the talk? — You know, as usual with this guy, premised on the typical Fregean confusion of semantics with psychology', told to us in full awareness that we share the 'confusion'. I think we find this annoying because, while an assertion is presented as something we are entitled to consider and reject, a presupposition is presented as something we already know and thus are not supposed to question; if so, the annoyance expresses the intuition corresponding for the case of presupposing to the one that Williamson appeals to for assertion.

well-phrased. In the case of assertion, there are, however, important considerations telling against 'regulative norms' accounts such as the one Hindriks favors, (GA), and in favor of normative accounts. There are well-known objections to Gricean accounts of speaker-meaning in general, of which (GA) is a special case for assertoric meaning, which strongly suggest that normative accounts are preferable.[15] Thus, the clerk in the information booth uttering 'The flight will depart on time', or the victim saying to his torturer 'I did not do it', or any of us saying to our neighbor in the lift 'Nice weather, isn't it?', may well lack the Gricean intentions that (GA) requires for them to assert, but they are asserting all right; any normative account would capture this, for, no matter their intentions, they are still committed to knowing what they say (or having justification for it, or being truthful).

I think that the case of informative presuppositions that we have examined at length in the previous section similarly tells against descriptive accounts of the phenomenon, and in favor of normative ones. Independently of the source (conventional, or otherwise) of the presupposition, the most that we can say is that the speaker 'presents himself' in such cases as if he thought that the presupposed proposition was in the common ground, exactly as the clerk in the information booth presents himself as if he cared about the information that his audience might receive. None of them need to have the attitudes that descriptive accounts ascribe them, and in fact in many cases they do not have them.[16]

Let us see now how this pattern reemerges when we consider some of the additional justification that Williamson provides for his specific normative proposal. First, he notoriously relies on intuitions about lottery cases, in which, knowing that you hold a ticket in a very large lottery, I assert 'your ticket did not win' only on the basis of

---

[15] Cf. Vlach (1981); Alston (2000: ch. 2); Green (2007: ch. 3)

[16] This is why Geurt's (1999: 11) normative characterization of speaker presupposition, 'a speaker who presupposes something incurs a commitment ... regardless whether he really believes what he presupposes', which is along the right lines, is doubtfully compatible with his Stalnakerian declarations, as indicated in a previous footnote.

the high probability of the utterance's truth (Williamson 1996/2000: 246-52). (KR') predicts, in accordance with our intuitions, that the speaker is doing something wrong. But presupposing the relevant proposition, as opposed to asserting it, sounds equally objectionable in those situations: 'You can throw away that losing ticket that you bought'. Second, Williamson argues that (KR') explains what is wrong in a version of Moore's paradox with 'know' instead of 'believe': *A*, and I do not know that *A* (1996/2000: 253-4). But we can easily obtain analogues of Moorean paradoxes when the speaker is presupposing, which would be similarly explained by the account I have proposed: 'It was John who infected the PC, and I do not know that anybody infected the PC'.[17]

As in the corresponding case of assertion – assuming (KR') – given the present characterization there will be many cases in which speakers make a mistake in presupposing something that in fact is not common knowledge, while intuitively they are not to be blamed. These cases can be treated along the lines suggested by Williamson for the corresponding cases involving assertion (1996/2000: 256-9). In some cases, it is reasonable for us to think that our interlocutors and we know something, even if we in fact do not; what we do is not permissible, but it is, we feel, exculpable. In some cases, additional values (saving someone from danger, enjoying a relaxed conversation) are at stake, allowing again for exculpation based on their contextual

---

[17] We can easily think of contexts in which nothing wrong would be felt with such an utterance, by analogy with other cases described in the literature as cases of presupposition 'disappearance' or even 'cancellation', as in the following variation on an example originally given by Keenan: 'You say that somebody infected the PC. It was not me who infected it, it was not Mary who infected it, it was not John who infected it . . . in fact, I do not know that anybody infected the PC'. Given that the presuppositions of clefts are, I think, conventionally triggered (cf. n. 13), I do not accept that they can be contextually cancelled the way that conversational implicatures can. I agree with Chierchia & McConnell-Ginet's (1990: 314-5) diagnosis of these cases: the presuppositions are (semantically speaking) still there; the speaker rhetorically uses their almost direct contradiction for the purposes of challenging and eventually changing the contextual assumptions. Cf. the account of accommodation below.

relative strength. We could easily provide an account of what goes on in Donnellan's 'the king in his countinghouse' example along these lines.

To give an account of what happens in the case of informative presuppositions on the basis of the present account is straightforward. Conventionally (and semantically, on the view suggested above about the semantics/pragmatics divide), whoever utters 'Who the heck would like to see that film?' is asking a question, but the speaker is in fact asserting something. Conventionally, and semantically, an utterance of 'Paul is a good friend' is an assertion that Paul is a good friend; in some contexts, it might be perfectly clear that the speaker is not making such an assertion, but in fact one with a contrary content. Conventionally, and semantically, 'Thanks for not browsing our magazines' is an expression of gratitude, but when we find an utterance of it in the train station kiosk, we know that its utterer was doing no such thing, but in fact making a request. Conventionally, and semantically, when George Eliot writes at the beginning of *Middlemarch* 'Miss Brooke had that kind of beauty which seems to be thrown into relief by poor dress' she appears to be presupposing the existence of a specific 'Miss Brooke' naming practice, on which she relies for the purpose of identifying a person about whose kind of beauty she makes an assertion; but in fact, she is not making either the presupposing or the asserting, she is just putting her audience in a position to imagine something. Finally, speakers who utter 'I cannot come to the meeting – I have to pick up my sister at the airport' or 'I am sorry I am late – my car broke down' conventionally and semantically presuppose that they have a sister and a car, respectively, but might very well in fact be doing no such thing – they might be providing their audiences with those pieces of non-controversial background information in a conveniently non-verbose way.

This is our diagnosis of the case of informative presuppositions, vis-à-vis the triad we used above to describe Stalnaker's difficulty: (i) semantically/conventionally, a presupposition is present; (ii) the speaker is not in fact presupposing; (iii) there is nothing inappropriate in it, exactly in the way that there is nothing such in all those analogous examples of indirection we have just mentioned.[18] As Karttunen (1974: 412) puts it, 'This is one way in which we communicate indirectly, convey matters without discussing them.' Stalnaker (1973: 451; 1974: 51-2) also accounts for these cases essentially in this way. We have seen that there are serious objections to his more recent assumption that the explanations are compatible with the non-existence of the 'mysterious relation X'.

There is no direct connection between a normative account of a speech act, and the existence of conventional means for performing it. There are indirect assertions, made without using conventional means for such a purpose (as in the previous example of the rhetorical question); our account of assertion must allow for that, as Williamson's normative account – which does not require any conventions for making assertions – does. The same applies to presupposing; as we have seen, speakers might presuppose without using conventional means for that, perhaps by means of indirect mechanisms like the one Grice described for conversational implicatures, perhaps by an even less linguistically dependent reliance on the capacity for rational inference of their interlocutors (as in the World Cup 2010 example). The normative account I have provided allows for it. However, it is perfectly natural to have conventional indicators that we are subjecting our behavior to specific rules, and perhaps the development of such conventional indicators is the only evolutionarily intelligible account for the existence of such a practice. Hence, from the present point of view, it is to be expected that languages have specific resources to (by default) indicate specific acts of presupposing.

I have left for the final paragraph a brief discussion of the consequences of the present account for our views concerning the nature of assertion. As Williamson notes, an account based on the weaker rules (TR) or (RBR) seems at first sight preferable: given that those rules are satisfied whenever the knowledge rule is, but not the other way

---

18 This is essentially the picture presented by von Fintel (2008: 151), as I mentioned above: 'the sentence plainly requires the context or common ground to be such that its presuppositions are satisfied ... But ... the norms for speakers are more subtle'.

around, it provides for a practice with fewer violations of its governing rule; some knowledge rule could then perhaps be explained as derived from (TR), together with considerations not specific to assertion. However, those rules, he argues (Williamson 1996/2000: 244-5), do not individuate assertion; alternative speech acts like conjecturing, reminding or swearing also involve one or the other.

Now we can see how the correctness of the account we have given for presupposing puts strain on Williamson's account of assertion, because it suggests that (KR) runs the same risk as (TR) and (RBR) according to him do, to wit, that of not properly individuating assertion. There is a difference between the rule we have invoked in order to characterize presupposing, and the knowledge rule: presupposing requires common knowledge, while asserting, according to (KR'), merely requires knowledge. But is this enough to distinguish them? I do not think so. If (KR') truly individuates assertion, and (SpP') presupposition, then, if presupposing p were correct in a given case, asserting it would also be correct in that case – or, at least, it would not be incorrect. This is, I think, clearly not acceptable: when it is correct to presuppose p, it is incorrect to assert it (putting aside non-default cases, such as 'making conversation', and so on).

Intuitively, it is relatively clear why Williamson's account is shown to be inaccurate, given an account of presupposition like the one I have proposed: assertion (unlike judgment) is a communicative act, whose function is to put audiences in a position to gain knowledge that speakers are in a position to impart. This is in fact, ultimately, the contrast that von Fintel's 'Hey, wait a minute!' test brings out; the complaint is appropriate for presupposed contents, because the audience is presented as knowing them already; it is inappropriate for asserted contents, because they are presented as having been put forward precisely for the benefit of the audience coming to know them. The three proposed rules for assertion we have considered, (KR), (TR) and (RBR), miss this communicative aspect of assertion; as I indicated at the beginning, they are, I think, good candidates for characterizing the internal act of judging, but not the communicative act of asserting. This is what the contrast we have been examining here with presupposing brings glaringly to the fore. I have made a proposal elsewhere (García-Carpintero 2004) to capture the communicative aspect of assertion in a normative framework, but a thorough examination must remain for further work.*

References

Abbott, B. (2008). Presuppositions and common ground. *Linguistics and Philosophy, 21,* 523–538.

Abusch, D. (2010). Presupposition triggering from alternatives. *Journal of Semantics, 27,* 37–80.

Alston, W. P. (2000). *Illocutionary acts & sentence meaning.* Ithaca: Cornell University Press.

Austin, J. (1962). *How to do things with words.* Oxford: Clarendon Press. Cit. in Austin, J. (1989). *How to do things with words.* (Second edition). Oxford; New York: Oxford University Press.

Bach, K. & Harnish R. M. (1979). *Linguistic communication and speech acts.* Cambridge, MA: MIT Press.

Beaver, D. (2001). *Presupposition and assertion in dynamic semantics.* Stanford: CSLI Publications.

Boër, S. E. & Lycan, W. (1976). *The myth of semantic presupposition.* Bloomington, Indiana: Indiana Linguistics Club.

Chierchia, G. & McConnell-Ginet, S. (1990). *Meaning and grammar.* Cambridge, MA: MIT Press.

Davidson, D. (1979). Moods and performances. In Margalit, A. (Ed.). *Meaning and use.* Dordrecht: D. Reidel.

---

* Financial support for my work was provided by the DGI, Spanish Government, research project FFI2010-16049 and Consolider-Ingenio project CSD2009-00056; through the award ICREA Academia for excellence in research, 2008, funded by the Generalitat de Catalunya; and by the European Community's Seventh Framework Programme FP7/2007-2013 under grant agreement no. 238128. The article was presented at a LOGOS seminar, and at conferences in Prague, Leuven and Lisbon; I thank the audiences there for comments and suggestions. Thanks to Ambròs Domingo, Max Kölbel, Josep Macià, Teresa Marques, Sven Rosenkranz and Philipp Schlenker for helpful discussion of some topics in this review, and to Michael Maudsley for the grammatical revision.

von Fintel, K. (2004). Would you believe it? The king of France is back! (Presuppositions and truth-value intuitions). In Reimer, M. & Bezuidenhout, A. (Eds.). *Descriptions and Beyond*, (pp. 269–296). Oxford; New York: Oxford University Press.

—— (2008). What is presupposition accommodation, again? *Philosophical Perspectives, 22*, 137–170.

García-Carpintero, M. (2000). A presuppositional account of reference-fixing. *Journal of Philosophy, XCVII*(3), 109–147.

—— (2001). Gricean rational reconstructions and the semantics/pragmatics distinction. *Synthese, 128*, 93–131.

—— (2004). Assertion and the semantics of force-markers. In Bianchi, C. (Ed.). *The semantics/pragmatics distinction*, (pp. 133–66). CSLI Lecture Notes. Chicago: The University of Chicago Press.

—— (2006). Recanati on the semantics/pragmatics distinction. *Crítica, 38*, 35–8.

Geurts, B. (1999). *Presuppositions and pronouns*. Amsterdam: Elsevier.

Green, M. (2007). *Self-expression*. Oxford; New York: Oxford University Press.

Heim, I. (1983). On the projection problem for presuppositions. *Proceedings of the West Coast Conference on Linguistics 2*, 114–126.

Hindriks, F. (2007). The status of the knowledge account of assertion. *Linguistics and Philosophy, 30*, 393–406.

Kadmon, N. (2001). *Formal pragmatics*. Oxford: Blackwell.

Karttunen, L. (1974). Presuppositions and linguistic contexts. *Theoretical Linguistics, 1*, 181–194. Cit. in Davis, S. (Ed.). *Pragmatics*, (pp. 406–416). Oxford; New York: Oxford University Press.

Lackey, J. (2007). Norms of assertion. *Noûs, 41*(4), 594–626.

Levinson, S. (1983). *Pragmatics*. Cambridge: Cambridge University Press.

Lewis, D. (1979). Scorekeeping in a language game. *Journal of Philosophical Logic, 8*, 339–359. Cit. in Lewis, D. (1983). *Philosophical Papers, vol. 1*, (pp. 233–249). Oxford: Oxford University Press.

Potts, C. (2007). Conventional implicature: A distinguished class of meanings. In Ramchand, G. & Reiss, Ch. (Eds.). *Oxford Handbook of Linguistic Interfaces,* (pp. 475–501). Oxford; New York: Oxford University Press.

Searle, J. (1969). *Speech acts.* Cambridge: Cambridge University Press.

Schlenker, P. (2010). Local contexts and local meanings. *Philosophical Studies, 151*(1), 115–142.

——— (ms). Maximize presupposition and Gricean reasoning. Manuscript. URL https://files.nyu.edu/pds4/public/. Accessed on August 6th, 2010.

Simons, M. (2001). On the conversational basis of some presuppositions. In Hasting, R., Jackson, B. & Zvolensky, Z. (Eds.). *Proceedings of Semantics and Linguistic Theory 11,* (pp. 431–448). Ithaca, NY: CLC Publications, Cornell University. Ithaca, NY.

——— (2003). Presupposition and accommodation: Understanding the Stalnakerian picture. *Philosophical Studies, 112,* 251–278.

——— (ms). Presupposition without common ground. Unpublished manuscript. URL http://www.hss.cmu.edu/philosophy/faculty-simons.php accessed on August 6th, 2010.

Stalnaker, R. (1973). Presuppositions. *Journal of Philosophical Logic, 2,* 447–457.

——— (1974). Pragmatic presuppositions. In Munitz, M. K. & Unger, P. K. (Eds.). *Semantics and Philosophy.* New York: New York University Press. Cit. in Stalnaker, R. (1999). *Context and Content,* (pp. 47–62). Oxford: New York: Oxford University Press.

——— (1978). Assertion. In Cole, P. (Ed.). *Syntax and Semantics 9,* (pp. 315–332). New York: Academic Press. Cit. in Stalnaker, R. (1999). *Context and content,* (pp. 78–95). Oxford; New York: Oxford University Press.

——— (1998). On the representation of context. *Journal of Logic, Language and Information, 7,* 3–19. Cit. in Stalnaker, R. (1999). *Context and content,* (pp. 96–113). Oxford; New York: Oxford University Press.

——— (2002). Common ground. *Linguistics and Philosophy, 25,* 701–721.

——— (2008). A response to Abbott on 'Presupposition and common ground'. *Linguistics and Philosophy, 21,* 539–544.

——— (2010). Responses to Stanley and Schlenker. *Philosophical Studies, 151*(1), 143–157.

Vlach, F. (1981). Speaker's meaning. *Linguistics & Philosophy, 4,* 359–91.

Weiner, M. (2005). Must we know what we say? *Philosophical Review, 114,* 227–51.

Williamson, T. (1996). Knowing and Asserting. *Philosophical Review, 105,* 489–523. Cit. in revised version as chapter 11 of Williamson, T. (2000). *Knowledge and its limits,* (ch. 11). Oxford; New York: Oxford University Press.

Yablo, S. (2006). Non-catastrophic presupposition failure. In Thomson, J. & Byrne, A. (Eds.). *Content and modality: Themes from the philosophy of Robert Stalnaker,* (pp. 164–190). Oxford: Clarendon Press.

Emma Borg
Minimalism and the Content of the Lexicon

1 Introduction

Minimal semantics is an approach which is primarily conceived of as a theory of the meanings of natural language sentences, namely as the thesis that a complete propositional content can be recovered for any well-formed natural language sentence given only a very limited appeal to features drawn from a context of utterance (see Borg 2004, Cappelen & Lepore 2005). That is to say, according to minimalism, propositional semantic content is something which attaches to sentences largely independently of the ways in which those sentences get used. However, although it is right to think of minimalism as a theory of sentence-level contents, we need to be careful that this doesn't obscure the fact that minimalism is also committed to non-trivial claims about the meanings of the words that go together to make up those sentences.

On the one hand, of course, it is well-known that minimalism is committed to the (anti-indexicalist) claim that there are only a limited number of genuine indexicals in natural language – roughly that, while words like 'this', 'that', and 'tomorrow' qualify as genuinely (i.e. syntactically and semantically) context-sensitive expressions, words like 'man' and 'fifty-two' do not.[1] In this respect, then, it is clear from the outset that minimalism makes overt claims about word meanings. However, minimalism is also committed to the denial of a more pervasive kind of lexical context-sensitivity, one which suggests that the meanings of words in general can only be settled within a context of utterance. According to this more pervasive kind of context-sensitivity (such as is found in Travis's occasionalism or Dancy's particularism; see Travis 1989, Dancy 2004) it is not that there are more *indexicals* in natural language than we might initially have supposed. Rather it is that giving the lexical content for an expression – i.e. fixing the contribution that a word makes to a larger unit in which it occurs – is something which can only occur relative to a specific context of utterance. On the minimalist model, on the other hand, since sentences are the bearers of semantic content (not utterances) words (barring genuine indexicals) are apparently required to make the same, stable contribution to all larger linguistic units in which they occur, regardless of the context of utterance. Furthermore, since word meanings need to be the kinds of things which, when plugged into the right kind of syntactic framework, give rise to truth-evaluable content, the minimalist assumption also seems to be that word meanings are, broadly speaking, externalist content, since we need world-involving content to get us to the level of truth-evaluable content (where this second assumption is specifically challenged within the internalist semantic framework, e.g. Chomsky 2000, Pietroski 2010).[2] In this article, then, I want to explore this minimalist model of word meaning, looking at what might push us away from such a stable, world-involving picture and what response the minimalist can make to the challenges we will explore.

The structure of the article is as follows: in section 2 I will sketch a definition of minimal semantics and outline some of the reasons one might have for wanting to be a minimalist. Then in section 3 I'll turn to the most prominent objections the minimalist faces and I will

---

1 For the indexicalist position see, e.g., Stanley (2000).
2 I will use the term 'broadly externalist' to indicate that the kind of appeal to the world envisaged here may be no more than what Rey 2005 terms 'weak externalism'.

give an overview of some of the lines of defence she might pursue. We will then focus on one specific challenge, namely the argument that minimalism cannot meet what I will call the 'internal' demands on a semantic theory. Section 4 will explore these internal demands in more detail and see how they might prompt us to expect a certain kind of account of lexical content (viz. one which sees the lexical entries for even simple, apparently atomic expressions as internally complex). Section 5 will then sketch some well-known problems for the kind of move to lexical complexity contemplated in section 4 and these concerns will prompt us to look for an alternative way to accommodate the phenomena in question, one which could preserve the idea that simple terms should have simple, atomic meanings. I will label the positive account I want to suggest here 'organisational lexical semantics' (OLS) and the claim will be, first, that adopting an account of word meanings along the lines of OLS allows minimalism to meet the relevant explanatory demands here and, second, that it might also allow the minimalist to resolve certain problem cases for her theory (namely, certain cases of apparent incompleteness, to be introduced in section 3). Thus I will conclude that there is an account of lexical content open to the minimalist which meets her requirements of being world involving and potentially non-complex, and yet which is also able to do the internal explanatory work required of a successful account of lexical and, following this, sentential content.

2 What is minimal semantics?

Minimal semantics as a theory derives its existence from formal accounts of linguistic meaning which suggest that semantic content attaches to formal, syntactically described items (like sentences), rather than to utterances, and which thus hold that the contextual input to semantic content is severely constrained.[3] In the contemporary arena, minimalism has grown up in opposition to theories like

---

[3] The connection between a commitment to a formal approach to semantics and limitations on the amount of context-sensitivity permitted in a language is discussed in Borg (forthcoming: chapter 1).

contextualism (see, e.g., Recanati 2004) and occasionalism (see, e.g., Travis 1989) which predict a much more pervasive role for pragmatics within the semantic domain. So, as noted above, minimalism maintains that propositional semantic content is a property of sentences and that it can be recovered given only minimal appeal to a context of utterance. In a little more detail, then, I take minimalism to be committed to four specific claims (as laid out in Borg forthcoming: chapter 1):[4]

(i) Semantic content for sentences is truth evaluable content.

(ii) Semantic content for sentences is fully determined by syntactic structure and lexical content: the meaning of a sentence is exhausted by the meaning of its parts and their mode of composition.

(iii) There are only a limited number of context-sensitive expressions in natural language.

(iv) Recovery of semantic content is possible without access to current speaker intentions.

It is the third claim which will be of particular interest in what follows.[5] For if minimalism maintains that sentences in general are capable of expressing truth-evaluable content and that what words contribute to larger linguistic units in which they occur is largely

---

4 It should be noted that the position defined by (i)–(iv) above differs in various ways from the 'insensitive semantics' given in Cappelen & Lepore (2005); see Borg (2007), Borg (forthcoming) for details.

5 As indicated in the introduction above, this clause is ambiguous. The way it standardly appears in discussions of minimalism (e.g. Cappelen & Lepore 2005) is as the claim that natural languages do not contain vast numbers of hidden or surprise indexicals, i.e. that Kaplan was more or less right in his list of indexical and demonstrative terms. However, (iii) can also be understood in a different way, as the denial of the occasionalist claim that word meanings themselves are context-sensitive (i.e. that working out what contribution 'red' makes to a sentence in which it appears is something which can only take place given a context of utterance). It is in this latter guise that (iii) will be of particular interest in what follows.

independent of the context of utterance, this would seem to suggest a fairly specific notion of word meaning. For sentences to have the properties minimalism suggests, then, it seems that word meanings must be both world-involving (to yield truth-evaluable content for sentences) and probably atomic.[6] Yet, according to at least some theorists (e.g. Chomsky 2000) any such model of word meaning is either impossible or irrelevant.[7] However, before we come to focus on this issue of word meaning, let us ask the more general question of why anyone might want to be a semantic minimalist in the first place. What motivation might we have for holding on to the conjunction of (i)–(iv)?

An initial point to note, I think, is that minimalism provides a pretty intuitive, simple theory of semantic content, and one which does fit with at least some of the intuitions which ordinary speakers have about linguistic content. Pre-theoretically the idea that the information a given sentence conveys is simply a function of, more or less, the words it contains and the way they are put together, seems quite appealing, as does the idea that (at least some) sentences are capable of conveying information which is true or false.[8] Furthermore, given the right context (i.e. one where subjects are asked to reflect on

---

6 Word meaning is 'probably' atomic for the minimalist as this would be the easiest way to ensure that words always make the same contribution to larger linguistic units in which they occur. Of course, word meanings could be complex and we might still simply stipulate that they always contribute the same content (either the same complete complex content or the same partial content) to larger units. However, as we will see, one significant motivation for positing lexical complexity is to allow different parts of the whole to be active in different contexts (e.g. to account for polysemy) and in general, once one allows that a simple word has a complex content, it is hard to see why one would then insist that a univocal content to be contributed on all occasions.

7 In what follows I will concentrate on the argument that an account of word meanings as atomic and externalist is irrelevant as explanatorily redundant. For discussion of Chomsky's challenge to the very possibility of externalist lexical content see Borg (2009b).

8 And, of course, if the meaning of a sentence is nothing more than the meanings of its parts and their mode of composition then the kinds of systematicity and productivity data stressed in Fodor & Lepore (2002) and elsewhere will be easily explained.

'literal' or 'strict' meaning) ordinary interlocutors can and do grasp the kinds of contents minimalism predicts. We are all used to the sarcastic or uncooperative response to something we have said which picks up not on obvious features of the conveyed content but instead insists on the minimal, literal interpretation of our words (e.g. responding to an utterance of 'There's nothing to eat' by pointing out the dried biscuit at the back of the cupboard, etc.). Children, legislators and philosophers often seem to operate with precisely the kind of strict, syntax-based model of meaning which minimalism suggests, so the readings the account predicts do match some of our ordinary intuitions about linguistic content.

On the other hand, however, adopting this kind of simplistic approach to semantic content does lead the minimalist to make predictions about semantic content which diverge from the attributions which ordinary speakers make to the things they say in conversational exchanges. So, for instance, minimalism claims that the sentence 'There is nothing to eat' means that *there is nothing to eat (in some universal domain)*. Yet of course what someone conveys when they utter this sentence is likely to be a much narrower content like *there is nothing to eat in the fridge* or *there is nothing appealing to eat in the kitchen*. Furthermore, this point is entirely general: take any sentence of natural language and minimalism is likely to predict a literal meaning for it which is at odds with the content likely to be conveyed by an utterance of that sentence. So why, the question becomes now, would anyone want an account of semantic content which departs so radically from our intuitions about what is said in conversational exchanges? Well, I think the answer to this question is two-fold.

First (as I tried to argue at length in Borg (2004: §2.5) and elsewhere) there are good reasons to think that it is simply a mistake to require a *semantic* theory to be answerable to intuitions about *speech act* content, for semantic content is one kind of thing (a repeatable, codifiable, rule-governed kind of thing) while speech act content is another kind of thing altogether (a potentially unrepeatable, nebulous, context-governed kind of thing). An utterance of the sentence 'Jill went to the store' can convey that she went to the store, or that she's been to the store recently, or that because Jill went to Mrs. Smith's store today there is now milk in the fridge, or any of an indefinite number of other things. Though clearly there must be a connection between the meanings sentences have and the things we can say using them – roughly, it must be in some way because sentence *s* means that *p* that we can use it to say *q* – still there is simply no reason to believe we can isolate some one (or just a few) of the things that can be conveyed by a sentence and treat them as yielding the literal content for that sentence.[9] Speech act content is, in the jargon, a massive interaction effect and thus the project of starting with intuitions about speech act content and trying to abstract out accounts of semantic content from there is doomed from the start. So, I would urge, the fact that minimalism predicts semantic contents which diverge from intuitive attributions of speech act content is not, in and of itself, any reason to impugn the theory.

The second reason for accepting minimalism despite the fact that it sets so little store by intuitions about speech act content is that moving away from an exclusively lexico-syntactic route to semantic content (which seems to be necessary if we want a semantic theory that better fits with speaker intuitions) would leave us (with apologies to Paul Churchland) all at sea in pragmatic space. If we dissolve the syntactic walls on what counts as semantic content we will be left with no way to reconstruct any walls at all. That is to say, we will lose all distinction between literal meaning and speech act content. If we open the door to let a little bit of (non-syntactically-triggered) pragmatic content inside the citadel of semantics we will, the claim is, inevitably be overwhelmed by a tsunami of pragmatic content, eroding entirely the semantics/pragmatics distinction. For there is simply no feasible criterion for making this distinction beyond the lexico-syntactic one. Thus, to the extent that we want to preserve a distinction between literal meaning and speaker meaning at all, we

---

9 I'd reject, then, the view of Soames (2002) and Cappelen & Lepore (2005) that minimal contents are those conveyed by *every* utterance of a sentence, holding instead that the minimal proposition which gives a sentence's meaning may not be asserted at all by a speaker uttering that sentence; see Borg (2007).

should simply be sanguine about the fact that semantic content fails to track speech act content.

It seems to me then that there are reasons to want the kind of strict, syntax-driven semantics which minimalism offers us, for it possesses intuitive appeal and offers a straightforward explanation of features of our linguistic comprehension like systematicity and productivity, together with the learnability of natural language.[10] Furthermore, contrary to some claims, the idea that semantics should capture all or even a significant amount of our intuitions about speech act content is, I think, ill-conceived. Instead we should recognise that semantic content and speech act content are two very different beasts, likely to be generated in two very different ways. Finally, if we jettison the lexico-syntactic borders on semantic content it seems we will be left unable to reconstruct a semantics/pragmatics divide at all.

3 The problems for minimal semantics

It seems, then, that there are reasons to want a minimal semantics but, as many theorists have objected, there are also arguments which seem to speak strongly against minimalism. I take the three key arguments here to be: first, what we might call 'the challenge of inappropriateness', second, the challenge of incompleteness, and third, the challenge that arises from semantic internalism.[11] According to the challenge of inappropriateness, there could be such things as minimal contents (contents recovered via lexico-syntactic features alone), but any such contents would be explanatorily redundant –

---

10 An additional motivation which I would stress is that only an intention-insensitive semantics like minimalism could fit within a computational, Fodorian module for linguistic comprehension and production (see Borg 2004: chapter 2).
11 Probably the best known form of argument against minimalism is the context shifting argument, whereby a sentence which doesn't initially seem relevantly context-sensitive is nevertheless apparently shown to be context-sensitive by revealing shifts in truth value following shifts in context of utterance (see Cappelen & Lepore 2005 for a clear statement). However this kind of argument form can be, and has been, deployed in the service of all three of the different challenges identified above, thus I don't include context shifting arguments under a separate heading.

they are not psychologically real and do no useful work in a semantic theory. Thus minimal semantics, while theoretically possible, is explanatorily impotent and should thus be abandoned (see here Recanati's 'quasi-contextualism', Recanati 2004: 86). On the other hand, according to incompleteness, minimal semantics is not even theoretically possible for there are a range of perfectly well-formed (not obviously indexical) sentences which fail to express propositions prior to significant appeal to a context of utterance. Problem cases here include gradable adjectives (e.g. 'Jack is tall' doesn't seem to express a complete proposition until we know from a context of utterance what kind of thing he is supposed to be tall for), weather predicates (e.g. 'It is raining' seems true or false only once a location for the rain is contextually supplied), along with many others (such as epistemic modals and expressions like 'ready' or 'enough').

Finally, the challenge from semantic internalism (like incompleteness) seeks to show that minimal semantics is not theoretically possible by undermining the minimalist assumption that well-formed sentences express propositional, truth-evaluable contents. Not this time because certain sentences seem incomplete without contextual input, but rather because sentences (as opposed to utterances) are simply not in the game of providing true/false content at all. On the internalist model semantic content is simply not world-involving in the way minimalism assumes, thus truth is the wrong kind of property around which to base an account of semantic content. Furthermore, as we will see, internalism stresses the kind of intra-linguistic work that a successful semantic theory should be required to do and it suggests that an approach like minimalism is not up to the explanatory challenge of capturing this intra-linguistic behaviour. Thus semantic internalism also issues in a challenge to the explanatory adequacy of minimalism (as inappropriateness does).

Now in other work I've tried to show that there are moves for the minimalist to make in the face of these significant and diverse challenges. So, for instance, Borg (2007) and Borg (2009a) try to provide an explanatory role for minimal propositions, against the challenge of inappropriateness, while Borg (2004) and Borg (forthcoming) try to address the challenge from incompleteness, suggesting that the minimalist has more explanatory moves available to her in the face of putative cases of incompleteness than might initially be thought. Finally in Borg (2009b) and Borg (forthcoming) I've tried to argue, against Chomsky's arguments for semantic internalism, that a weak externalism in semantics is both possible and necessary, and thus that minimalism is warranted in incorporating an externalist account of the meaning of at least some expressions (so that, say, at least part of the semantic content of a proper name is given by the thing in the world it picks out, and at least part of the meaning of a predicate like 'red' is given by the property in the world to which it refers or by the set of objects in the world which satisfy it). However, these extant responses leave unaddressed the final challenge issued by internalism above, namely that minimalism is explanatorily inadequate as it is unable to accommodate the internal, or intra-linguistic, demands on an adequate semantic theory. Thus it is this challenge that I want to concentrate on in the remainder of this article.

4 The internalist (intra-linguistic) burden on semantics

The challenge is, then, that minimalism, with its broadly externalist assumptions about the meanings of at least certain primitive expressions and about the kinds of concepts which can be deployed within a semantic theory (e.g. reference and truth), is destined to fail to capture certain facts which any adequate semantic theory is required to capture. So what, we might ask, is this intra-linguistic burden which the minimalist is supposed to be unable to shoulder? Well, I think there are four main features which internalists want to highlight here.

First, it is clear that a semantic theory must explain both the possible and impossible readings for natural language sentences. So, consider the following well-known examples:

(1)   a. Jack is too clever to catch Jim.

       b. Jack is too clever to catch.

(2) a. Jill is eager to please.

   b. Jill is easy to please.

Here, despite the surface similarities of each pair of sentences, very different readings are required. For while Jack and Jill are the agents of (1a) and (2a) respectively, in (1b) and (2b) they do not play this role at all (with (1b) stating that Jack is too clever *for someone* to catch, while (2b) is read as claiming that Jill is easy *for someone* to please). However, if we want to explain these differences in thematic roles it looks as if we will need to appeal to more than the syntactic structure of the sentence and the denotational content of the terms involved – knowing, say, just that 'easy' picks out the property of *being easy* doesn't seem to help here (see Pietroski 2005: 263-4). Instead, then, it seems we need to know something about how the content of a term can affect the structure of a sentence, and this seems to suggest that the lexical content for the terms involved should be construed more richly than as simple word-denotation pairs.

This idea that explaining the syntactic behaviour of expressions and the readings that sentences admit of requires us to look beyond the denotational content of a term is reinforced by considering other patterns of syntactic distribution. For instance, consider the kind of evidence about English verb behaviour collected by Levin (1985, 1993), and surveyed in Pinker (2007: 103-7) (from whom the following examples are taken). First, consider conative constructions such as 'Jill cut at the rope'. Here we find that some expressions participate in the conative form while others resist it:

Claudia kicked at the cat.

Vince hit at the dog.

* Nancy touched at the cat.

* Rhonda broke at the rope

It seems that conative constructions are admissible with verbs like 'hit' or 'cut' but that they are ill-formed with verbs like 'touch' or 'break'. The difference between verbs which enter the conative ('hit', 'chip', 'chop', etc.) and those which don't ('kiss', 'pat', 'rip', 'smash', etc.) seems to be, as Pinker (2007: 103) puts it, that "the eligible verbs signify a kind of motion resulting in a kind of contact". That is to say, 'hit', 'kick' and the other participating verbs care about the *kind* of motion which precedes the contact – something is a kick or a hit not merely if it makes a specific kind of contact but also if it involves a certain kind of motion beforehand. Verbs like 'touch' and 'break' on the other hand are not sensitive in this way. All that matters for touching or breaking is the end result – the kind of contact made with an object not the movement that led to that contact. Or again, take the following alternation:

> I hit the wall with the bat.
>
> I hit the bat against the wall.
>
> She bumped the table with the glass.
>
> She bumped the glass against the table.

This alternation resists verbs of breaking and of touching:

> I cut the rope with the knife
>
> * I cut the knife against the rope.
>
> She touched the cat with her hand.
>
> * She touched her hand against the cat.

In these cases participating verbs involve motion followed by contact (as in the conative construction) but not motion followed by contact followed by a specific effect (cutting, or breaking, say), nor contact without motion, i.e. without prior change of location (as in kissing or touching). The suggestion is then that there are non-arbitrary patterns of syntactic distribution for natural language expressions (see Levin 1993 for many more examples of this kind) and, prima facie, this is the kind of thing we might expect a semantic theory to explain and predict. However, it also seems clear that a theory which treats the lexical content of expressions as exhausted by their denotational content will be unable to capture these non-arbitrary patterns. Nothing in the claim that 'cut' means *cut* seems able to explain why 'I cut at the chain' is admissible but '*I cut the knife against the chain' is not. So, simple externalist axioms for words look problematic in the face of data concerning the syntactic interactions of expressions: saying that 'easy' picks out the property of being easy, or that 'hit' picks out the property of hitting, seems totally inadequate to explain the kinds of interpretations these expressions admit of and the kinds of complex intra-lexical relations they enter into.

Furthermore, it seems that such axioms are also shown to be inadequate by consideration of certain intuitively semantic relations, such as synonymy, analyticity, entailment, and polysemy. For instance, intuitively it seems we want a semantic theory to reveal when two terms are synonymous, e.g. showing that 'vixen' means the same as 'female fox'. Clearly, however, this is something which goes beyond a straightforward appeal to denotation, since two expressions can have the same extension (indeed, necessarily the same extension) and yet still fail to be synonymous: 'cordate' and 'renate' agree in extension, yet they do not mean the same thing. So the synonymy of 'vixen' and 'female fox' can't simply be a result of the fact that every vixen is a female fox and vice versa. Rather to capture the synonymy here it seems that we want an analysis of the meaning of 'vixen' which shows it as somehow containing the elements *female* and *fox*, yet clearly this would be to reject the idea that word meanings are given simply via denotation.

Just as a broadly externalist account of word meaning seems destined to miss the synonymy of certain terms, so it will also miss the analytic nature of certain inferences. For instance, take the move from 'x is a bachelor' to 'x is an unmarried man', or from 'x is red' to 'x is coloured'. In each case the moves are intuitively analytic, they seem to be guaranteed just by the meanings of the terms involved. Yet it is not clear how this intuitive analyticity could possibly be captured by a theory that claimed that word meanings are exhausted by their referential properties, for nothing in the claim, say, that 'red' picks out the property of *redness* seems to underwrite an analytic inference from 'x is red' to 'x is coloured'. Or again, it seems we can infer from

'x chased y' to 'y was followed by x', or from 'x is a dog' to 'x is a mammal', yet any classical account of validity which looks just to the logical form of the sentences paired with the denotational properties of the expressions involved will apparently miss the intuitive validity of these arguments.

A third semantic relation which is relevant here is that of polysemy, i.e. words with a single surface presentation and multiple meanings where those meanings seem related to one another in non-arbitrary ways. So, consider the concrete and abstract senses of a term like 'book', as in 'the book weighs two pounds' versus 'the book is in every shop in the country', or the different interpretations of 'good' in 'a good car' versus 'a good child', or the different senses of 'keep' in 'keep a pet', 'keep the money' or 'keep a crowd happy' (see Jackendoff 1993: 37-9). Or again, there seems to be a quite general mechanism (sometimes referred to as 'the universal grinder') which allows a count noun to become a mass term (so, from Pinker 2007, 'she loved her cat' and 'after reversing, there was cat all over the driveway'). Prima facie, then, it seems we should expect a semantic theory to capture the relations of meaning we witness amongst polysemous terms and the general mechanisms which seem to underpin their introduction. Yet, as Pustejovsky (1995: 53-4) notes '[f]or all of these cases, [referential lexical axioms] would simply list the alternative structures along with their apparently distinct but related meanings. The fact that these senses are so related, however, suggests that this approach is missing the underlying generalization behind these syntactic forms'. Capturing these generalisations will, he suggests, push us away from a simple denotational account of word meaning and towards a view of lexical meanings as complex, structured entities.

The final problem I want to raise for the kind of simple, referential lexical axioms under consideration here is that of so-called 'impossible words': these are words which do not occur in any natural language, despite their having apparently cogent meanings. So for instance, there is no natural language verb 'to cow', such that we could say:

*It cowed a calf,

meaning that *a cow had a calf* (the example is from Hale and Keyser 1993: 60). Or again, although we can say 'Mary broke the desk', there is no verb 'blik' where 'the desk bliked Mary' means that the desk was broken by Mary. As Johnson (2004) notes:

> The absence of the word *blik* does not appear to be an accident, in the way that it is an accident that there is no noun that picks out one's tallest friends relatives. Instead, the absence of the verb *blik* appears to be due to the more general fact that whenever a transition verb of English expresses a relation between the doer of an action and the thing that is acted upon... the former is the subject of the verb and the latter is the object. (Johnson 2004: 334)

Clearly, if it is not an accident that natural language fails to contain words like 'cowed' and 'blik' then some explanation of these absences is required, but once again, if word meanings are given simply in terms of denotation, then it is unclear how we are to meet this explanatory demand. Nothing in the claim that the meaning of a verb is given by the relation in the world that it picks out reveals why, in a sentence of the form '*x* Vs *y*', *x* is always the subject and *y* is always the object.

So, the claim is that any externalist account of lexical semantics is destined to neglect the very real internalist burden on a semantic theory. That is to say, such an account will fail to predict or explain what readings can and cannot be given for sentences, it will fail to predict or explain the complex patterns of syntactic distribution we witness for natural language expressions, it will fail to capture intuitively semantic relations like synonymy, analyticity and polysemy, and it will fail to explain why 'impossible words' are impossible. When we turn to examine the work a semantic theory must do what we find is that it is not to be done by appeal to how words connect to objects (i.e. not by a semantic theory that contains lexical axioms like ['e' refers to *e*]) but rather by an appeal to the complex structures and information which lie behind the apparently simple surface form of the word. That is to say, what these arguments point towards is the need to treat word meanings not as brute, atomic entities but as complex, structured entities, allowing that the precise configuration of complex properties a word contributes to the larger unit in which it occurs can differ across different contexts of use.[12] Thus we find accounts like inferential role semantics in philosophy and lexical semantics in linguistics which treat word meanings as complex bundles of more primitive features.[13] However, rather than look now in detail at specific theories of lexical complexity and see how exactly they can accommodate the intra-linguistic burden on semantics, I want to turn instead to look at the general concerns which it seems can be raised

---

12 There is an important caveat here: in what follows I will be pursuing (and ultimately rejecting) the suggestion that to properly accommodate the internalist burden on semantics one requires complex lexical contents, rather than atomistic, externalist ones. However an alternative response (pursued by Pietroski 2010) is to treat the conceptual content required as non-complex but also non-externalist. Thus Pietroski proposes I-concepts (to be utilized within a Chomskian I-language) which are simple monadic concepts, associated with terms like 'easy' and 'eager', derived from complex concepts but stripped down to some sort of world-independent core. These I-concepts can then combine with other monadic concepts to yield the semantic content of a sentence – a non-truth-evaluable, internalist content capable of displaying genuine sensitivity to the complex linguistic interactions required by our language. It seems that the Pietroskian model would provide a model of meaning which could fit within the occasionalist approach, providing that stable, constant element of content (the element of 'white' which makes it appropriate for speaking of snow but not coal, as Travis tends to put it) but where this content falls short of determining literal truth-conditions for sentences. We thus have two available models here: on one (as in the text above) word meanings are complex, holistic things and context is required to fix or adjust the elements from that complex that are contributed to an utterance on any given occasion. On the other, word meanings are atomic, internalist things and context is required to flesh out these thin, rather spectral entities into something truly world-involving and ultimately (for complete utterances) truth-evaluable. Concerns with the Pietroskian model seem to turn on the nature of these I-concepts themselves (just what content do they have; how, for instance, should we distinguish the I-concept for 'blue' and that for 'red'?) and on the feasibility of internalist semantics itself. These concerns would take us too far afield here, thus I will not address them further in what follows (for further discussion, see Borg forthcoming: chapters 4 and 5).
13 For inferential role semantics, see Horwich (1998), Harman (1989), Brandom (2000), and for lexical semantics see Jackendoff (1983, 1993) and elsewhere, Pustejovsky (1995), Chomsky (2000), Pinker (2007), amongst many others.

for any account which endorses lexical complexity. For while such accounts undoubtedly do hold out the promise of accommodating some (or all) of the intra-linguistic burden, it seems that they may do so at a price.[14]

5 Lexical complexity: some problems and a solution

The move to treat even simple expressions as possessing complex meanings is, as noted, a well-established one, but the problems any such move faces have also been well-discussed, primarily in a series of vociferous attacks from Jerry Fodor and Ernie Lepore. A first point to note (stressed by Fodor, Fodor and Garrett 1975: 527) is what we might term 'the problem of residual meaning': that is to say, it is unclear that we can in fact dissolve simple word meanings into a conjunction of more basic parts since the meanings of most words seem to contain an undecomposable element. What, we might ask, can we add to the notion of *colour*, other than the notion of *red* itself, to get the meaning of the term 'red'? Secondly, it seems that complex meanings and simple terms are likely to display different behaviour in complex contexts. For instance, as Fodor (1970) points out, one might be tempted to define 'kill' as *cause to die*, yet while it seems fine to say that 'Mary caused Bill to die on Wednesday by shooting him on Monday', it seems far less acceptable to say that 'Mary killed Bill on Wednesday by shooting him on Monday'. Finally, the main charge which Fodor and Lepore lay at the door of theories advocating lexical complexity is that they are bound to fail compositionality constraints. If, for instance, the meaning of an expression like 'dog' contains an element like *typical pet* (as, say, prototype theory would allow), then this is an element which will not be contributed to certain larger expressions in which the term appears, such as 'wild dog'.[15] Now, of

---

14 The question of how much of the intra-linguistic burden specific theories are able to accommodate is explored somewhat further in Borg (forthcoming: ch. 5).
15 This would mean, as they argue in Fodor & Lepore (2002), that someone could know the meaning of the complex 'wild dog' *without* knowing the meaning of

course, advocates of lexical complexity have responded to these objections, arguing that Fodor and Lepore have misunderstood the nature of their accounts (see, e.g., Pinker's (2007: 100-1) objection that the analyses in lexical semantics are not akin to dictionary definitions) and have misunderstood the demands of compositionality (see, e.g., Pagin & Pelletier 2007).

However, what I want to highlight here is one underlying feature of this debate, for it is important to note that all of the objections which Fodor and Lepore level against lexical complexity concern the idea that simple words have meanings which *decompose*, i.e. that lexical complexity is synonymous with the breaking up of word meanings into simpler constituent parts. However, it seems that not all accounts of lexical complexity need take this form. For instance, the notion of meaning postulates given by Carnap (1952) is apparently an account of lexical complexity without decomposition (for on this model there are word meanings and *in addition* logical relations which serve to connect certain lexical contents, e.g. the meaning postulate that $\forall x[red(x) \rightarrow coloured(x)])$.[16] It seems entirely possible, then, to maintain the idea that simple words have simple meanings whilst allowing that the framework into which they slot is itself a complex, cross-categorising system and thus that additional lexical complexity emerges at this point (external to the meaning of a word). On this sort of model of lexical complexity, which I will label 'organisational lexical complexity' ('OLS'), the additional information emerges as part of the organisational structure of the lexicon, telling us *something about* the meaning of words but where this information is in addition to, and extraneous to, the meaning of a particular linguistic item.[17] In this way, it would be possible to adopt a broadly referential account of word meaning (in at least some cases) but posit an additional level

---

'dog', something which compositionality concerns seem to show should not be permitted.

16 For a more recent endorsement of meaning postulates, see Partee (1995).

17 To borrow Fodor's (1998: 63) terminology, the proposal is that lexical items *have* complex semantic features but not that lexical items *are* bundles of these features.

of lexical organisation which would be capable of grouping word-meaning pairs into different categories.[18] So, for instance, a noun like 'dog' could perhaps be marked as, say, +/−AGENT, +ANIMATE OBJECT (utilizing the kind of properties in play in other varieties of lexical semantics), but these properties of the expression would not constitute part of the word's meaning, indicating instead the *kind* of expression the word is by revealing the categories into which it falls. The additional content emerges then not within the meanings of words themselves but within the organisation of the lexicon.[19]

Of course, there are many questions any account like this would need to answer: most fundamentally, I think, the question of which properties figure as categorising properties of the lexicon and why? (This question is discussed somewhat further in Borg forthcoming: chapter 5.) However, even whilst acknowledging that crucial details are pending we can begin to see how such an approach might accommodate the internal burden on semantics which we outlined in the previous section. So, for instance, an advocate of OLS might seek to explain the very different meanings for 'Jack is eager to please' versus 'Jack is easy to please' by positing information associated with the key terms which would be responsible for the construction of the logical forms of sentences in which they appear. These rules would tell us (perhaps, as suggested by Kent Bach, p.c, because 'easy' is marked as a property of events and 'eager' as a property of persons)

---

18 Collins (forthcoming) briefly considers, and rejects, an apparently similar approach which he refers to as 'split lexical items'. His concern with the approach he considers is that it treats one element as giving the meaning of an expression and the other as purely non-semantic, structural information. His objection then is that structural information also contributes to our understanding of meaning for expressions. This objection would not, I think, hold against the current proposal, which sees both 'structural' and atomic elements as part of the lexicon, i.e. as part of our understanding of expressions broadly construed.

19 There are clear parallels here to the approach of 'semantic nets' in AI, see, e.g., Simmons (1973), and indeed to certain varieties of lexical semantics (namely those which preserve a clear role for the 'root' element of an expression, see Levin & Rappaport Hovav 2005 for discussion). I introduce the label 'organisational lexical semantics' not, then, because I think of the position as startlingly new, but rather because I want to make explicit the commitments of this kind of approach to lexical semantics (i.e. to stress it's anti-decompositional and structural nature).

that in ⌜*x* is easy to please⌝ we have a suppressed subject and a vocalised object, yielding the reading *it is easy for someone to please x*, while in ⌜*x* is eager to please⌝ we have a vocalised subject and suppressed object yielding the reading *x is eager to please someone*. In this way, though 'easy' simply means *easy*, and all that is required to understand the term per se is to grasp the concept of *easiness*, still full competence with the term entails understanding how the logical form of sentences containing these terms are constructed. In this way, the advocate of OLS might hope to explain possible and impossible interpretations of sentences whilst still retaining the idea that the meanings of apparently simple words are given by simple atomic concepts. Or again, it might be right to treat 'hit' as a +MANNER OF MOTION, +CONTACT expression and having these properties would see 'hit' as being assigned to the same lexical category as words like 'kick' and 'chop'. However, on the current account, it would nevertheless be possible to know the meaning of 'hit' (e.g. know that 'hit' refers to *hitting*) without knowing these additional facts (i.e. without knowing that 'hit' is a +MANNER OF MOTION verb). Someone who didn't know these additional facts would thus be likely to make mistakes about the kinds of syntactic environments in which the term could appear, e.g. mistakenly holding that 'Jack hit at Jill' is improper. But these would be errors in a subject's competence with an expression, they would not be revelatory of an error concerning their grasp of the meaning of the term. In this way, the patterns of syntactic distribution noted in section 4 could be explained and predicted on the basis of an expression's lexical category and profile, without us treating word meanings themselves as complex.[20]

---

[20] We might also note that the concern, raised at the start of this section, that definitions always miss some aspect of word meaning drops out of the picture here for, to repeat, there is nothing definitional about the current approach. Word meanings are non-decomposed primitives not definitions (dictionary or otherwise), so there is no question of something being missed in the meaning. Now, the flip side of this is obviously that we can't explain the way in which the meanings of new terms are acquired in terms of learning definitions. Thus the current picture must, it seems, follow Fodor in claiming that word meanings are not learnt. However, as Fodor himself has stressed, not being learnt is not the same thing as being there at birth. For instance, it may be that word meanings are

OLS, then, seems to hold out the promise of being able to accommodate at least some of the internalist burden on semantics, though it is also important to note that it doesn't hold out the promise of capturing it all. Specifically, the kinds of properties which have particularly exercised philosophers in this area – properties like synonymy, analyticity and entailment – are not likely to be explained (or at least explained in their entirety) on the OLS model.[21] For instance, the entailment from 'Jack is a bachelor' to 'Jack is an unmarried man' will not, on this model, be made valid either by the meanings of 'bachelor' and 'unmarried man' nor by the associated properties the expressions possess within the lexicon (for, whatever properties OLS treats as structuring properties of the lexicon, these properties will not, it seems, have the kind of content required to underpin classic analytic entailments). In these kinds of cases then, an advocate of this model would, it seems, have to follow Fodor (1998: 74) in locating the support for such moves within the world (as a necessary relationship between properties) rather than within the language (as a feature of meaning). It seems to me, however, that while recognising that this sort of structural approach to lexical complexity cannot explain everything laid at the door of an adequate semantic theory in section 4, nevertheless it can shoulder enough of the burden to rebut the claim of explanatory inadequacy here. If this is right, then an approach to sentence meaning like minimalism can still maintain that word meanings are the kinds of simple, world-involving things which, when appropriately threaded together, give rise to genuinely truth-evaluable content *without* thereby giving up on the need to explain significant aspects of the internalist burden.

In closing, then, I'd like to note one final feature of the OLS model which might be attractive to the would-be semantic minimalist, for such an approach seems to hold out the promise of a distinctive explanation of certain instances of the problem of incompleteness

---

acquired through our transactions with the world, which trigger the acquisition of concepts, in which case word meanings are not learnt but neither are they innate (in the sense of 'being there from birth').

21 For discussion of the inferences an OLS model might be able to capture see Borg (forthcoming: ch. 5).

(as raised in section 3). Recall that the challenge of incompleteness is that there are well-formed (not relevantly indexical) sentences which nevertheless apparently fail to express complete propositions prior to the provision of information from a context of utterance. So consider 'Jack is ready': here it seems that the content delivered by the syntactically realised elements of the sentence (the words 'Jack', 'is' and 'ready' plus the sentence structure) fail to deliver a complete proposition. The problem is that the content *Jack is ready* is held not to be a genuine propositional content – it is thought not to be truth-evaluable until we know, from the context of utterance, just what Jack is ready to do. Yet, according to the minimalist, this sort of contextual contribution to propositional semantic content is outlawed unless 'ready' is (as seems unlikely) a genuine indexical.

It seems, however, that the minimalist who embraces something like OLS might pursue a different analysis of the problem here. For OLS could allow that 'ready', although its meaning is simply given by the property in the world to which it refers, is nevertheless categorised within the lexicon as a two-place expression. That is to say, it *requires*, as part of its lexical grouping, both a subject and an object. If this were the case then, although the second argument might remain unvocalised at the surface level (as in the above example) nevertheless it would still be marked at the level of logical form, being placed there via the properties of the expression type (as marked by its lexical categorisation). What we would have at the level of logical form for the sentence in question is then something akin to *there is something/some event for which jack is ready*.

There may, however, be an immediate concern here, for one might object that this kind of move cannot be consistent with a position like minimalism. Instead this idea of unvocalised syntactic material may be thought to be part and parcel of views opposed to minimalism like indexicalism and contextualism. However, I think this kind of concern is in fact ungrounded. A first point to note is that the kind of move suggested above would not be equivalent to treating 'ready' as an indexical, for on this model 'ready' always makes exactly the same contribution to any larger unit in which it occurs, it never literally means *ready for lunch* in one context and *ready to take the exam* in another. Instead such enriched readings will always, just as minimalism predicts, count as pragmatically conveyed contents rather than as literal meanings. A second point to note is that minimalism should not be construed as the thesis that all semantically relevant material must be explicitly represented at the surface level – after all this kind of view would be shown to be false by any genuine instance of ellipsis (e.g. the question and answer context where *A* asks 'Does Jack like dogs?' and *B* replies 'Jack does', thereby expressing the proposition that *Jack does like dogs*). Instead it seems to me that minimalism should be understood primarily by the claims, first, that lexicon and syntax fully determine propositional semantic content and, second, that not all or even almost all expressions are indexicals or context-sensitive in other, less overt ways. Furthermore it should rule out one-off intuitions about speech act content as providing legitimate reasons for making semantic or syntactic claims. Yet all of these claims are consistent with the adoption of the kind of OLS manoeuvre considered above.

Minimalism, as I construe it, was born in the movement to treat context-shifting arguments as irrelevant in discussions about the determination of semantic content. Yet what might motivate a move, via OLS, to allow hidden context-insensitive argument places with respect to expressions like 'ready' is certainly *not* a desire to cleave more closely to judgements of speech act content. Rather it would be a desire to capture correctly the syntactic behaviour of these expressions, recognising that simple, externalist lexical entries cannot be the whole story in accounts of the content of the lexicon. Yet once we recognise that, to do what a theory of lexical semantics needs to do (in terms of capturing data about possible and impossible readings, syntactic distribution, etc.) we need an additional level of lexical complexity, then the door is at least open to a minimalist account which takes seriously certain intuitive judgements of language users (namely the incompleteness intuitions appealed to in section 3).[22]

---

22 Furthermore, note that the intuitions which are relevant here are not the kind of one-off, on-the-fly intuitions about speaker meaning appealed to in context-shifting arguments. Rather they are type-level intuitions about the meanings

Finally, note also that the claim that these additional argument places are not obvious at the surface level is only partially correct. Of course they are not explicitly vocalised but, on the OLS account, they are explicitly provided by the terms in the sentence: it is because 'Jack is ready' contains the two-place expression 'ready' that it is to be understood as *Jack is ready for something*. Thus adopting this kind of OLS move takes us, it seems, only a very small step indeed away from the idea that minimalism takes the semantic content of a sentence to be something which can be read straight from its surface form.

6 Conclusion

As noted at the outset of this article, minimal semantics is a theory of sentence-level contents yet, clearly, any view about the nature of sentence meanings will have significant repercussions for one's view of word meanings. Specifically, for the minimalist, the contribution a term makes to a larger linguistic unit in which it occurs must (generally) be context-independent and word meanings must be world-involving (to make it possible for sentences to express truth-evaluable content). However, this view of lexical content (as atomic, broadly externalist content) is challenged by what I've here called the internalist or intra-linguistic burden on semantics. That is to say, the minimalist model of word meaning seems destined to fail to explain features like the possible and impossible readings of sentences, the apparently non-arbitrary patterns of syntactic distribution which words display, the impossibility of certain words in natural languages, and paradigm semantic relations like synonymy, analyticity and polysemy. Instead it may be thought that what is required to explain these kinds of features is a notion of word meanings as bundles of simpler features such as is found in lexical semantics or in inferential role semantics. Yet any such model seems to sit uncomfortably within a minimalist

---

of terms in our language (e.g. our sense that 'ready' is incomplete without two arguments) and it is clear that even the most austere formal semantic theory will need to let in some kind of appeal to what speakers think about and do with their words in the course of constructing a lexicon for a natural language (see Borg 2005).

framework, where words always make a constant contribution to larger units, irrespective of the context they find themselves in. Such a move also faces independent worries, such as those raised by Fodor and Lepore concerning the apparent impossibility of defining words and the difficulty of meeting compositionality constraints.

Instead, then, I've tried to sketch an alternative variety of lexical complexity here, one which turns on lexical organisation rather than on lexical decomposition. I've argued that any such model would fit comfortably within the overarching minimalist framework (maintaining the idea that the meaning of a simple broadly referential expression is simple and broadly referential) whilst still allowing the minimalist to capture (at least a significant proportion of) the internalist burden. Furthermore, as noted in closing, such an approach might be of additional benefit to the minimalist since it might allow her to pursue an alternative explanatory route in the face of certain cases of putative incompleteness, arguing that, for some expressions, the appearance of incompleteness is only superficial since features of the expression's lexical category ensure additional argument places at the level of logical form. To conclude, then, though it is right to think that minimalism makes certain assumptions about the nature of word meanings, it is wrong, I believe, to suggest that these assumptions necessarily result in an explanatorily inadequate semantic theory. Minimalism can, via an approach like OLS, capture that part of the internalist explanatory burden which it may be truly correct to lay at the door of semantics.

References

Borg, E. (2004). *Minimal semantics*. Oxford: Clarendon Press.
—— (2005). Intention-based semantics. In Lepore, E. & Smith, B. (Eds.). *The Oxford Handbook of Philosophy of Language*, (pp. 250–267). Oxford; New York: Oxford University Press.
—— (2007). Minimalism versus contextualism in semantics. In Preyer, G. & Peter, G. (Eds.). *Context sensitivity and semantic minimalism: essays on semantics and pragmatics*, (pp. 546–571).

Oxford; New York: Oxford University Press. Reprinted in Ezcurdia, M. and Stainton, R. (Eds.). *The semantics-pragmatics boundary in philosophy*. Oxford: Oxford University Press.

———— (2009a). Minimal semantics and the nature of psychological evidence. In Sawyer, S. (Ed.). *New waves in philosophy of language*, (pp. 24–40). Palgrave.

———— (2009b). Must a semantic minimalist be a semantic internalist? *Proceedings of the Aristotelian Society, Supplementary Volume LXXXIII*, 31–51.

———— (forthcoming). *Pursuing Meaning*. Oxford; New York: Oxford University Press.

Brandom, R. (2000). *Articulating reasons: An introduction to inferentialism*. Cambridge, MA: Harvard University Press.

Cappelen, H. & Lepore, E. (2005). *Insensitive semantics*. Oxford: Blackwell.

Carnap, R. (1952). Meaning postulates. *Philosophical Studies, 3*, 65–73.

Collins, J. (forthcoming). Impossible words again; or why beds break but not make. *Mind & Language*.

Chomsky, N. (2000). *New horizons in the study of language and mind*. Cambridge: Cambridge University Press.

Dancy, J. (2004). *Ethics without principles*. Oxford; New York: Oxford University Press.

Fodor, J. and Garrett, M. (1975). The psychological unreality of semantic representations. *Linguistic Inquiry, 4*, 515–531.

Fodor, J. (1970). Three reasons for not deriving 'kill' from 'cause to die'. *Linguistic Inquiry 1*(4) (October 197), 429–438.

———— (1998). *Concepts: Where cognitive science went wrong*. Oxford; New York: Oxford University Press.

———— (2000). *The mind doesn't work that way*. Cambridge, MA: MIT Press.

Fodor, J. & Lepore, E. (2002). *The compositionality papers*. Oxford; New York: Oxford University Press.

Hale, K. & Keyser, S. (1993). On argument structure and the lexical expression of syntactic relations. In Hale, K. and Keyser, S. (Eds.). *The view from building 20: essays in honour of Sylvain Bromberger*, (pp. 53–110). Cambridge, MA: MIT Press.

Horwich, P. (1998). *Meaning*. Oxford; New York: Oxford University Press.
Jackendoff, R. (1983). *Semantics and cognition*. Cambridge, MA: MIT Press.
—— (1993). *Languages of the mind: Essays on mental representation*. Cambridge, MA: MIT Press.
Levin, B. & Rappaport Hovav, M. (2005). *Argument realization*. Cambridge: Cambridge University Press.
Pagin, P. (2006). Meaning holism. In Smith, B. & Lepore, E. (Eds.). *The Oxford handbook of philosophy of language,* (pp. 213–232). Oxford; New York: Oxford University Press.
Pagin, P. & Pelletier, J. (2007). Content, context and composition. In Preyer, G. and Peter, G. (eds.). *Context sensitivity and semantic minimalism: Essays on semantics and pragmatics,* (pp. 25–62). Oxford; New York: Oxford University Press.
Partee, B. (1995). Lexical semantics and compositionality. In Osherson, D. (General Ed.). *Invitation to Cognitive Science*. In Gleitman, L. & Liberman, M. (Eds). *Part I: Language,* (pp. 311–360). 2nd edition. Cambridge: MIT Press.
Pietroski, P. (2005). Meaning before truth. In Preyer, G. & Peter, G. (Eds.). *Contextualism in philosophy: Knowledge, meaning, and truth,* (pp. 255–302). Oxford; New York: Oxford University Press.
—— (2010). Concepts, meanings and truth: First nature, second nature and hard work. *Mind & Language, 25*(3), 247–278.
Pinker, S. (2007). *The stuff of thought*. London: Penguin.
Pustejovsky, J. (1995). *The generative lexicon*. Cambridge, MA: MIT Press.
Recanati, F. (2004). *Literal meaning*. Cambridge: Cambridge University Press.
Rey, G. (2005). Mind, intentionality and inexistence. *Croatian Journal of Philosophy, 5*, 389–415.
Stanley, J. (2000). Context and logical form. *Linguistics and Philosophy, 23*, 391–424.
Travis, C. (1989). *The uses of sense: Wittgenstein's philosophy of language*. Oxford; New York: Oxford University Press.

— 4 —

Anne Bezuidenhout

Contextualism and Information Structure: Towards a Science of Pragmatics

1 Introduction

In a recent article (Bezuidenhout 2009), I argue that the debate between contextualists and minimalists is largely terminological and that people in these two camps are mostly arguing at cross-purposes. The most plausible versions of contextualism are empirical theories concerned to give an account of the processes involved in natural language production and comprehension. Many minimalists, on the other hand, are diehard anti-psychologists, who believe that formal semantics can and should be conducted without reference to psychology. However, some minimalists, such as Borg (2004), have tried to take on contextualists on their own turf, by arguing for a form of psychological minimalism. In the article mentioned above, I laid out both conceptual and empirical evidence against psychological minimalism. Conceptually, when one explores the idea of a minimal meaning or concept, it dissolves into incoherence. On the empirical side, far from its being the case that contextualist processes lead to a breakdown in communication, as has been claimed by Cappelen &

Lepore (2005), it is when communicators are prevented from relying on anything but minimal meanings that comprehension breaks down.

In this current article, I continue to explore some of the empirical grounds for thinking that language comprehension depends crucially on contextual processes. I hope to show that if one takes information-structural facts into consideration (i.e., facts about how information is 'packaged' in a particular communication), principles emerge that can explain how comprehenders can so rapidly and generally unerringly understand what a speaker is saying. Bezuidenhout (2009) showed how conversational topic constrains pragmatic modulation. Here I focus on the role of discourse coherence relations in such modulation. In particular, I show that discourse relations can help resolve ambiguities, play a role in pronoun reference resolution, and guide pragmatic enrichment processes.

A secondary aim is to establish that these influences are systematic and amenable to scientific investigation. I trust it is clear why it is interesting and important if I can convince the reader of this. It would show that pragmatic modulation is a constrained process, not some sort of 'anything goes' process where a speaker can make things up at whim, as Cappelen & Lepore (2005) have suggested is the problem with contextualist processes. In section 2, I lay out the evidence that knowledge of discourse relations constrains pragmatic modulation. In section 3, I answer some minimalist objections that could be raised against my claims to have shown that pragmatic modulation is affected systematically by discourse-level factors and that it is amenable to scientific investigation.

2 The role of discourse relations

Discourse coherence relations are relations holding between the contents of consecutive utterances in a conversation. These relations are sometimes explicitly signaled by discourse connectives, which give comprehenders a clue as to how the utterances in a discourse are hooked up to each other. Discourse connectives are words and phrases such as 'however', 'yet', 'nevertheless', 'after all', 'since', 'because', 'so', 'as a result', etc. In some cases, information about discourse coherence relations is implicit in the conversational context and must be inferred from other background information, such as knowledge about the type of conversational context that is currently operative – is this for example a context in which someone is narrating a series of events or is the speaker attempting to give an explanation for something or is she attempting to justify her behavior? But whether implicitly or explicitly signaled, what discourse coherence relations do is to relate the content of one utterance to the content of another either as a reason for, or an elaboration on, or a contradiction of, etc. what has previously been conveyed. Different theorists have identified different sets of coherence relations, but most theorists' lists contain at least a subset of the following relations: EXPLANATION, RESULT or CONSEQUENCE, EVIDENCE, NARRATION, ELABORATION, BACKGROUND, VIOLATED EXPECTATION, PARALLEL, and CONTRAST. See Hobbs (1979), Mann & Thompson (1988), Asher & Lascarides (1996), Kehler (2000).[1]

In particular, what I hope to show is that discourse coherence considerations constrain processes of disambiguation, pronoun resolution and free enrichment. I will discuss these three pragmatic processes in order.

Disambiguation

It is relatively easy to show that knowledge of discourse relations can help resolve *lexical* ambiguities. For example, Asher & Lascarides (1996) show how discourse-level information can interact with lexical information in the process of lexical disambiguation. Consider the following two discourses:

(1) The judge asked where the defendant was. His barrister apologized, and said he was at the pub across the street. The court bailiff found him slumped underneath *the bar*.

---

1 Hobbs (1979) introduced the label 'coherence relation'. However, other expressions have been used in the literature, including 'rhetorical relation' and 'discourse relation'. I will treat these as synonymous expressions.

(2) The judge asked where the defendant was. His barrister apologized, and said he was at the pub across the street. But in fact the court bailiff found him slumped underneath *the bar*.

Asher and Lascarides argue that the ambiguous term 'bar' will be resolved in favor of the pub meaning in case (1), because this is a narrative story, and if we see the sentences in the discourse as connected via the relation NARRATION, we will assume that the events are described in their temporal sequence and the last mentioned location of the defendant was the pub. On the other hand, the speaker's use of 'but' in (2) signals that an assumption is being challenged. Thus the contents of the discourse segments will be related via the rhetorical relation VIOLATED EXPECTATION. In this case the term 'bar' will be interpreted in its courtroom sense, since the pub location will have been ruled out as the defendant's location.

It is also possible to use discourse-level information to resolve *structural* ambiguities. Take, for example, sentences containing prepositional phrases that exhibit high versus low attachment ambiguities, as in (3) below:

(3) John shot the man with the rifle.

This is ambiguous as to whether the prepositional phrase (PP) contains information about the instrument of the action of shooting (high attachment) or whether it modifies the NP 'the man' (low attachment) – the 'high' and 'low' referring to whether the PP is attached to a node higher or lower in the tree structure. (See Figure 4.1 below)

Consider the following two contexts. In (4), the relation of RESULT holds between the two utterances and the structural ambiguity is resolved in favor of the low attachment option. In (5), the relation of NARRATION holds and the ambiguity is resolved in favor of the high attachment option:

(4) John shot the man with the rifle. (So) he dropped the rifle and ran.

High attachment

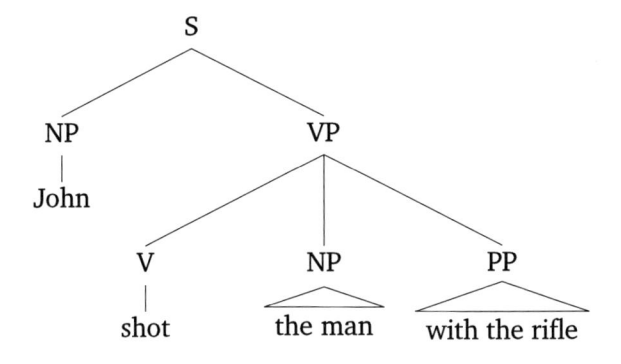

Low attachment

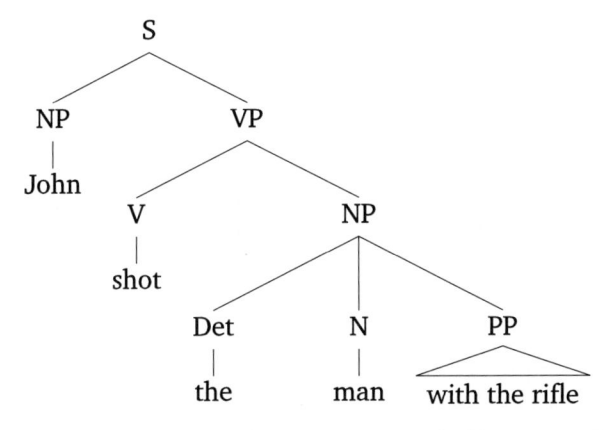

Figure 4.1: Structure trees showing prepositional phrase attachment ambiguity.

(5) John shot the man with the rifle. (Then) he dropped the rifle and ran.

In these cases it is not only the structural ambiguity that must be resolved. The referent of the 'ambiguous' pronoun 'he' in the second clauses of (4) and (5) must be resolved too.[2] One could argue that once the pronoun reference is resolved correctly, the structural ambiguity is automatically resolved. This is true. However, the fact that 'he' gets resolved in these ways is due to information about which discourse coherence relation holds between the events described in the two clauses, as will be demonstrated more fully in the following section. Thus, knowledge of discourse coherence relations can aid structural ambiguity resolution, even if only indirectly.

Pronoun resolution

In my discussion of pronoun resolution, I will confine my attention to deictic and simple anaphoric uses of pronouns. To resolve the reference of a pronoun, the interpreter has to select an appropriate referent from the set of entities available in the discourse context. A speaker's use of a pro-form such as 'he' or 'she' to refer to an entity carries a presupposition that the referent is at least weakly familiar. An entity is weakly familiar if knowledge of its existence is part of the conversational common ground or is entailed by information in that common ground.[3] See Roberts (2004) for details.

---

2 In the psychological literature that I discuss below, it has become standard to talk of pronoun ambiguity when there are two or more candidate referents in the context that match the semantically encoded gender and number information associated with the pronoun. In the case of (4) and (5), John and the man both possess the features [+male][+singular] that are semantically associated with 'he'. I prefer the term 'referential indeterminacy', but will continue to talk of pronominal ambiguity, so that my usage conforms to that in the literature I am relying on in this present discussion.

3 I will set aside for the time being issues having to do with informative presuppositions and the vexed issue as to whether we need to invoke a notion of presupposition accommodation to account for such presuppositions. This would matter if there were felicitous cases of pronoun uses that referred to entities that were not weakly familiar before the time of utterance.

Now, there may be several entities in the discourse context that are weakly familiar. However, they probably will not all be equally salient at any one moment. Linguists generally agree that, at any moment in a conversation, discourse entities can be ranked in order of salience and that by using a pro-form a speaker is signaling an intention to refer to the highest ranked member of this set. This is one of the central ideas in Centering Theory, a computational linguistic framework for understanding how conversational topics are established and then maintained or shifted as a conversation evolves. See Grosz et al. (1995) for details. Gundel et al. (1993) also defend the idea of salience rankings of discourse entities. They propose a Givenness Hierarchy (GH); this specifies the appropriate form of expression to use to refer to an entity, depending on the entity's position in the GH. When a speaker uses a pro-form, she signals to the audience that the referent is not merely weakly familiar (which would license the use of a definite expression such as a proper name or definite description) but currently in focus. The idea of a salience ranking of entities and an associated ranking of types of referring expressions is defended also in Ariel (1990).

For current purposes it is not necessary to adjudicate the merits and demerits of these competing proposals. What I am taking from these various theorists is just the idea that not all discourse entities are equally salient at any one moment in a conversation and that if a speaker chooses to use a pronoun, the assumption is that the referent is highly salient to the audience at that point in the conversation. So to resolve the pronoun's reference, the audience must pick the currently most salient discourse entity. What I am interested in here are the factors at work making one entity more salient than all others at any one moment. I am going to suggest that a consideration of discourse coherence is one such factor.

In this article I am trying to show that discourse coherence relations play a role in various sorts of pragmatic processes. I am *not* claiming that discourse coherence is the only factor at work. There are many other factors that have to be taken into consideration. For example, I already noted that Bezuidenhout (2009) discusses the role of conversational topic in pragmatic modulation. When it comes to pronoun resolution, many factors have been proposed to play a role in making an entity salient.

For instance, Gernsbacher & Hargreaves (1988) showed that the first-mentioned entity in a discourse enjoys a processing advantage. A competing effect is the so-called recency effect, which gives a boost to the last-mentioned entity, presumably because the activation of information about that entity in working memory lingers temporarily. Others, such as Gordon et al. (1993), have shown that the grammatical category of the expression used to refer to an entity has an effect on salience. Entities referred to by subject expressions seem more salient than those referred to by direct or indirect object expressions, at least in English. This is presumably because, in English, subject position is the default position for placing information that is currently topical, and topical entities are salient.

There are other linguistic and paralinguistic means to bring entities into the foreground and into focus. Speakers use a variety of focusing mechanisms, such as cleft constructions, as well as strategies such as the preposing (left-dislocation) of expressions, the use of contrastive stress or special intonation contours, etc. Some examples are given below:

It-cleft: 'It was Mary who broke the vase.'
   This brings Mary into focus.

WH-cleft: 'What Mary broke was the vase.'
   This brings the vase into focus.

Left-dislocation: 'Mary, she is someone you can trust.'
   This brings Mary into focus.

Contrastive stress: 'MARY you can trust.'
   This brings Mary into contrastive focus with some other (less trustworthy) discourse entity.

Rising intonation contour: 'You can trust Mary.'

This brings Mary's trustworthiness into contrastive focus with other of Mary's features (e.g., her likeableness: 'You can trust Mary even though she's not very likeable').

Such information-structural considerations have been thoroughly discussed by linguists such as Birner & Ward (1998), Erteschik-Shir (2007), Lambrecht (1994).

Semantic information, such as the thematic role of the entity, has an effect on salience too. An entity that plays the agent role may in certain contexts be more salient than one that plays a patient role, regardless of the grammatical category of the expression used to refer to the agent (that is, agency can make an entity salient whether the entity is referred to by a subject or object expression). Similarly, the stimulus that brings about an experiential state in an individual may in certain contexts (such as explanatory contexts) be more salient than the experiencer. And in contexts where a transfer is enacted, the goal entity may be more salient than the source entity.

The way in which information about thematic roles helps in pronoun resolution has been experimentally investigated in the context of what has become known as the 'implicit causality bias' of certain 'interpersonal' verbs. One of the first such studies was reported by Garvey & Caramazza (1974) and there is still a thriving literature on the topic. Articles addressing the issue of implicit causality and pronoun resolution include Brown & Fish (1983), Au (1986), Garnham et al. (1992), McKoon et al. (1993), Gordon & Scearce (1995), Stevenson et al. (2000), Arnold (2001), Koornneef & van Berkum (2006) and Kehler et al. (2007).

Many of these studies have collected data using various permutations on a basic completion task. Participants are asked to supply completions for fragments of the following form, where 'V' is a transitive verb belonging to the class of 'interpersonal' verbs:[4]

(6)　　John V'ed Sam because he _____.

---

[4] These verbs have been a target of implicit causality studies because many of those engaged in this research are social psychologists, although more recently cognitive psychologists have become interested in the issue too.

Some studies have used discourse connectives other than 'because', such as 'so', 'and', 'whereupon', and 'next'. And some have included a condition in which no discourse connective is used and there is a full stop before the pronoun. The clause prior to the one containing the pronoun always introduces two characters into the discourse. In most studies these are characters of the same gender, so that the following pronoun is 'ambiguous'. However, some studies use characters of different genders so that the pronoun is unambiguous, since the gender information semantically associated with the pronoun provides the information needed for resolving the referent of the pronoun (on the assumption that the referent is one of the two individuals introduced by the previous sentence, and not some third discourse entity). In some studies the fragments may be embedded in slightly longer scene-setting discourses.[5]

The 'interpersonal' verbs of interest include both transitive action verbs (which introduce events that have both an Agent and a Patient) and transitive state verbs (which introduce states that involve both a Stimulus and an Experiencer). The state verbs used in implicit causality studies are transitive verbs that belong to the class of what Levin (1993) calls psych-verbs. She writes: 'The transitive psych-verbs ... fall into two classes according to whether the experiencer is the subject (the *admire* verbs) or the object (the *amuse* verbs).' (Levin 1993: 189) On the other hand, the action verbs that have been studied belong to the class of what Levin (1993) calls judgment verbs, and include verbs such as *criticize, forgive, mock, praise* and *scold*.

In experiments using the basic completion task, it has been found that with psych-verbs of the *amuse* sub-class, people are more likely to construct completions where the pronoun is taken to co-refer with

---

5 And some studies have ended the fragment with the discourse connective (i.e., have not included the pronoun). In these studies, the completions supplied by participants include ones that contain no pronouns, as well as ones that contain no expressions that refer back to either of the two characters mentioned in the first clause. Nevertheless, when some sort of singular referring expression *is* used, the experimenter can look to see how frequently such expressions are used to refer to either the subject entity or the object entity introduced by the first clause. (See next note).

the subject of the preceding clause, whereas with verbs of the *admire* sub-class, it is more likely that the pronoun is taken to co-refer with the object of the preceding clause. This indicates which of the entities people are more likely to assume is causally responsible for the state described in the first clause. Thus verbs in the former sub-class are said to be NP1-biased verbs and the latter to be NP2-biased verbs, meaning that the former have an implicit causality bias that favors the subject entity as the cause, whereas the latter sub-class is biased towards the object entity as the cause.[6]

Brown & Fish (1983) argue that these findings support their hypothesis that the implicit causality bias of such state verbs favors the entity that plays the thematic role of Stimulus. As can be seen from the examples, below, NP1 biased verbs are ones where the subject is the Stimulus, whereas NP2 verbs are ones where the object is the Stimulus. So the Thematic Role account seems more fundamental than an appeal to subject- versus object-entity biases.

(7) NP1 bias: John$_{(Stimulus)}$ amused Paul$_{(Experiencer)}$ because he _____.

(8) NP2 bias: John$_{(Experiencer)}$ admired Paul$_{(Stimulus)}$ because he _____.

Brown & Fish (1983) also predicted that the action verbs they studied would show an NP1 bias, and they argued that the underlying explanation in this case was that Agents are preferred as causes. In completion tasks where participants saw fragments such as the following, they were more likely to construe the pronoun as referring to the subject:

(9) NP1 bias: John$_{(Agent)}$ harmed Paul$_{(Patient)}$ because he _____.

---

[6] By 'subject entity' I mean the entity referred to by the proper name occupying subject position in the first clause. Similarly for the term 'object entity'.

Again, the thematic role explanation seems more fundamental than an explanation that appeals to grammatical category biases, such as subject or object biases.

With respect to the class of interpersonal action verbs, completion tasks have not always supported Brown & Fish's (1983) finding that these verbs show an NP1 bias. Au (1986), for example, found that some of these verbs in fact show an NP2 bias. Her own diagnosis is that these action-verbs fall into two sub-categories, depending on whether they describe actions that are performed in response to an earlier action of the Patient or are ones that could be spontaneously initiated by the Agent. Thus in (9) it is plausible to imagine that John initiated the action of harming Paul without any provocation from Paul. However, in (10) below, in order for John to felicitously praise Paul, Paul must have done something praiseworthy, and so John can be seen as reacting to rather initiating something.

(10) NP2 bias: John$_{(Reactor)}$ praised Paul$_{(Prompt)}$ because he _____ .

In addition to completion tasks, studies of implicit causality have also used probe tasks, as well as reading and listening tasks using various 'online' data collection methods, including self-paced reading, eye-movement monitoring, ERP monitoring, and eye tracking using the Visual World paradigm.

In probe studies, participants are presented with completed sentences based on the sorts of frames illustrated in (7)–(10) above. At various points (such as after the discourse connective, after the pronoun, or at the end of the sentence), participants are presented with the name of one of the characters introduced in the first clause (John or Paul in my examples). The time it takes people to judge whether that name occurred earlier in the sentence is measured. It has been found that people take longer to identify the name of a character if that character is not the one supported by the implicit causality bias of the verb. That is, for NP1 biased verbs, people are facilitated in identifying the name of the subject entity, whereas with

NP2 verbs the facilitation favors the name of the object-entity. See McKoon et al. (1993).

Garvey & Caramazza (1974) hypothesized that if sentences containing biased verbs are presented with completions going against the implicit causality bias of these verbs, people will take longer to process these sentences compared with ones whose completions support the implicit bias. Consider the following pair of sentences:

(11) The mother punished her daughter because she admitted her guilt.

(12) The mother punished her daughter because she discovered her guilt.

Both (11) and (12) are coherent sentences. However, 'punish' is an NP2-biased verb. So, given that the pronoun 'she' in (12) is co-referential with the *subject* term in the first clause, (12) is resolved in a way that goes against the implicit causality of 'punish'. Subsequent studies using methods that allow measures of online processing have confirmed Garvey & Caramazza's prediction that sentences such as (12) take longer to process than sentences such as (11). For example, the G-C prediction has been confirmed in online production tasks by Guerry et al. (2006), in self-paced reading tasks by Stewart et al. (2000), in an eye movement monitoring study by Koornneef & van Berkum (2006), and in an ERP study by Ferretti et al. (2009), although the last-mentioned study was focused on transfer verbs (such as 'give' and receive') rather than the interpersonal verbs discussed above.

Although this does not get discussed as much, Au (1986) also looked at biases for *consequences* in addition to biases for causes. This has been picked up more recently by Stewart et al. (2000) and Crinean & Garnham (2006). By focusing on sentences using the discourse connective 'because', most studies have ignored biases for consequences. Using a different connective may bring out a different bias. Thus consider these variants of (7)–(10):

(7*) John$_{(Stimulus)}$ amused Paul$_{(Experiencer)}$ so he _____ .

(8*) John₍Experiencer₎ admired Paul₍Stimulus₎ so he _____.

(9*) John₍Agent₎ harmed Paul₍Patient₎ so he _____.

(10*) John₍Reactor₎ praised Paul₍Prompt₎ so he _____.

Here the use of the discourse connective 'so' points to what resulted from the state or event described in the first clause, and thus people are likely to focus on the entity that was acted on (namely the Experiencer or the Patient).[7] One might think that the consequence bias is just the opposite of the causality bias, so that verbs with an NP1 causality bias will have an NP2 consequence bias and vice versa. And, in fact, in experiments using completion tasks, this is just what is found for the psych-verbs illustrated in (7*) and (8*).

However, the action verbs behave a little differently. The ones belonging to the 'harm' sub-category, which have an NP1 causality bias (in favor of Agents), do indeed have an NP2 consequence bias (in favor of Patients). But Crinean & Garnham (2007) provide evidence that the verbs belonging to the 'praise' sub-category pattern differently. They have both an NP2 causality bias *and* an NP2 consequence bias. Crinean & Garnham explain this by positing that 'praise'-type verbs blend features of both action verbs and psych-verbs. The subject of a 'praise'-type verb (in active form) refers to an entity that is a reactor, and in that sense the subject entity is a little like an Experiencer, who is acted on by a Stimulus, explaining why these verbs have an NP2 causality bias. On the other hand, the subject entity also plays an agentive role, since reacting still is a form of acting. Hence the object entity is acted upon. Thus the consequence bias will favor the object entity, resulting in an NP2 consequence bias.

---

7 Stevenson et al. (2000) found that their participants did not always construe 'so' as indicating the relation RESULT, but sometimes construed it as short for 'so that' and thus as indicating the relation PURPOSE. E.g., 'John handed the plate to Bob so _____' might be completed either as 'John handed the plate to Bob so he put it in the dishwasher' (RESULT) or as 'John handed the plate to Bob so that he could balance his glass on it' (PURPOSE). Either way, the pronoun is resolved in favor of NP2 for a transfer verb such as 'handed to'.

The claim made by many of those who believe that interpersonal verbs carry causality and consequence biases, is that these biases help resolve pronoun reference, because the bias focuses one of the arguments of the verb. However, as should be plain from the above discussion, it is not the verb bias by itself that does the focusing, but this bias together with the discourse coherence relation indicated by the discourse connective. Whether it is the causality or consequence bias that will operate depends on the use of 'because' or 'so'. Once the bias is triggered, this will focus either the subject or object entity, depending on whether the relevant verb bias is an NP1 or NP2 bias. So at the very least, we have to assume that verb bias and discourse coherence considerations work together to help in focusing an entity and hence in aiding pronoun resolution. (And as we've also seen, thematic role information plays a role too, rather than mere grammatical category information).

Stevenson et al. (2000) disagree with this. They see entity focusing and discourse coherence as independent matters, and they identify two competing theories of pronoun resolution based on these notions. They call these the Focusing and Relational Hypotheses respectively.

According to the Focusing Hypothesis (FH), pronoun resolution requires a focused entity and both verbs and connectives have focusing properties. Action and transfer verbs direct attention to the endpoint of the described event and thus make the entity associated with the endpoint salient (namely, the Patient with actions and the Goal with transfers). State verbs have no default focus, since states have no endpoints encoded in the semantics of the verbs describing them. Connectives also have focusing properties. 'Because' directs attention to the cause of the previously described event, 'so' to its consequence, 'so that' to its purpose, 'whereupon' to its temporal successor, etc. Using one of these connectives with a state verb can transform the state into an event and can thus bring an entity into focus. For example, with 'so', the Experiencer will be brought into focus and with 'because', the Stimulus will be brought into focus. Action and transfer verbs, as already mentioned, have a default focus on the endpoint of the described event, and adding a connective can either support this default focus or attenuate it, by focusing on some other aspect of the event, such as the event's cause. Stevenson et al. (2000) claim that the findings from Stevenson, Crawley & Kleinman (1994), as well as the findings of the three new studies they report, favor the FH. (These studies are all ones using continuation tasks).

The Relational Hypothesis (RH) claims that the function of discourse connectives is not to focus on an individual participating in an event but to provide information about 'the coherence relation holding between two described eventualities' (Stevenson et al. 2000: 230). The RH argues that the referent of a pronoun is determined by the choice of coherence relation and not by what is in focus. Thus it appears to be a prediction of the RH that a pronoun's referent could be resolved in favor of a non-focused entity. Stevenson et al. (2000) claim that their Study 3 provides evidence against the RH, since they claim to have shown that when the focused entity is not the one determined by the coherence relation, it will be the focused entity that is selected as the referent, and not the entity determined by the coherence relation.

However, Stevenson et al.'s interpretation of their findings can be challenged. The discourse connective used in their Study 3 was 'next'. Participants had to complete fragments of the following sorts:

(13) Patrick criticized Joseph. Next he _____.

(14) Joseph was criticized by Patrick. Next he _____.

Stevenson et al. assume that the RH is committed to the claim that 'next' always invokes the discourse coherence relation NARRATION, and that this relation favors the Agent as the referent of the pronoun.[8] On the other hand, they claim that the focused entity will be the first-mentioned entity because 'next' favors a temporal rather than a causal

---

8 I assume the idea is that in a narration there is typically a character whose actions and exploits are being reported and so the default assumption is that succeeding utterances will continue the narrative thread about this agent (unless some signal has been given that the view-point has changed to that of some other character or perhaps to that of an omniscient narrator).

reading. (Why exactly a temporal reading favors first-mentioned entities is never explained). What they found was an apparent preference for the first-mentioned entity as the referent of the pronoun. However, an analysis of the continuations supplied by participants showed that readers did not always construe the relation picked out by 'next' as NARRATION. Readers sometimes construed the relation as RESULT. When one looks at the data just for the NARRATION continuations, it is clear that pronoun resolution favors the Agent, just as predicted by RH. When readers understood 'next' as signaling RESULT they resolved the pronoun in favor of the Patient, which again is consistent with the RH.

Stevenson et al. (2000) nevertheless construe these results as favoring their own FH, on the grounds that the pronoun is first resolved in favor of the first-mentioned (focused) entity and then, *after the fact*, readers select a discourse coherence relation that is in line with the thematic role of this entity (i.e., depending on whether it is an Agent or Patient). However, it seems to me that they can't have things both ways. If the first-mentioned entity is in focus because 'next' triggers a temporal rather than causal reading of the verb (p. 247), then it can't be that after the fact readers opt for a causal reading of 'next'! It is more plausible to conclude that 'next' is ambiguous as to whether it picks out the relation of NARRATION or RESULT. Furthermore, when NARRATION is selected, the referent is *not* always the first-mentioned entity, contra FH.

Thus I conclude that semantic considerations (such as the thematic roles of discourse entities and the semantic biases of verbs) and considerations of discourse coherence (as encoded in discourse connectives or implicitly signaled by background information) work together to constrain pronoun resolution. Arnold (2001) and more recently Koornneef & van Berkum (2006) have defended this sort of multiple constraint view.

Kehler et al. (2007) on the other hand argue that discourse coherence is the main driver of the effects that have been found in studies of implicit causality. They argue that effects that may seem to be driven by verb biases and thematic role considerations are merely epiphenomena – byproducts of processes sensitive to discourse-level considerations of coherence. There are at least two reasons for being skeptical that discourse coherence by itself explains pronoun resolution. The first reason is that discourse coherence concerns 'relations that hold between two described eventualities', as Stevenson et al. (2000: 230) put it. But then how can considerations of discourse coherence help with pronoun resolution? How do we get from information about relations between events to information that can help with the salience ranking of entities? I am inclined to agree with Stevenson et al. (2000: 258) that what connects event-level information to the entity-level is that entities play roles in these events. So, making the connections between levels that are necessary to bring discourse coherence to bear on pronoun resolution *presupposes* knowledge of the thematic roles that entities play. That in turn means that the effects of such knowledge cannot be relegated to the status of epiphenomena.

Secondly, if what appear to be semantic biases are indeed byproducts of coherence facts, it ought to be impossible to dissociate these apparently semantic effects from coherence factors. However, it seems likely that these factors are dissociable. If it could be shown that people show a preference for one entity over another as soon as the verb is encountered and before the discourse connective is processed, this would be evidence of dissociation between verb bias and discourse relation bias and would count against Kehler et al.'s (2007) claim that such semantic biases are merely epiphenomenal. Pyykkönen & Järvikivi (2010) report on a Visual World study that shows just such an early effect of verb bias.

Free enrichment

I turn finally to a discussion of how discourse coherence considerations can play a role in processes of free enrichment. I assume this will be the case that most interests philosophers. The sorts of examples I will be focusing on have not, so far as I am aware, attracted the attention of experimental psychologists. However, there has been a fair amount of attention paid by experimental psychologists to related pragmatic processes.

For example, there have been several recent empirical studies of metonymy, which have tried to understand the processes involved in the interpretation of expressions like 'Dickens' in sentences of the form of (15) and (16), where on one reading it picks out the man Dickens and in the other the writings of the man. See Frisson & Pickering (2001, 2007):

(15) As a young girl, my great-grandmother met Dickens.

(16) As a young girl, my great-grandmother read Dickens.

There has also been a fair amount of attention paid to what Jackendoff (2002) calls 'enriched composition'. One type of phenomenon that has been studied under this rubric is 'aspectual coercion', a phenomenon described and analyzed by Pustejovsky (1998). For example, the verb 'finish' subcategorizes for a following event-nominal. Yet in (17) below, the noun phrase 'the book' does not pick out an event. Thus the interpreter is coerced into searching the discourse context for an appropriate event; was it the reading of the book, or the writing of the book, or the printing of the book, etc. that John finished? See McElree et al. (2001, 2006); Pickering et al. (2006) for reports on experimental investigations of coercion:

(17) John finished the book.

In the philosophical literature, there has been a great deal of debate as to whether or not there really is such a thing as free enrichment, and I do not intend to enter into that debate here. Critics of the notion have argued that what seem to be cases of semantic underdetermination calling for free enrichment are in fact cases falling under what Carston (1988) calls the Linguistic Direction principle. The principal way that the notion of free enrichment has been challenged is by positing the presence of hidden variables, reducing such cases to ones that resemble the pronoun cases I've already discussed. For present purposes I am simply going to assume that there are cases requiring pragmatic processes that seem to be interestingly different from the indexical and ambiguity cases I've already discussed. (I have tried to defend this claim in Bezuidenhout (2002).)

The cases I have in mind are cases involving contextuals, such as 'local' and 'foreign', and cases of verbs such as 'come' and 'go' that encode a perspective or point of view (POV) that must be contextually resolved. I will show that the pragmatic enrichment/modulation required to interpret utterances containing such expressions is helped by knowledge of discourse coherence relations.

Consider the following mini-discourses involving the contextual expression 'local':

(18) John was in his hotel room in downtown Toronto and planned to take the tram to Brockton because he wanted to visit a local pub before flying back to the US the next day. The pub proved to have all the neighborhood charm that the guidebook promised.

(19) John was in his hotel room in downtown Toronto and planned to take the tram to Brockton. However, he wanted to visit a local pub before flying back to the US the next day. So he never got to visit the charming neighborhood the guidebook promised.

The discourse relations EXPLANATION and VIOLATED EXPECTATION make a big difference in interpretation of 'local' in (18) and (19). In (18), the speaker's use of the connective 'because' signals that a feature of the planned trip to Brockton is about to be explained. Hence, 'local' picks up the pub in Brockton as the locus. In (19), 'however' signals that some expectation about the planned Brockton trip is about to be violated, and this blocks Brockton as a location for the pub, and hence the pub in downtown Toronto becomes the locus for 'local'.

I hypothesize that part of what discourse connectives do is provide information about the perspective from which the discourse is to be understood. Coherence relations such a NARRATION and ELABORATION indicate that some protagonist's point of view will continue to be relevant or operative in the next discourse segment. Relations such as EXPLANATION and RESULT also maintain a point of view, but differ in being either backward- or forward-looking. Relations such as PARALLEL and CONTRAST switch points of view, either to a contrasting entity or to an entity of equal status whose point of view will be maintained alongside the one previously operative.

Just as contextual expressions require anchoring in a point of view, so too do verbs such as 'come' and 'go'. When we interpret sentences containing such expressions, we must recover from the discourse context something about the locus that is either the endpoint (with 'come') or the starting point (with 'go') of the action. As before, I claim that knowledge of discourse relations can help with the identification of this locus. Consider the following examples (not perfect ones, I realize) using the verb 'come':

(20) John texted Bill because a DEA agent came to visit.

(21) John texted Bill; as a result a DEA agent came to visit.

When the discourse relation is EXPLANATION, the locus of the action of coming is John's location, whereas when it is RESULT, the (preferred) locus of the action of coming is Bill's location.

3 Minimalist objections and responses

In this section I want to address three objections raised by Horisk (2009) on behalf of defenders of minimalism. The first objection is that a minimalist can accept what I say about the role of discourse relations in disambiguation and pronoun resolution, at least for those cases in which the discourse relation is explicitly signaled by a discourse connective. The second objection is that I seem to be supposing that discourse connectives have semantically stable meanings, and if so, my arguments seem to be more friendly to the minimalist than to the contextualist. The third objection is that most of the experimental work I cite draws conclusions from data collected by the presentation of decontextualized sentences to experimental participants. Thus this data shows that language comprehension is possible even without contextual support. I answer these objections in turn.

Minimalism and the multiple constraint view

Is it true that the psychological minimalist can accept the kind of multiple constraint view I've been arguing for, according to which pragmatic processes of disambiguation, pronoun resolution and free enrichment are constrained by information from multiple levels, including discourse-level information? Horisk (2009) is more circumspect; obviously minimalists will reject the notion of free enrichment, so we should narrow the question to focus just on disambiguation and pronoun resolution. Moreover, any pragmatic modulation that is constrained by discourse level information that is not explicitly signaled by a discourse connective cannot be compatible with minimalism, since the minimalist is allowed to appeal only to semantically encoded information. However, even when we narrow the focus in these two ways, it is unclear that psychological minimalists can accept the multiple constraint view advocated in section 2.

For one thing, the sorts of pragmatic modulation processes described above are all local pragmatic processes that contribute pragmatically modulated contents to the incremental interpretive process. Thus the final understanding of a speaker's utterance will be composed out of modulated contents, not minimal ones. The psychological minimalist on the other hand wants to argue that a complete minimal proposition with un-modulated contents is extracted first and that pragmatic and discourse-level information operates only in a secondary way on this minimal proposition. This is the view defended by Borg (2004). It is important for Borg to argue in this way, because she does not want to grant that pragmatic processes intrude into fixing truth-conditional content. In general, minimalists do not want to allow for the idea of enriched composition; that is, the idea that interpretive processes compose modulated meanings to arrive at a pragmatically enhanced truth-conditional content.

I believe that Horisk (2009) is misled into thinking that the multiple constraint view is more compatible with minimalism than it is because of an ambiguity in the phrase 'semantic content'. I have been using this phrase throughout this article to refer to semantically encoded content, which is the content associated with lexical items and that I assume is context-invariant (or at least relatively stable across contexts). Such semantically encoded meanings (e.g., the meanings associated with the semantically biased verbs that were the topic of section 2 above) constitute one sort of constraint on pragmatic modulation, along with information from other levels of language (such as syntactic, phonological and informational-structural levels). A commitment to such stable meanings is not anti-contextualist. What *is* anti-contextualist is the notion that semantically encoded information *by itself* is sufficient to determine truth-conditional content. This is the view defended by Borg (2004) and that I claim is inconsistent with the multiple constraint view defended in this article. Many philosophers want to reserve the term 'semantic content' for truth-conditional content. In this sense of semantic content, of course the contextualists want to say that it varies across contexts. But none of the empirical work I cited in the previous section is compatible with the view that truth-conditional content is invariant across contexts, and hence none of that work is minimalist-friendly, contra Horisk (2009).

The semantics of discourse connectives

In section 2, I seemed to be assuming that discourse connectives such as 'because', 'as a result', 'so', etc. have semantically stable meanings, and Horisk (2009) argues that this is more friendly to minimalists than to contextualists. Once again, this objection trades on the ambiguity of the phrase 'semantic content' mentioned in the previous subsection. Of course it is compatible with contextualism and the multiple constraint view I was advocating to think that discourse connectives have semantically stable encoded contents, just as is the case with any lexical item. Semantically encoded contents are just one input into the incremental process of interpretation; information from other sources is needed too, including discourse-level information.

However, Horisk (2009) may intend her second objection in a slightly different way. This alternative objection is that a contextualist must allow that the meanings of discourse connectives can undergo pragmatic modulation, just as any other semantically encoded content can undergo such modulation (e.g., via processes of enrichment, loosening, transfer, type coercion and other such local pragmatic processes).[9] I appear to be assuming that discourse connectives are not subject to such modulation, and hence, if we assume that a contextualist must agree that every lexical item is subject to pragmatic modulation, I must be going against contextualism.

With respect to discourse connectives, I am inclined to accept the view advocated by Relevance Theorists, such as Blakemore (2002). According to this view, discourse connectives encode procedures rather than concepts. This means that their contribution to interpretation is completely different from the contribution of expressions such as nouns, verbs, adverbs, adjectives and some prepositions, which *do* encode concepts. For example, consider:

(22) S_1 because S_2.

(23) p_1 and p_2 and p_2 is the cause of p_1.

Suppose that 'S_1' and 'S_2' as uttered in context C express the propositions p_1 and p_2 respectively. According to a conceptualist/representationalist view, (22) expresses (23). The representationalist assumes that 'because' encodes the concept of one event's being the cause of another. The proceduralist view, on the other hand, assumes that 'because' encodes an instruction to the interpreter to process the speaker's utterance in a context in which the event represented by p_2 is a cause of the event represented by p_1. On this view, there is no higher-order representation of this causal fact in the hearer's discourse model. Events are simply ordered in a certain sequence and causal (e.g., agentive) properties are assigned to event participants but there is not in addition a causal fact added to the model over and above the properties assigned at the object-level. In Bezuidenhout (2004), I argue that procedures must be executed without an intervening level of representation on pain of an infinite regress of representations. I cannot digress here to lay out that argument. For

---

9 For discussion of such local pragmatic processes, see Carston (2002), Recanati (2004), Jackendoff (2002), Pustejovsky (1998), and Nunberg (1995).

present purposes, however, it is sufficient to note that if discourse connectives encode procedures rather than concepts, then one would not expect them to be subject to pragmatic modulation. But if so, there is a way to be a contextualist and yet to accept that discourse connectives are not subject to pragmatic modulation.

This proceduralist account would avoid Horisk's second objection. However, for the sake of argument, let us suppose that the representationalist view is correct and that discourse connectives encode concepts, in particular, relational concepts. Thus 'because' will represent the concept EXPLAINS(X,Y), 'however' the concept VIOLATES EXPECTATION(X,Y), etc. Even though the modulation of the meanings of discourse connectives was not the focus of my remarks in section 2, I see no reason for thinking that such modulation never occurs. Consider a discourse connective that has been much discussed, namely 'but'. This has at least two distinct uses, one in which it is more or less synonymous with 'however' in signaling a violated expectation, as in (24) and (25) below, and another in which it signals a contrast, as in (26) below:

(24) Jack is in his office, but you can't see him right now.

(25) Jill is poor but honest.

(26) Jill is tall but her sister is short.

It is relatively easy to see how context could modulate the meaning of 'but'. For example, out of the blue one is likely to understand (25) as challenging a background assumption of the hearer's (or of some other contextually salient group) to the effect that poor people are generally dishonest. However, the assumption being challenged can change depending on context. Consider the following two contexts:

> Context 1: Suppose a criminal gang is planning a bank heist and they want to bribe someone on the inside to help them gain access to the safe. They are considering targeting one of the junior bank tellers, who might be more susceptible to bribery than other bank employees,

for various reasons. Someone suggests Jill and someone else replies by uttering (25). Here 'but' challenges the assumption that Jill will be susceptible to bribery. There need be no assumption about poor people in general being dishonest. Perhaps the gang is even operating with the assumption that lowly bank employees in general are an honest bunch. The assumption being challenged is that Jill's honesty can be overcome for a price.

Context 2: Suppose that a drug cartel is trying to recruit villagers to be part of a drug-running operation. They are looking for a ruthless person who won't think twice before performing even the most heinous acts. There is an assumption that the villagers in general are an honest bunch; however, the hope is that there will be one amongst the bunch who can serve the cartel's needs. Someone suggests Jill and someone else replies by uttering (25). Here the 'but' challenges the assumption that Jill is the hoped for dishonest villager.

Thus I do not accept the idea that discourse connectives are never subject to pragmatic modulation. Inasmuch as they encode concepts, these concepts are as context-sensitive as any others.

Contextualism and experimentation

The third objection Horisk (2009) raises is that the experimental evidence I have cited in support of the multiple constraint view depends largely on data collected by presenting experimental participants with sentence fragments or pairs of sentences, without rich supporting discourse contexts. Yet participants were able to produce completions for the fragments and comprehend the sentence pairs in systematic ways, without apparent difficulty. This might be thought to lend support to the minimalist and show that contextualism is mistaken.

However, minimalists can take no comfort in these experimental results. The systematic ways in which people understood the experimental items provide us with evidence that interpretations are sensitive to discourse-level information as soon as it becomes available in the incremental process of interpretation. This counts against minimalists such as Borg (2004) who argue that pragmatic and discourse-level information is only taken account of in a secondary way, once a complete minimal proposition is recovered.

Secondly, while it is true that the contexts presented were minimal, it is not true that they were absent altogether. Even mini-discourses consisting of two sentences will prompt interpreters to access lexical, syntactic, phonological, informational-structural, and world knowledge. As language comprehenders, we rely on our cognitive abilities to fill in and fill out the schematic meanings that are semantically encoded in a speaker's utterances. These abilities are not shut down even in the highly artificial experimental environments constructed by psycholinguists, which is a good thing, because otherwise there would be no way to scientifically investigate the processes of language production and comprehension. Just as protons don't lose their natures (e.g., turn into fairy dust) in the artificial environments created in particle accelerators, so too our cognitive processes maintain their integrity, even in the unusual linguistic environments created by experimental psychologists. If well designed, these experimental manipulations can give us a glimpse into the workings of these contextual processes that are ordinarily hidden from view.

4 Conclusion

What I hope to have convinced the reader of is that there are some very systematic factors at work in processes of pragmatic modulation, which are amenable to scientific study, and which have in fact already been studied rather thoroughly by experimental psychologists, using a variety of experimental tasks and methodologies. Thus philosophers who are inclined to throw their hands up and say that contextualism is a bad theory because pragmatic processes are too undefined and wooly and that contextualism is thus committed to an 'anything goes' theory of content, should reconsider. I do agree that pragmatic processes are complex and governed by multiple constraints. But that does not mean that we need to despair of ever treating these processes scientifically. There may be a lot of trial and error on the path to understanding, but the end result will be worth the effort.

References

Ariel, M. (1990). *Accessing noun-phrase antecedents*. London: Routledge.
Asher, N. & Lascarides, A. (1996). Lexical disambiguation in a discourse context. In Pustejovski, J. & Boguraev, B. (Eds.). *Lexical semantics: The problem of polysemy,* (pp. 69–108). Oxford: Clarendon Press.
Arnold, J. E. (2001). The effect of thematic roles on pronoun use and frequency of reference continuation. *Discourse Processes, 31*(2), 137–162.
Au, T. (1986). A verb is worth a thousand words: The causes and consequences of interpersonal events implicit in language. *Journal of Memory and Language, 25,* 104–122.
Bezuidenhout, A. (2002). Truth-conditional pragmatics. *Philosophical Perspectives 16,* 105–134.
────── (2004). Procedural meaning and the semantics/pragmatics interface. In C. Bianchi (Ed.). *The semantics/pragmatics distinction,* (pp. 101–131). Stanford: CSLI Publications.
────── (2009). Contextualism and the role of contextual frames. *Manuscrito: Revista Internacional de Filosofia, 32,* 59–84.
Birner, B. & Ward, G. (1998). *Information status and non-canonical word order in English*. Amsterdam: Benjamins.
Blakemore, D. (2002). *Relevance and linguistic meaning: The semantics and pragmatics of discourse markers*. Cambridge: Cambridge University Press.
Borg, E. (2004). *Minimal semantics*. Oxford: Oxford University Press.
Brown, R. & Fish, D. (1983). The psychological causality implicit in language. *Cognition, 14,* 237–273.

Capelen, H. & Lepore, E. (2005). *Insensitive semantics*. Oxford: Blackwell.

Caramazza, A., Grober, E., Garvey, C. & Yates, J. (1977). Comprehension of anaphoric pronouns. *Journal of Verbal Learning and Verbal Behavior, 16*(5), 601–609.

Carston, R. (1988). Implicature, explicature, and truth-conditional semantics. In R. Kempson (Ed.), *Mental representations: The interface between language and reality,* (pp. 155–181). Cambridge: Cambridge University Press.

——— (2002). *Thoughts and utterances*. Oxford: Blackwell.

Crinean, M. and Garnham, A. (2006). Implicit causality, implicit consequentiality and semantic roles. *Language & Cognitive Processes, 21*(5), 636–648.

Erteschik-Shir, N. (2007). *Information structure: The syntax-discourse interface*. Oxford: Oxford University Press.

Ferretti, T., Rohde, H., Kehler, A., & Crutchley, M. (2009). Verb aspect, event structure and coreferential processing. *Journal of Memory and Language 61*, 191–205.

Frisson, S., & Pickering, M. J. (2007). The processing of familiar and novel senses of a word: Why reading Dickens is easy but reading Needham can be hard. *Language and Cognitive Processes 22*, 595–613.

Frisson, S.P., & Pickering, M. J. (2001). Obtaining a figurative interpretation of a word: Support for underspecification. *Metaphor and Symbol, 16*, 149–171.

Garnham, A., Oakhill, J., & Cruttenden, H. (1992). The role of implicit causality and gender cue in the interpretation of pronouns. *Language and Cognitive Processes,7* (3-4), 231–255.

Garnham, A., Traxler, M., Oakhill, J., & Gernsbacher, M. A. (1996). The locus of implicit causality effects in comprehension. *Journal of Memory and Language, 35*(4), 517–543.

Garvey, C., & Caramazza, A. (1974). Implicit causality in verbs. *Linguistic Inquiry, 5*, 459–464.

Garvey, C., Caramazza, A. & Yates, J. (1975). Factors influencing assignment of pronoun antecedents. *Cognition, 3*, 227–243.

Gernsbacher, M. & Hargreaves, D. (1988). Accessing sentence participants: The advantage of first mention. *Journal of Memory & Language, 27*, 699–717.

Gordon, P., Grosz, B. & Gilliom, L. (1993). Pronouns, names, and the centering of attention in discourse. *Cognitive Science, 17*, 311–347.

Gordon, P. C., & Scearce, K. A. (1995). Pronominalization and discourse coherence, discourse structure and pronoun interpretation. *Memory & Cognition, 23*(3), 313–323.

Greene, S. B., & McKoon, G. (1995). Telling something we can't know: Experimental approaches to verbs exhibiting implicit causality. *Psychological Science, 6*(5), 262–270.

Greene, S. B., McKoon, G., & Ratcliff, R. (1992). Pronoun resolution and discourse models. *Journal of Experimental Psychology: Learning, Memory, and Cognition, 18*(2), 266–283.

Grosz, B., Joshi, A. & Weinstein, S. (1995). Centering: A framework for modeling the local coherence of discourse. *Computational Linguistics 21*, 203–226.

Guerry, M. Gimenes, M., Caplan, D. & Rigalleau, F. (2006). How long does it take to find a cause? An online investigation of implicit causality in sentence production. *The Quarterly Journal of Experimental Psychology, 59*(9), 1535–1555.

Gundel, J., Hedberg, N. & Zacharski, R. (1993). Cognitive status and the form of referring expressions in discourse. *Language, 69*, 274–307.

Hobbs, J. (1979). Coherence and coreference. *Cognitive Science, 3*, 67–90.

Horisk, C. (2009). Comments on Bezuidenhout's 'Information structure and the S/P interface', delivered at a conference on the Challenge of Contextualism, held at Queens University, Kingston, Ontario, September 11-13, 2009.

Jackendoff, R. (2002). *Foundations of language: brain, meaning, grammar, evolution.* Oxford: Oxford University Press.

Kehler, A., Kertz, L., Rohde, H., & Elman, J. (2007). Coherence and coreference revisited. *Journal of Semantics 25*, 1–44.

Koornneef, A. & van Berkum, J. (2006). On the use of verb-based implicit causality in sentence comprehension: Evidence from self-paced reading and eye-tracking. *Journal of Memory & Language, 54*(4), 445–465.

Lambrecht, K. (1994). *Information structure and sentence form: topic, focus and the mental representations of discourse referents.* Cambridge: Cambridge University Press.

Levin, B. (1993). *English verb classes and alternations: A preliminary investigation.* Chicago: University of Chicago Press.

Mann, W. & Thompson, S. (1988). Rhetorical structure theory: Toward a functional theory of text organization. *Text, 8*(3), 243–281.

McElree, B., Pylkkänen, L., Pickering, M.J., & Traxler, M. (2006). The time course of enriched composition. *Psychonomic Bulletin & Review, 13,* 53–59.

McElree, B., Traxler, M., Pickering, M. J., Seely, R, & Jackendoff, R. (2001). Reading time evidence for enriched composition. *Cognition, 78,* B17–B25.

McKoon, G., Greene, S. B., & Ratcliff, R. (1993). Discourse models, pronoun resolution, and the implicit causality of verbs. *Journal of Experimental Psychology: Learning, Memory, and Cognition, 19*(5), 1040–1052.

Nunberg, G. (1995). Transfers of meaning. *Journal of Semantics, 12,* 109–132.

Pickering, M. J., McElree, B., Frisson, S., Chin, L., & Traxler, M. (2006). Aspectual coercion and underspecification. *Discourse Processes, 42,* 131–155.

Pickering, M. J., & Majid, A. (2007). What are implicit causality and consequentiality? *Language and Cognitive Processes, 22*(5), 780–788.

Pustejovsky, J. (1998). *The generative lexicon.* Cambridge, MA: MIT Press.

Pyykkönen, P. & Järvikivi, J. (2010). Activation and persistence of implicit causality information in spoken language comprehension. *Experimental Psychology, 57*(1), 5-16.

Recanati, F. (2004). *Literal meaning*. Cambridge: Cambridge University Press.

Roberts, C. (2004). Pronouns as definite. In Reimer, M. and Bezuidenhout, A. (Eds.). *Descriptions and beyond*, (pp. 503–543). Oxford: Oxford University Press.

Stevenson, R., Knott, A., Oberlander, J., & McDonald, S. (2000). Interpreting pronouns and connectives: Interactions among focusing, thematic roles and coherence relations. *Language and Cognitive Processes, 15*(3), 225–262.

Stewart, A., Pickering, M. & Sanford, A. (2000). The time course of the influence of implicit causality information: Focusing versus integration accounts. *Journal of Memory & Language, 42*(3), 423–443.

Traxler, M., McElree, B., Williams, R. S. & Pickering, M.J. (2005). Context effects in coercion: evidence from eye-movements. *Journal of Memory and Language, 53*, 1–25.

— 5 —

Agustín Vicente & Fernando Martínez-Manrique
Lexical Concepts: From Contextualism to Concept Decompositionalism

1 Introduction: stability and polysemy

There are two puzzles that any mentalistic account of meaning has to address, the puzzle of *stability* and the puzzle of *polysemy*. The puzzle of stability is how it is possible for a word to retain basically the same meaning across contexts, such as 'wall' in 'red wall', 'brick wall' or 'big wall'. The puzzle of polysemy is how it is possible for a word to have a number of different but apparently related senses in different contexts, such as 'keep' in 'keep money', 'keep quiet' or 'keep Jack happy'. *Decompositionalism* is a thesis about word meaning, and its attractiveness lies in the fact that it can provide a common and simple solution for both puzzles.[1] Broadly characterised,

---

1 There are different ways to envision decompositionalism. A classical model is componential semantic theory (Katz & Fodor 1963), and more recent ones come from lexical and generative semantics (Cruse 1986, 2000; Moravcsik 1990; Bierwisch and Schreuder 1992; Jackendoff 1992, 2002; Pitt 1999; Pustejovsky 1995; Wierzbicka 1996). What they have in common is that they regard word meanings as structured mental entities. They differ, among other respects, on the nature of the components (e.g., lexical or sublexical units), the type of

decompositionalism says that words stand for structured complexes of representational elements. The kind of decompositionalism we advocate further claims that each word is associated with a molecular representational structure that consists of a variable combination of components with a more or less stable core. The core accounts for the stability of word meaning, while the variable part allows the instantiation of different related senses.

Alternative accounts of stability and polysemy tend to downplay one notion or the other. One such alternative, *conceptual atomism* (Fodor 1998) accepts that words express concepts, but rejects that concepts have structure. So a word like 'keep' expresses a concept like KEEP,[2] and this concept does not decompose into other elements. Stability is explained by taking that each word meaning corresponds to a context-independent atom that, by definition, retains its sense across different contexts. Polysemy, in contrast, appears (almost) as a spurious phenomenon: the responsibility for the different meanings of the different expressions in which 'keep' occurs is to be found in the different contexts provided by the expressions themselves, not in differences between the underlying conceptual structures that account for 'keep'.[3]

Another alternative (e.g. Travis 2000) rejects that there is some context-independent element in the mind that corresponds to the meaning of a word. Polysemy here is taken as the norm rather than

---

decomposition involved (e.g., definitional or variable), and the representational levels involved (e.g., semantic or conceptual). Here we will defend the view that word meanings (or lexical concepts) are complex sublexical concepts and, crucially, that they have a variable structure. Thus, our claim will be that only a 'cluster decompositionalism' (see Vicente 2010) can adequately account for the puzzles of stability and polysemy.

2   We follow the convention of writing names of concepts in small capitals, words in single quotes, and (only when possible ambiguities arise) world properties in italics.
3   Here we are following Fodor (1998), where he accounts for the putative polysemy of 'keep'. It is unfair, however, to say that Fodor considers that polysemy is totally spurious: Fodor & Lepore (2002) hold (a) that some cases of polysemy such as 'bake' ('bake a cake' vs. 'bake a potato') are special cases of ambiguity, and (b) that some other cases ('want' in 'I want a beer' vs. 'I want to have a beer') are not instances of polysemy but of ellipsis. We will discuss these ideas later on.

the exception (Cohen 1985: 131), and stability of word meaning is not based on a stable correspondence with certain mental structures but on the existence of similar uses of the word in the past. So when a word seems to have the same sense across different utterances what actually happens is that the context of utterance is pretty much the same in all the cases.

Atomism accounts for stability in terms of something that is represented in mind (stable word meanings) but rejects a similar explanation for polysemy. Radical contextualism moves in the opposite direction: it accounts for polysemy in terms of some semantic potential[4] but seeks a different explanation for stability. Decompositionalism diverges from both positions in its commitment to an explanation in terms of mental representations for stability and polysemy.[5]

In this article, we want to offer a general defence of decompositionalism by arguing against conceptual atomism. We will show how the current stronger version of conceptual atomism (Fodor's) is associated to a problematic thesis, the Disquotational Lexicon Hypothesis (DLH). This thesis will have to be dropped in order to obtain an account of lexical meaning capable of explaining polysemy. The argument we are going to offer is based on the phenomenon of what has been called 'semantic underdeterminacy', which in part shows how deep and ineliminable polysemy is. Then we will argue that a decompositionalist theory is in a better position to account for the semantic underdeterminacy challenge. Thus, we will try to show that

---

4 This might be, in principle, a set of mental representations. Yet, there are reasons to doubt that extreme contextualism (such as Travis 2000) is compatible with representationalism.

5 The picture gets complicated once we consider the kind of mental representations involved. One possibility, call this conceptual decompositionalism, is to admit a single level of representation, in which word meanings are complexes of conceptual elements (Jackendoff 2002). A second possibility, call this the two-level theory, is to distinguish two representational levels, one for meanings (the semantic level), and another for concepts (the conceptual level). Now, it is possible to be either decompositionalist or atomist about the semantic level. Some componential semanticists (Bierwisch & Schreuder 1992) can be regarded as decompositionalist two-level theorists, while an atomistic two-level position is assumed by authors such as Levinson (2001, 2003) and probably by Carston (2002). In this article we will be concerned only with single-level accounts.

contextualism does have some implications about the issue of lexical structure.

2 Atomism and Semantic Underdeterminacy

Fodor's conceptual atomism assumes that the function of language is the expression of thought. Just as a sentence expresses a fully propositional thought, we can say that its component words express the component concepts of that thought. This is a position that shares widespread assumptions about the relation between language and thought (cf. Cruse 2000; Murphy 2002), and that are commonplace in the decompositionalist side (e.g., Jackendoff 1992). In addition, both atomism and the decompositionalism we want to argue for agree that there is a bottom rock of conceptual elements, that is, a set of *primitive concepts* from which all other concepts are obtained. Where Fodor parts company with decompositionalism is on the relation between word meanings and concepts.

Atomism is the thesis that concepts have no structure. The exception, of course, comes from *complex* concepts, i.e., those concepts that are obtained by composition of two or more concepts. In principle, this view is compatible with different positions regarding the relation between words and concepts: it could be either a one-to-many relation, with a word expressing a complex concept; or it could be many-to-one, as in the case of idioms. Yet, Fodor contends that this relation is (almost) one-to-one, i.e., barring idioms, each word usually expresses one concept. Fodor has been arguing for this idea for a long time, but he has expressed it more explicitly in his Disquotational Lexicon Hypothesis (DLH), according to which the concept a word expresses can be captured by disquoting and capitalising it. Thus, the DLH holds that there is a one-to-one relation between words and concepts and that the latter are atomic. In contrast, decompositionalism holds that (most) lexical units express in fact complex concepts, which are obtained from a set of primitive sublexical concepts, and this set is much smaller than the set of lexical units. If we call lexical concepts those concepts that are expressed by lexical units, what decompositionalism claims is that *most* lexical concepts are not primitive, while atomism is the thesis that almost *all* lexical concepts are nonstructured primitives.

Another consequence of the DLH is the invariability of word meaning: a word, like 'keep', expresses the same concept in all contexts – i.e., the concept KEEP. The responsibility for the different meanings of the different expressions in which 'keep' occurs is to be found in the different contexts provided by the expressions themselves, not in differences among the underlying conceptual structures that account for 'keep'. This shows how atomism can easily account for stability of meaning. It also allows us to make sense of Fodor's troubles with polysemy, which make him oscillate between claiming that 'there is no such thing as polysemy' (Fodor 1998: 53) and trying to explain it away, either as ambiguity or as something which 'belongs not to the theory of content but to the theory of logical form' (Fodor & Lepore 2002: 116).

The role that DLH plays in conceptual atomism is unclear. On the one hand, it may be regarded as a condition that simplifies the picture and safeguards lexical concepts against the complications that arise in alternative versions of conceptual atomism. On the other hand, it may be a consequence of the way words and concepts relate in the informational semantics that Fodor endorses. At any rate, we are going to argue that its inability to cope with polysemy makes DLH a dispensable principle. What we are going to show is that there is a route from semantic underdeterminacy to polysemy, with the consequence that DLH –and with it (single-level) conceptual atomism– will have to be abandoned.

The clash between underdeterminacy and disquotationalism

Semantic underdeterminacy (henceforth SU) is the thesis that linguistic meaning is not enough to determine the truth-conditional content of what is said by a sentential utterance, to which end the interpreter always has to add pragmatic factors (Bach 1994; Recanati 2001, 2004; Sperber & Wilson 1986, 1995; Carston 2002). This is especially conspicuous in the case of utterances containing demonstratives, like 'that book is heavy', but many other expressions follow the same pattern. For instance, Recanati argues that utterances with the expression 'John's car' do not have a determinate value until we take into account what sort of relation between John and the car the speaker has in mind. Whether it is a relation of 'ownership' or 'drivership' or 'being the car John bet on' or any one of numerous other possibilities, is something that can only be determined by looking at the wide context, so truth conditions cannot be ascertained until this is taken into account. As opposed to the narrow context, which is limited to a short list of contextual parameters, the wide context includes any element of the interaction between speaker and interpreter (e.g., perceptually salient elements, previously uttered sentences, their common personal histories, and so on) that can make a particular semantic value more accessible than any other candidate. In other words, we cannot turn the relation of John to his car into a semantic rule, because there is no rule that can tell us which of the possible elements will be most accessible on each occasion.

Carston (2002) argues that both referential and predicative terms are sources of underdeterminacy. For a start, proper names should be treated as indexicals whose rule is not 'pure' (it roughly says 'this name refers to the contextually prominent bearer of it'). But even the reference of complete definite descriptions depends on the context, which can be the actual world, a possible world, or even a belief world. In addition, examples such as 'the kettle is black', 'the table was covered with butter' and 'Hugo is a sailor' (Travis 1985; Carston 2002), where 'black', 'covered with butter' and 'sailor' may apparently mean a variety of things, suggest that underdeterminacies also arise with regard to the semantic value of predicates.[6]

It is fair to say that defenders of *semantic minimalism* (Borg 2004; Cappelen & Lepore 2005) object to those conclusions. They agree that semantics underdetermines what a speaker means while contending

---

[6] This claim will be revised later on, for it seems reasonable to say that what we have in some of these cases is not an underdeterminacy in the semantic values of predicates but an underdeterminacy – or better, an indeterminacy – in the composition rules.

Lexical Concepts

that there is also a sense in which sentences express the same truth-conditional meaning across contexts. This is the so-called minimal proposition that, according to those authors, is as determined with respect to truth conditions as it can be. To take an example, 'an utterance of "A is tall" expresses the proposition *that A is tall* and it is true just in case A is tall' (Cappelen & Lepore 2005: 155). Now, we do not wish to enter this dispute or provide more ammunition for the contextualist side. Rather, we will assume that contextualism is right. What we want to do is to extend the conclusions from the argument of SU to the dispute between decompositionalism and atomism.

Our claim is that if SU is such a widespread phenomenon, then Fodor's conceptual atomism is in trouble to account for lexical concepts. In fact, if there is hope for any atomistic theory, it will have to be without the Disquotational Lexicon Hypothesis. Here is the structure of our argument:

(i) If the truth conditions of sentential utterances are semantically underdetermined, then sentential utterances do not have literal meanings.

(ii) If sentential utterances do not have literal meanings, and if literal meanings of words are understood as concepts that correspond one-to-one to the words, then (some of) the utterances' component words do not have literal meaning either.[7]

(iii) The Disquotational Lexicon Hypothesis posits that, in most cases, there is a one-to-one correspondence between words and concepts, and entails that there are literal meanings for words (namely, their corresponding concepts).

(iv) Hence the DLH is false.

Let us examine each step of the argument.

---

7 A more accurate phrasing of this premise would be this: if sentential utterances do not have literal meanings, then for every sentential utterance there is at least one component lexical item which is not a pure indexical and whose semantic value is partly determined by the context.

Premise (i): SU and literal meaning for sentential utterances

This is the first claim we want to argue for:

(i) If the truth conditions of sentential utterances are semantically underdetermined, then sentential utterances do not have literal meanings.

We must begin by noting that literal meaning is not an easy notion to unpack. In its most general sense, it corresponds to a meaning that is constant across all contexts of utterance. When applied to sentential utterances, the usual idea is that a sentence has a *propositional content* that is totally determined by semantic values and rules of language alone. Given that the notion of a 'rule of language' itself can be interpreted with varying degrees of liberality, it is possible to entertain different variations on the idea of literalness. Yet we will take it that there are two key elements in this idea: (1) the literal meaning of a sentential utterance is truth-conditional,[8] and (2) it is determined by compositional linguistic (i.e., non-pragmatic) fixed rules applied to the meaning of the utterance's component expressions. On the other hand, and most importantly, in the mentalistic framework that we assumed right from the beginning, we concur with the opinion of those (Recanati and Carston among them, but also advocates of semantic minimalism) who have contended that the notion of literal meaning that is at stake is a *psychologically realistic* one. In representational terms, this means that whatever one thinks of the theoretical role that literal meaning might play in linguistics, it should also correspond to some representational structure that is constructed in the hearer's mind at some step of the interpretive process. Notice that this reading is especially relevant to Fodor's enterprise. As a downright supporter of the mentalistic, conceptualist view of meaning, he is heavily concerned with providing a psychologically realistic account.

Our point, then, is that if SU is a general phenomenon there cannot be (a mental structure corresponding to) a truth-conditional

---

[8] Although, see Bach (2005).

literal meaning for most, if not all, sentential utterances ever made. As suggested above, the alleged reason is that sentential utterances would not have determinate truth-conditions until pragmatic factors are taken into account. Hence composition of linguistic elements cannot provide by itself a truth-conditional proposition.[9] Now, one may object that even if this were true about many sentences as they are *actually* uttered, it does not necessarily apply to most sentences that one can *potentially* utter. In other words, there may be eternal sentences, or sentences relevantly similar to eternal sentences, which do have literal meanings in the required sense. So the objection is that even if we have shown that a good number of our sentential utterances are semantically underdetermined, we still fall short of showing that they do not have literal meanings in general. This seems to be an important point, because if there were eternal sentences, then it seems there could be literal meanings for words, and our argument would not run from premise (i) to premise (ii).

Imagine that for any underdetermined utterance it is possible to find another one that explicitly, or literally (i.e., without any contextual aid) expresses the same proposition that the former expresses aided by contextual information. For instance, imagine that the underdetermined 'John's car is empty' is translatable into 'the car John owns has nobody inside' and that the latter has a literal meaning. Then, it seems, we are in a position to claim that 'own', 'inside', etc. have a literal meaning, namely, OWN, INSIDE, etc. Words would not always express the same concepts (perhaps they would rarely do), but the meaning of a word could be an atomic concept.

We want to argue against the existence of such eternal sentences, but first we want to point out that the recourse to eternal sentences may not be particularly helpful for the atomist defending the DLH. For

---

9 This claim has to be qualified. An utterance of a sentence such as 'John's car is empty' can be said to have some truth-conditional and compositional (and context-independent) meaning, such as *a thing that is said to be a car (real car, toy car, or whatever) that is in some close relationship to someone presumably called 'John' is relevantly empty*. We would say that these are not the truth conditions of the utterance, and are sympathetic to those who regard this meaning as non-propositional.

suppose that 'John's car is empty' is a highly ambiguous expression, which may mean that the car John owns has nobody inside, that the car John likes has nothing in it, etc. Then the genitive and 'empty' would not stand for single atomic concepts; rather, it seems that if there is, e.g., such an EMPTY concept, it must be decomposable, depending on the context, into NOBODY INSIDE, or NOTHING IN IT, etc., that is, complexes of the concepts encoded by words in putative eternal sentences. Inasmuch as semantic underdeterminacy is general enough, we would then have that the stock of primitive concepts is considerably smaller than the lexicon of English. So the atomist would be ill advised to hold onto eternal sentences, given that it looks like a sure road to decompositionalism.

Now, the discussion about eternal sentences is long and sustained (Quine 1960; Katz 1981; Wettstein 1979; Recanati 1994; Carston 2002). Defenders of eternal sentences claim that defenders of generalised underdeterminacy owe us a principled reason to hold that all sentences resemble their examples. On the other hand, defenders of the generalised underdeterminacy thesis take it that in the absence of an example of an eternal sentence, we should assume that all sentential utterances do in fact resemble their favourite cases of underdeterminacy. One of the most thorough defences of generalised underdeterminacy is due to Carston (2002), where she argues against the following 'principle of effability' as formulated (and also rejected) by Recanati:[10]

> For every statement that can be made using a context-sensitive sentence in a given context, there is an eternal sentence that can be used to make the same statement in any context. (Recanati 1994: 157)

---

10 Another moderate version of this claim can be found in Bach (2005: 28): 'for every sentence we do utter, there is a more elaborate, qualified version we could utter that would make what we mean more explicit'. The 'elaborate version' is closer to what is literally meant, but it is unclear whether he conceives of it as a version that is always perfectible (in which case there would not be eternal sentences as such).

Carston argues that there are no such things as eternal reference and eternal predication given that all referential and predicative terms are open to contextual variation. In other words, any referential term can be used to refer to an actual object, a possible object, or a belief-world-object, while predicative terms are always interpreted according to a 'certain understanding', as Travis, another defender of ineffability would put it (Travis 2000).

It seems to us that this point can be illustrated by means of Culicover and Jackendoff's (2004) Mme. Tussaud's examples. These authors persuasively argue that any proper name can be referring either to a person/object (its bearer) or to some iconic representation of it, such as a picture or a statue. For instance, 'Ringo is the Beatle that I like the most' may mean either that the actual drummer of the Beatles is the musician (or person) that I like the most, or that Ringo's statue at Mme. Tussaud's is the statue of a Beatle that I like the most. Now, think about the more precise formulation 'The statue of Ringo is the one I like the most'. This should clarify the possible ambiguity, but does it? Well, it clarifies *that* ambiguity, but this new sentence happens to be ambiguous itself, for we could be speaking either about the statue of Ringo or about a picture of it (we took pictures of all the statues and the picture of Ringo's statue happens to be the best). Culicover and Jackendoff sum up the lessons of these examples in the following *statue rule*:

> The syntactic structure NP may correspond to the semantic/conceptual structure PHYSICAL REPRESENTATION (x) where x is the ordinary interpretation of NP. (Culicover & Jackendoff 2004: 371)

This rule is by itself enough to jeopardise effability. But it is probably just one source of variation among many others (e.g., a belief-world rule that enabled an NP to refer to a mental representation of its usual reference, or the already noted context sensitivity of predicative terms).

Carston (2002) proposes that the reason why natural language is so unspecific is due to the evolutionary precedence of mind-reading abilities over language, which made it otiose to develop a precise medium of communication. That may be too speculative, but it goes some way into trying to provide a principled reason against effability. However, perhaps it is not needed: as things stand, we take it that the burden of proof should be on the defender of eternal sentences.

Premise (ii): SU and atomic literal meaning for words

The second premise we want to argue for is:

(ii) If sentential utterances do not have literal meanings, and if literal meanings of words are understood as concepts that correspond one-to-one to the words, then (some of) the utterances' component words do not have literal meaning either.[11]

We now claim that the SU of sentential utterances puts in jeopardy the possibility that lexical items (words, for short) have literal meanings themselves, when these are understood as concepts that correspond one-to-one to words. In the mentalistic framework we are assuming, the literal meaning of a word will be understood as the context-independent mental representation that it *encodes*.

Arguably, some of the examples about semantic underdeterminacy presented above apply in a straightforward manner to words. For instance, the claim is that 'Ringo is the Beatle that I like the most' is underdetermined partly because, due to the statue rule 'Ringo' is underdetermined itself. But doubts about the generalisability of this case arise more naturally for words. We are going to examine several possibilities in which the idea that words have literal meaning is fleshed out in a way that favours conceptual atomism, i.e., possibilities in which the literal meaning of a word is understood as an *encoded atom* that corresponds one-to-one to the word. Our rejection of such possibilities will rely on a simple argument: if words' literal meanings are understood as encoded atoms, then it will normally be possible to construct eternal sentences out of them; but since eternal sentences are suspect, so are literal meanings for words.

---

[11] This claim has to be qualified according to what we say later about the indeterminacy of composition rules.

The main idea is this: suppose that for each word there is an encoded atom that constitutes the word's literal meaning. Suppose that we construct a sentence in which every component word expresses precisely its encoded meaning. Suppose that there are rules of composition that operate on those encoded meanings so as to obtain a proposition – i.e., a truth-conditional structure. Then the meaning of this sentence is composed just by the encoded meanings of its words, according to certain rules of composition. But this is precisely what it takes to obtain an eternal sentence. So literal meanings for words entail the possibility of eternal sentences.

Let us examine two objections that might block the path from premise (i) to premise (ii). First, it is possible to say that words *encode* concepts in a one-to-one way, and that underdeterminacy effects are due to the fact that words can be used to *express* an open range of concepts. Second, we have shown a path from literal meanings of words to the existence of eternal sentences that depends crucially on certain rules of composition operating on meanings so as to obtain a proposition. But now it is possible to argue that semantic underdeterminacy, either of sentences or phrases, is due to the undeterminacy of the rules of composition. This way one could still hold that the parts (the words' meanings) are not underdetermined themselves. Let us examine these two positions in turn.

The encoded/expressed distinction

A key idea in Relevance Theory (Sperber & Wilson 1998; Wilson 2003) is that words *encode* concepts in a one-to-one way, even though they can *express* an open range of them. The inexistence of literal meanings for sentential utterances could be explained by holding that those various concepts that words can express are not lexicalised. To put it in simple terms, even though 'empty' encodes the concept EMPTY, an utterance of 'empty' does not express this concept, but a concept related to *having no people inside*. This second concept need not be lexicalised. This way one avoids being finally committed to effability in the sense mentioned above. Explaining how we go from the encoded concepts to the expressed ones is the task of the new field of 'lexical pragmatics' (Wilson 2003). Basically, lexical pragmatics has to explain core processes such as narrowing and loose talk or broadening, by which we modulate the extension of a given encoded concept so as to obtain a non-lexicalised concept. Sperber and Wilson (1998) claim that these non-lexicalised concepts are *ad hoc* concepts built on-line from encyclopaedic knowledge in order to meet the requirements of communicative relevance. However, in their view these concepts would be *just as atomic as encoded concepts are*, not just complexes of encoded concepts. Now, we think that a problem arises for this thesis regarding the role assigned to *encoded* concepts, and their relation to *ad hoc* concepts.

First of all, the commitment to encoded conceptual atoms as the starting point of the interpretive process seems to bring about the possibility of truth-conditional literal meanings for at least some sentences – that is, the possibility of some eternal sentences. RT's preferred explanation is that *ad hoc* concepts are obtained inferentially from encoded concepts. The starting point of such an inference is a representation *made (compositionally) out of encoded concepts*. That is, the necessary steps for inference to take place would be, first, decodification of words onto their encoded concepts, and, crucially, their composition into a structured representation. Some of these representations would be propositional templates: this would be the case of representations corresponding to sentences with indexicals, free variables, gradable adjectives, etc. However, in many cases the representation obtained should be fully propositional: the conceptual representation corresponding to, say, 'some leaves are green' would putatively be SOME LEAVES ARE GREEN. But such a representation would in effect constitute the literal meaning of the sentence, and this is exactly what the argument from SU denied, as claimed in premise (i). It seems that such *full* compositions (i.e., those that result in truth-conditional representations) are in this model plentiful: all that is needed is (1) an encoded concept for each of the sentences's components, and (2) a rule of composition that results in truth conditions. This being so, barring indexical expressions and the saturation of free variables, literalism (or, in any case, the DLH) at the level of the lexicon brings in its wake a kind of minimalism, i.e., the existence of propositions in a first stage of processing. This amounts to a denial of the underdeterminacy thesis.[12]

In fact, there is a general problem concerning *ad hoc* concepts. We are told that encoded concepts or literal meanings are modulated, so that their extensions are narrowed or broadened, but arguably the best way to make sense of modulations is by explaining them as concept compositions. Take 'that is a red pen': if RED gets modulated into RED WRITING, it is precisely because it turns out to express RED WRITING. That is, we do not really understand why *ad hoc* concepts in this picture could or should be atomic. We lack the space to go into some detail here (we do it elsewhere: see Vicente & Martínez Manrique 2010), but it seems to us that the concept ANGEL*, expressed in 'Mary is an angel' (to take another well-known example of concept broadening), is exhausted by the composition of concepts like KIND, GOOD and others. Now, if this were so, there would be even more encodable propositions than expected, for most utterances would encode a proposition and perhaps express another, which would be in turn encoded by a different sentence.

Underdeterminacy of rules

One may argue that the semantic underdeterminacy of sentences is due not to any underdeterminacy in their constituents but to the way rules of composition work. It might seem plausible to say that, e.g., 'the ink is blue' (Travis 2000) is underdetermined (it may write blue, or it may be look blue while writing black) because it is not specified how 'blue' is supposed to modify 'ink'. That is, 'blue' means BLUE and 'ink' means INK, and what makes the sentence underdetermined is the indeterminacy of the composition rule. This would also explain why 'some leaves are green' is underdetermined even though its components have, apparently at least, corresponding encoded concepts.

---

12 Moreover, and following this thread: given that 'some leaves are green' does not have determinate truth conditions (see Travis 1996), which of the possible propositions that it can express would it encode? There seems to be no principled answer to this question.

We want to address this objection even though we doubt that it is a popular one. Orthodoxy has it that composition rules follow syntactic information, compositionality principles stating that the meaning of a whole is a function of the meaning of its parts and its syntactic structure. The syntactic structure of 'blue ink', or of 'the ink is blue' is not ambiguous, so the composition rule cannot be either. The same goes for noun + noun complexes, such as 'oil alarm'. The rule says that the first noun modifies the second: there is no ambiguity in that. So the underdeterminacy of the sentence 'this is a new oil alarm' must have another cause.

However, one might want to depart from orthodoxy here, and claim that semantic composition rules do not track syntactic structure. Perhaps there are properly semantic rules, so that adj + noun or noun + noun constructions are underdetermined because it is not determined which of the various possible semantic rules we have to follow in a given case. Sometimes an adjective such as 'blue' modifies its head by being applied to its referent considered as a physical object, while other times its modification is applied to what its referent typically does. This seems to be compatible with the fact that 'blue', as most of the words, encodes a conceptual atom.

Now, the problem with this position is that it probably hides a trap to the atomist. For the best explanation for the variation in the composition rules is that meanings are complexes, such that, e.g., an adjective may be applied to different parts of the complex. That is, if composition rules worked as suggested, then it seems that concepts would need a certain inner structure. There must be information within the concept about what the things that fall under it are for, or even what kind of thing they are: if PEN is decomposable into at least PHYSICAL OBJECT, and, say, USED FOR WRITING (though this is a rough proposal: WRITING should be decomposable in other basic concepts), then it is possible to explain that there are at least two rules of composition that can be applied to RED PEN. In contrast, it seems difficult to explain how the atomic RED can be applied in various ways to the atomic PEN: if RED applies to PEN, it seems all that you can possibly have is the complex RED PEN, whose denotation is the intersection of red things and pens.

To sum up, it is open to the atomist to argue that the semantic underdeterminacy of sentences does not establish the semantic underdeterminacy of some of its parts, since sentential underdeterminacy may be caused by indeterminacy of rules. However, if this path is taken, it will probably have to be at the price of conceding that concepts have some kind of internal structure all the same. Furthermore, it will have to be conceded that, lacking contextual information, it is indeterminate which parts of the decomposition have to be activated. One possible reading of the latter point is that, lacking contextual information, what the word means is underdetermined. However, this reading may seem a bit too forced. What happens if rules are indeterminate, under this account, is that part of the concept comes to the fore, but clearly, the word does not mean *just* that part of the concept. So we can say that if some SU of sentential utterances is due to indeterminacies in composition rules, then the DLH is clearly false in its atomistic assumptions. It is a matter of interpretation whether rule indeterminacy by itself falsifies the thesis about the relation of words and concepts: it sounds reasonable to say that, in the 'red writing pen' and 'red looking pen' readings, 'pen' does not express the same concept, but it can also be said that, for all the discussion shows, it does.[13] In both cases, it means something like PHYSICAL OBJECT USED FOR WRITING, although the different parts of the complex may be differentially active.

So this is as far as our argument goes. Before closing this section, there is still another atomist alternative that we do not want to leave unmentioned. Recall from section 1 that Fodorian atomism relies on the existence of a single level, the conceptual level, to capture what words encode or express. Now, if we differentiate semantic and conceptual levels, it is possible to put forward an atomistic model without the burden of DLH. The idea, in a nutshell, is to posit the existence of semantic entities that encode word meanings, while leaving the solution of semantic underdeterminacies in the hands of

---

13 Note that, contrary to appearances, the polysemous word on this account would be 'pen' and not 'red'. Thus, this account is in contradiction with accounts such as Rotschild and Segal's (2009) and Kennedy and McNally's (forthcoming), which try to explain Travis cases by resorting to different analyses of colour terms.

the conceptual, pragmatically-driven device. Levinson (1997, 2003) has offered a number of reasons in support of such a distinction, while Carston (2002) has speculated on the possibility that word meanings appear in mind not as concepts but as 'concept schemas or pointers to conceptual space' (Carston 2002: 360; see also Bierwisch & Schreuder 1992). We do not have the space to develop and criticise two-level theories in this article[14] but we think that they share some of the problems noted above. For instance, the troubles RT has in accounting for the relation between encoded and *ad hoc* concepts reappear in Carston's two-level version when it comes to explain the relation between entities at the semantic and conceptual levels. In addition, two-level theories have their own specific problems. One of them is to explain in what sense semantic entities are different from conceptual ones (see Martínez Manrique 2010). Another is to avoid needless redundancy, as it seems to arise from positing a layer of concepts onto which semantic representations immediately map (Levinson 2003) – a layer which does in fact mirror the semantic level.

3 Decompositionalism, polysemy and underdeterminacy

We began this article claiming that a mentalistic account of word meaning has to account for stability and polysemy. If we force our hand towards stability we find radical atomism, which envisions a mind endowed with context-independent representations that correspond closely to words. If we emphasise polysemy we run into radical contextualism, which cannot find representational structures that match up with word meanings in a stable way. The decompositionalism we argue for tries to find a way to navigate between

---

[14] We do it elsewhere: for a criticism of two-level accounts related to points addressed in this article see Vicente & Martínez Manrique (2010); for a general criticism of the cogency of semantic representation as a distinct representational kind see Martínez Manrique (2010).

those extremes. It shares with atomism the representationalist principle that sentences express thoughts that are ultimately composed of primitive context-independent conceptual elements. It shares with contextualism a *principle of context*: words express concepts only in context (both linguistic and extralinguistic) and what they express depends partially on it. Joining both principles we get a picture in which mental representations of word meanings consist of a cluster of primitive concepts with perhaps a basic, more or less stable core, and a number of variable components that can be adjoined or removed depending on particular contexts of utterance.

Primitives may include 'traditional' semantic features (Bierwisch & Schreuder 1992), as well as more general conceptual elements. The latter may include concepts of basic kinds that mature in the toddler's mind, such as OBJECT (Spelke 1990), AGENT (Bloom 2004), or GENERIC SPECIES (Atran 1998), basic relations, such as CAUSATION; categories, such as EVENT, PLACE or PROPERTY (Jackendoff 2002), etc. Obviously, the list has to be taken with caution. In particular, the fact that one cannot help using names for concepts must not lead one to conclude that they correspond to meanings of the respective words ('object', 'cause', etc. Rather, they are fairly abstract atoms that compose to make up more familiar concepts, which, in correspondence, are said to *de-compose*.

Now, decompositionalism fares clearly better than atomism in accounting for the variability of meanings. Let us go back to the principle of context: what we said is that words express concepts only in context (both linguistic and extralinguistic) and what they express depends partially on it. How can it happen? The decompositionalist has a simple explanation: a word typically stands for a complex of concepts, but the complex may be variable, i.e., it may vary from token to token (of that word-type). At this point, it is possible to adopt either a cluster theory, where every component is in principle removable, as long as there are enough that stay, or a more classical theory, according to which there is a permanent or essential nucleus and a constellation of joinable concepts. In any case, there is variability because words do not stand for simple concepts, but for alterable complexes of simple concepts.

On the one hand, we have simple explanations for the polysemy of words such as 'keep'.[15] According to Jackendoff (1992), the word 'keep' in 'Susan kept the money' stands for a concept that can be (roughly) decomposed into CAUSE and STATE OF POSSESSION THAT ENDURES OVER TIME, in the structure CAUSE [STATE OF POSSESSION THAT ENDURES OVER TIME]. The decomposition of 'keep', however, is not univocal: in different contexts it can stand for notions such as causing the endurance of a state of location ('keeps the car in the garage'), causing the endurance of a state of commitment ('keeps a promise'), etc. Although Jackendoff's proposal may well be too rough and rudimentary, it is easy to see that decompositionalism provides us with the essentials to explain both stability and polysemy: there is something permanent to the different uses of 'keep' (so 'keep' cannot stand just for any concept), but there is also something that can change. A simple way to explain how 'keep' can take these different meanings is by holding that most 'keep' meanings have a common structure: CAUSE [STATE OF x THAT ENDURES OVER TIME], which implies that there is a free variable within the structure that has to be saturated. How do we assign a value to such a variable? The idea would be: by resorting basically, or in a large part, to information located in lexical entries, such that 'in the garage' activates STATE OF LOCATION THAT ENDURES OVER TIME as a complement of CAUSE, and 'money', in the absence of a locative, activates STATE OF POSSESION THAT ENDURES OVER TIME. In addition, decompositionalism is not committed to the idea that CAUSE is a *necessary* component of the meaning of 'keep'. There may be contexts in which the causative element is absent (e.g., intransitive uses such as 'an apple that keeps'), but that share a number of other typical conceptual elements (e.g., ENDURE OVER TIME) sufficient to regard the expressed concept as another sense of 'keep' (rather than a homonymous word).

On the other hand, decompositionalism also has the resources to deal with cases of SU that can be taken to arise from indeterminacies

---

15 This is also clearly the case for examples of alleged narrowings and broadenings: a meaning gets narrowed down if some concepts are adjoined to it; it is broadened if some concepts are removed from the complex.

in construction rules. As we have explained above, the indeterminacy that affects an example such as Travis's (2000) 'blue ink' may be explained by saying that INK is a complex of concepts, perhaps put together in what Pustejovsky (1995) calls 'a *qualia* structure' (say, DENSE LIQUID STUFF USUALLY USED FOR WRITING), and that the modifier 'blue' can modify either some or all of these. Thus, when 'blue' is applied to DENSE LIQUID STUFF 'blue ink' means 'blue in its external aspect', when it is applied to the telic *qualia* FOR WRITING, it means 'blue in its writing', etc.

Second, decompositionalism has – and atomism lacks – resources to deal with the distinction between polysemy and homonymy. Consider an example from Pustejovsky (1995) discussed by Fodor & Lepore (2002): 'bake' is typically regarded as polysemous because it is used with different but *related* senses, such as 'bake a cake' (*create*) vs. 'bake a potato' (*heat up*). In contrast, homonymous words, such as 'bank' in 'bank a plane' and 'bank a check', are those that have different *unrelated* meanings. Psycholinguistic tradition takes it that homonymous words have separate entries in the mental lexicon, while part of the debate is whether the different senses of polysemous words are also separately listed or it is possible to generate them from a common representational core.[16]

Fodor and Lepore follow the tradition with respect to 'bank', but they contend that 'bake' is an ambiguous word that behaves the same way in the expressions in which it occurs, i.e., it may refer either to *create* or to *heat up* in 'bake the cake', 'bake the potato' or 'bake the knife'. The reason why the latter two cases sound funny in the *create* sense is 'something you know about the world, not something you know about words: namely, that you can't make a knife or a potato by baking it. If you didn't know this, you would hear the ambiguity, as indeed you do in "John is baking something"' (Fodor & Lepore 2002: 107). This explanation strikes us as odd, because if it were correct, we could extend it to homonymous words, i.e., one could argue that

---

[16] See Taylor (2003b) for an overview of the debates concerning polysemy. The currently prevalent view seems to favour the 'common representation' thesis, but for psycholinguistic experimental work in support of the 'separate senses' view of polysemy see Klein & Murphy (2001, 2002).

every occurrence of 'bank' is ambiguous between *manoeuvre* and *deposit*, the difference lying in how the world is with respect to things such as planes and checks. This might be all coherent if one held that 'bake' and 'bank' behave similarly, homonymy being thus the norm. But this is not what Fodor and Lepore hold, given that they endorse the view that 'John baked the potatoes and Mary the cookies' makes sense while '*John banked the check and the plane' does not.[17]

Indeed, Fodor and Lepore do not try to provide an account of polysemy, but to show that it is a multifarious phenomenon with no single unified explanation. In their view, there are lots of 'residual cases' of words with meanings that 'can partially overlap in all shorts of ways, so there are all shorts of ways in which polysemous terms can differ from mere homonyms. Nothing in the literature convinces us that there are powerful generalizations to state' (Fodor & Lepore 2002: 116). What we contend is (a) that this way they leave too many (paradigmatic) cases with no explanation at all, and (b) that decompositionalism provides the outline of such an explanation.

Let us restate what it is that begs for an explanation: there are words whose different senses strike us as related, namely 'bake', and others with unrelated senses, namely 'bank'. Psycholinguistic research puts this impression on trial and, more often than not, gives us grounds to think that both classes of words are represented in different ways and have different processing effects. The reasons why a word belongs to one class or the other may be, if one wants

---

[17] They propose this as a sort of test to tell polysemy from homonymy (see their fn. 9), probably following Zwicky & Sadock's (1975) zeugma test for polysemy. The fact that they use a test for polysemy as a test for homonymy makes it suspect. But leaving that aside, the test does not seem to embody a robust criterion, as neither does Zwicky and Saddock's. On the one hand, paradigmatically homonymous words may pass the test when the context is weird enough to allow unusual combinations of words. For instance, one can imagine a scenario in which one banks a plane in the same sense as one banks a check (e.g., a world in which you can carry your old plane to a bank as if it were cash) and vice versa (e.g., a world in which you can pilot giant checks, say, as if they were flying carpets). On the other hand, seemingly polysemous words, such as 'unchain', may not pass it: 'John unchained his bike and the storm' is doubtfully meaningful following Fodor and Lepore's standards.

to put it in these terms, metaphysically grounded – the processes referred to by 'bank' are grossly different while those referred to by 'bake' have some commonalities. But the answer is clearly insufficient. It is not only that the denoted processes are partly common, partly different; it is also a fact that interpreters *notice* the commonalities and differences. So they must have the means to represent them in their respective thoughts. Those are the representational elements that the decompositionalist tries to provide. Moreover, decompositionalism allows for the distinction between polysemy and homonymy to be one of degree: homonymous words would be those that express representational structures with almost no components in common, and the elements with which they combine (in each of the senses) come typically from separate sets, e.g., the words with which 'bank' combines in the sense of *manoeuvre* do not (in general) overlap with words with which it combines in the sense of *deposit*. Atomism, as we have tried to show, has a bad time telling polysemy from homonymy, and it hesitates between making the former collapse onto the latter (and endorsing thus an enormous mental lexicon that lists every word sense separately and adds a new entry for each new sense extension), and simply denying the phenomenon of polysemy as such.

4 Conclusion

The decompositionalist program has been defended as the best account available of phenomena such as argument structure (Levin & Rappaport Hovav 2005; Pinker 2007), impossible words (Johnson 2004), coercion (Jackendoff 2002), polysemy (Jackendoff 1992; Pustejovsky 1995), the typical semantic relations such as entailments, synonymy and antonymy, and the very compositionality of semantics (Jackendoff 2002).[18] Here we have tried to offer a new line of attack on its main rival, atomism. We have argued that atomism in any of

---

[18] See Pitt (1999) for other merits of decompositionalism to account for intuitive semantic properties, reference fixing, informal inference, and language understanding.

its versions cannot cope with the contextualist challenge. This is significant, because some of the most influential current contextualists are atomist. A cluster decompositionalism is, in our view, a much more commendable position for contextualists: it offers a much better explanation of variability both of word meanings and of sentence meanings.*

References

Atran, S. (1998). Folkbiology and the anthropology of science: Cognitive universals and cultural particulars. *Behavioral and Brain Sciences, 21,* 547–609.

Bach, K. (1994). Conversational impliciture. *Mind & Language, 9,* 124–162.

——— (2005). Content ex machina. In Szabó, Z. G. (Ed.). *Semantics versus pragmatics,* (pp. 15–44). Oxford; New York: Oxford University Press.

Bierwisch, M. & Schreuder, R. (1992). From concepts to lexical items. *Cognition, 42,* 23–60.

Bloom, P. (2004). *Descartes' baby.* New York: Basic Books.

Borg, E. (2004). *Minimal semantics.* Oxford; New York: Oxford University Press.

Cappelen, H. & Lepore, E. (2005). *Insensitive semantics: A defense of semantic minimalism and speech act pluralism.* Oxford: Blackwell.

Carston, R. (2002). *Thoughts and utterances.* London: Blackwell.

Cohen, J. (1985). A problem about ambiguity in truth-conditional semantics. *Analysis, 45,* 129–134.

Cruse, D. A. (1986). *Lexical semantics.* Cambridge: Cambridge University Press.

Cruse, D. A. (2000). *Meaning in language.* Oxford; New York: Oxford University Press.

Culicover, P. and Jackendoff, R. (2004). *Simpler syntax.* Oxford; New York: Oxford University Press.

---

* Research for this article has been funded by the Spanish Government (project FFI2008-06421-C02). Special thanks are due to Begoña Vicente.

Fodor, J. (1998). *Concepts*. Oxford; New York: Oxford University Press.

―――― (2001). Language, thought and compositionality. *Mind & Language, 16*, 1–15.

Fodor, J. & Lepore, E. (2002). The emptiness of the lexicon: Reflections on Pustejovsky. In Fodor, J. & Lepore, E. *The compositionality papers,* (pp. 89–119). Oxford: Oxford University Press. (Revised from the version published in *Linguistic Inquiry, 29,* 269–288.)

―――― (2005). Out of context. *Proceedings and Addresses of the APA, 78*(2), 3–20.

Jackendoff. R. (1992). *Languages of the mind*. Cambridge, MA: MIT Press.

―――― (2002). *Foundations of language: brain, meaning, grammar, evolution*. Oxford; New York: Oxford University Press.

Johnson, K. (2004). From impossible words to conceptual structure: The role of structure and processes in the lexicon. *Mind & Language, 19,* 334–358.

Katz, J. J. & Fodor, J. A. (1963). The structure of a semantic theory. *Language, 39,* 170–210.

Katz, J.J. (1981). *Language and other abstract objects*. Oxford: Blackwell.

Kennedy, C. & McNally, L. (forthcoming). Color, context and compositionality. *Synthese*.

Klein, D. E. & Murphy, G. L. (2001). The representation of polysemous words. *Journal of Memory and Language, 45,* 259–282.

―――― (2002). Paper has been my ruin: Conceptual relations of polysemous senses. *Journal of Memory and Language, 47,* 548–570.

Levin, B. & Rappaport Hovav, M. (2005). *Argument realization*. New York: Cambridge University Press.

Levinson, S. (1997). From outer to inner space: Linguistic categories and non-linguistic thinking. In Nuyts, E. & Pederson, J. (Eds.). *Language and conceptualization,* (pp. 13–45). Cambridge: Cambridge University Press.

―――― (2003). Language and mind: Let's get the issues straight. In Gentner, D. & Goldin-Meadow, S. (Eds.). *Language in mind,* (pp. 25–45). Cambridge, MA: MIT Press.

Martínez Manrique, F. (2010). On the distinction between semantic and conceptual representation. *Dialectica, 64*(1), 57–78.

Moravcsik, J. M. (1990). *Thought and language.* London: Routledge.

Murphy, G. L. (2002). *The big book of concepts.* Cambridge, MA: MIT Press.

Pinker, S. (2007). *The stuff of thought.* London: Penguin Books.

Pitt, D. (1999). In defense of definitions. *Philosophical Psychology, 12,* 139–156.

Pustejovsky, J. (1995). *The generative lexicon.* Cambridge, MA: MIT Press.

Quine, W. V. O. (1960). *Word and object.* Cambridge, MA: MIT Press.

Recanati, F. (1993). *Direct reference.* Oxford: Blackwell.

―――― (1994). Contextualism and anti-contextualism in the philosophy of language. In Tsohatzidis, S. (Ed.). *Foundations of Speech Act Theory,* (pp. 156–166). London: Routledge.

―――― (2001). What is said. *Synthese, 128,* 75–91.

―――― (2004). *Literal meaning.* Cambridge: Cambridge University Press.

Rothschild, D. & Segal, G. (2009). Indexical predicates. *Mind & language, 24,* 467–493.

Spelke, E. (1990). Principles of object perception. *Cognitive Science, 14,* 29–56.

Sperber, D. & Wilson, D. (1986). *Relevance: Communication and cognition.* Cit. in 2nd edition (1995). Oxford: Blackwell.

―――― (1998). The mapping between the mental and the public lexicon. In Carruthers, P. & Boucher, J. (Eds.). *Language and thought: Interdisciplinary themes.* Cambridge, MA: MIT Press, 184–200.

Taylor, J. R. (2003a). *Linguistic categorization.* Oxford; New York: Oxford University Press.

―――― (2003b). Polysemy's paradoxes. *Language Sciences, 25,* 637–655.

Travis, C. (1985). On what is strictly speaking true. *Canadian Journal of Philosophy, 15*, 187–229.
—— (1996). Meaning's role in truth, *Mind, 105,* 451–466.
—— (2000). *Unshadowed thought.* Cambridge, MA: Harvard University Press.
Vicente, A. (2010). Clusters: On the structure of lexical concepts. *Dialectica, 64*(1), 79–106.
Vicente, A. & Martínez Manrique, F. (2010). On relevance theory's atomistic commitments. In Soria, B. & Romero, E. (Eds.). *Explicit communication: On Robyn Carston's pragmatics.* London: Palgrave McMillan.
Wettstein, H. (1979). Indexical reference and propositional content. *Philosophical Studies, 36,* 91–100.
Wierzbicka, A. (1996). *Semantics: primes and universals.* Oxford; New York: Oxford University Press.
Wilson, D. (2003). Relevance and lexical pragmatics. *Rivista di Linguistica / Italian Journal of Linguistics, 15.2,* 273–291.
Wilson, D. & Sperber, D. (2002). Truthfulness and relevance. *Mind, 111,* 583–632.
Zwicky, A. & Sadock, J. (1975). Ambiguity tests and how to fail them. In Kimball, J. (Ed.). *Syntax and semantics, 4,* (pp. 1–35). New York: Academic Press.

Isidora Stojanovic

Referring With Proper Names: Towards a Pragmatic Account

1 Introduction

Proper names have been undoubtedly one of the most discussed topics in philosophy of language; whether this is deservedly so is not among my present concerns. The motivations that are driving this article are not so much proper names *per se*, as the issue of how they fit into a more general framework of meaning, reference and content that I have been trying to develop in recent years (e.g. in Stojanovic 2005, 2008). So far, my main focus has been on indexicals, which are often thought of, following Kaplan's (1977) influential work, as directly referential expressions *par excellence;* that is, expressions that contribute their reference, and nothing but their reference, to semantic content. Against the mainstream view, I have held that all there is to semantic content is the lexically encoded content; in particular, I have argued that the things and individuals referred to with the help of indexical pronouns, while being relevant to determining truth value, are neither part of semantic content nor otherwise involved in determining semantic content (cf. Stojanovic 2009). In section 2, I will briefly survey some motivations for this view, and explain how I see the interplay between reference, meaning and content in the case of indexicality. It should be noted that while it is central to my proposal that (indexical and demonstrative) reference does not reach into semantic content, I have no qualms with the sheer idea that reference can be part of content – or, alluding to the famous exchange between Frege and Russell, that Mont Blanc, with all its snowfields, may be a constituent of a proposition. But this leaves me with something of a dilemma: when it comes to names, which, too, are often thought of as directly referential expressions *par excellence*, are there reasons to depart from the mainstream Kripkean-Kaplanian view?

Following the one horn of the dilemma, we might say that, unlike indexicals, names are indeed directly referential and contribute their reference, and nothing but their reference, to semantic content. Following the other horn of the dilemma, we might say that, as with indexicals, the things and individuals referred to with the help of names are neither part of semantic content nor otherwise involved in determining semantic content. The latter horn of the dilemma gives rise to further ramifications, depending on how we think of meaning – and, more precisely, of the lexically encoded meaning – in the case of proper names. The various options related to the question of whether names have meanings and, if they do, what their meanings are like, will be explored in section 3, as well as the question of what kind of (logical) inferences proper names give rise to. The discussion of those two questions will pave the way to distinguishing, in sections 4 and 5, three views that are all compatible with the idea that (indexical) reference does not reach into content:

(i) the mainstream Kripkean-Kaplanian referentialist view of names;

(ii) the perhaps equally mainstream descriptivist view of names, which further bifurcates into, on the one hand, the classical Fregean-Russellian view, on which some non-trivial description may be associated with a given name (e.g. 'the teacher of Alexander the Great' for the name 'Aristotle'); and, on the other, the so-called metalinguistic view, on which, for any name N, the associated description is 'the bearer of N';

(iii) the off-stream view, which I have dubbed the *pragmatic* view, on which names contribute neither reference nor any kind of meaning to any semantic level – rather, names are merely pragmatic devices that help the hearer figure out what the speaker is talking about, and may therefore be relevant to determining truth value, but have no impact on semantics.

The goal of my article, then, is to clarify these views, and explain how each of them can fit into the more general picture outlined in section 2. Although I will not try to come up with any decisive argument for or against any of those views, I have great sympathy for the pragmatic view, hence my secondary goal in this article will be to show it to be a very plausible view, notwithstanding appearances.

2 Removing (demonstrative) reference from semantic content

In previous work, I have argued that all there is to semantic content is the lexically encoded content, hence that the things referred to with the help of demonstrative and indexical pronouns, not being themselves part of the pronoun's lexical meaning, are not part of the semantic content associated with the sentence in which the pronoun occurs. This does not mean, though, that the things referred to are not relevant to determining truth value. Thinking of it somewhat formally, semantic content may be represented by a function from a sequence of parameters that, along with possible world and time parameters, include parameters of *individuals*, into truth values. To illustrate the idea, suppose that I say, pointing at Tareq:

(1) He is a doctor.

My proposal, on a first approximation, is that the semantic content of (1) is a function from sequences (world, time, individual, $p_4 \ldots p_n$) to truth values, a function that returns value True if and only if i is a doctor in w at t (leaving the remaining parameters $p_4 \ldots p_n$ unspecified, as they have no impact on the truth value in the case of (1)). So, with a sentence like (1), the semantic content will yield a truth value only once it has been given a world, a time, and *an individual* to be evaluated at. And normally, our judgments of truth concerning (1) will rely on evaluating the semantic content associated with (1) at Tareq, since he is the person about whom I am talking, as well as at the time at which (1) is uttered and at the world that we are in. The crucial point is that Tareq is no more part of the semantic content of (1) than are the world and the time of evaluation.

As already emphasized, removing reference from semantic content does not mean removing it altogether from the entire picture. To the contrary, reference still plays an important role in the account that I am proposing. I take it that communication presupposes that we should be able to convey information *about* people and things around us, and that this, in turn, strongly suggests that we should be able to *refer* to those things *directly*. Here is an example of what I take to be a paradigmatic case of direct reference. Suppose that we have just tasted together a certain dish, and I simply say:

(2) Delicious!

I will be referring to that very dish, and will be saying *of that dish* that it is delicious. Or, to take another example, suppose that I say:

(3) I'm ready!

To determine the truth value of (3), one must determine who spoke, and what the world is like, viz. whether that person is ready, but of course, one must also determine which action or event (3) is about; e.g. if I am ready for lunch, but not ready to send off a job application, it is crucial to know whether it is the lunch or the job application that I am talking about in (3). And this, I take it, is something to which I would be referring directly.

Examples (2) and (3) illustrate a form of reference that makes it possible to talk about a particular thing or event without having to use any expression for it, reference that relies entirely on the non-linguistic contextual setting in which communication takes place. It is this form of reference that I take to be direct reference *par excellence*. Reference supported by words like pronouns is merely parasitic on this other, more basic form of reference.

It is easy to confuse direct reference with the use of indexicals. A possible explanation of why indexicals are so often taken to be devices of direct reference is that in theorizing about them, philosophers often focus on those uses on which indexicals do no interesting semantic or pragmatic work – rather, they merely 'articulate' the reference. Suppose that the following are uttered in the same situations in which (2) and (3) were uttered:

(4)   This is delicious!

(5)   I'm ready for it.

These appear to be equivalent ways of expressing the same thing as in (2) and (3).[1]

However, the conclusion that one might be tempted to draw, to the effect that 'this' in (4) and 'it' in (5) must be contributing their reference to semantic content (for what else could they possibly contribute?), is clearly unwarranted. Rather than think of direct reference as a by-product of *direct-referentiality*, which would be a semantic property of a certain class of expressions, I propose that we view direct reference as, first and foremost, *referring directly*, which is an action performed by the speaker, and is, therefore, a pragmatic phenomenon. It does not require the speaker to use any expression that would stand for the thing referred to, and when it is accompanied by the use of an indexical, the speaker will typically use the indexical in order to help her audience figure out what it is to which she, *qua* speaker, is referring. The idea is that the way in which indexicals help figuring out what is being referred to, is by constraining the range of potential referents by means of constraints lexically encoded in

---

[1] Note, however, that (5) sounds rather odd in situations in which the bare 'I'm ready' is fine; that is, situations in which there is no linguistic antecedent for the pronoun 'it' and no event contrasted with the one for which I say that I'm ready. On the other hand, the use of 'this' in (4) comes more naturally, since it is justified from the standpoint of syntax alone.

their meaning. To illustrate the idea, suppose that we are looking at a certain couple, Tareq and Aysha, and I tell you:

(6)   He is a doctor.

The 3rd person pronoun 'he' has only a very poor lexical meaning. All that is lexically encoded is that the person referred to should be *male*. But even this information, rather uninteresting in itself, is doing something useful in communication. It helps you, *qua* hearer, figure out that it is Tareq rather than Aysha that I am referring to, since he is the one who, among the things or people to whom I *might* be referring in the situation at stake, satisfies most saliently the condition associated with the pronoun 'he'.

What I hope to have done is to give you some idea about the interplay between reference and the use of indexicals, so let me now turn to the notion of semantic content to see where and how it fits into the picture. Recall the case in which, in reference to the dish we've just tasted, I simply say 'delicious'. The suggestion is that the semantic content in this case is simply a property; namely, deliciousness.[2] The object to which that property is attributed, that very dish, is not part of semantic content. Rather, it is that with respect to which semantic content will be normally evaluated for a truth value, just as it will be evaluated for a truth value at a certain time and with respect to a certain state of affairs (or a possible world).

On a first approximation, the same story might go for the case in which, in reference to Tareq, I say:

(7)   He is a doctor.

---

[2] Let us, for the sake of simplicity, pretend that deliciousness is indeed a property, i.e. a one-place predicate that applies to the object said to be delicious and does not require any other argument. Beware, though, that this simplification obliterates the fact that what is delicious to me need not be delicious to you. In other words, it would be more accurate to consider deliciousness as a *relational* property: something can be delicious with respect to some agents without being so with respect to others. For discussion, see Stojanovic (2007).

Ultimately, I would like to defend this proposal. But a question immediately arises: what is going to be the difference between the semantic content associated with (7) and that associated with:

(8)   She is a doctor.

The simple story, which, for reasons that will become clear shortly, I call the 'exclusive' view, gives a simple answer: there is no difference!

This answer will probably be met with some reluctance. More likely, one could think that, assuming that indexicals do not contribute reference to semantic content, they must contribute something else, hence presumably the constraints lexically encoded in their meaning. I call this the 'inclusive' view, since it holds that the semantic content associated with a sentence that contains an indexical *includes* the constraints encoded in the indexical's lexical meaning, while the exclusive view holds that it doesn't. But how is one to run the inclusive view? On a first approximation, one might suggest that the semantic content associated with (7) corresponds to a function that takes an individual, a time, a world, etc. and returns True if that individual is a doctor *and male* at that time and in that world, and False otherwise.

This straightforward proposal will not work, though, for (at least) two reasons. The first one has to do with the interaction between indexicals and intensional operators (such as the various modal, temporal and epistemic expressions), viz. the fact that if one embeds (7) under, say, the possibility operator, what one is concerned with is whether there is a possible state of affairs in which Tareq is a doctor, whether or not Tareq is also male (i.e. satisfies the descriptive material lexically encoded in 'he') in that state. The problem can be solved by using the mechanism of *double indexing*, that is, by taking semantic contents to be functions that take as arguments not just one time and one world, but rather, a pair of times and a pair of worlds, the first of which are the 'designated' time and world (the now and the actuality), the second of which are the time and the world deployed in the recursive truth clauses of non-indexical temporal and modal operators.

The second reason why the straightforward proposal won't work is that if we evaluate the semantic content associated with (7) at, for example, Aysha, it will return False (since Aysha isn't a *he*). But then, assuming the usual truth clause for negation, the following will be true when evaluated at Aysha:

(9) It's not the case that he is a doctor.

Yet if I utter (9) in reference to Aysha, whom let us furthermore suppose to be a doctor, I will not be speaking truly. To solve this problem, one had better take the semantic content associated with (7) to be a *partial* function, namely, a function that takes an individual i, a pair of times (t^*, t) and a pair of worlds (w^*, w), and returns True if i is male at t^* and w^* and i is a doctor at t and w, returns False if i is male at t^* and w^* and i is not a doctor at t and w, and simply does not return anything (i.e. is undefined) if i fails to be male at t^* and w^*.[3]

Turning to the exclusive view, it holds that the semantic content of (7) just is the property of being a doctor, i.e. a total function that takes an individual, a time and a world (or sequences thereof), and returns True if the individual at stake is a doctor at the time and in the world of evaluation, and False otherwise. In other words, on this view, indexical and demonstrative pronouns do not contribute anything to semantic content. The semantic content of (7), if evaluated at Aysha, would thus return True if Aysha is a doctor, even though she is female. The lexical meaning of 'he' in (7) would, then, intervene at a *post-semantic* stage, at which semantic content gets evaluated for a truth value. Its role would be to indicate that only individuals who satisfy the lexically encoded constraint (i.e. who are male) may be plausibly taken as values for the parameters at which the content of (7) is to receive its truth value. By way of an analogy, suppose that I utter the sentence in (7) in a situation in which, as we have been talking

---

[3] This move will be familiar from formal theories of presupposition. Indeed, I believe that the most attractive variant of the inclusive view is that which construes the constraints lexically encoded in the meaning of pronouns as presuppositions (albeit of a special sort).

about Khaled, Tareq comes in. To determine whether what I say is true, you need to evaluate the semantic content associated with (7) at an individual, and you have narrowed down your choices to Khaled and Tareq, but you still don't know which one to give preference to – for you don't know whether I'm talking about Tareq or Khaled. Now suppose that, as I say (7), I also make a pointing gesture towards Tareq. Then this gesture serves as a device to indicate that it is Tareq, rather than Khaled, at whom I want you to evaluate this content for its truth value. So then, just as such pointing gestures intervene at a post-semantic stage, to indicate at whom one could plausibly evaluate content for a truth value, so do the constraints lexically encoded in indexicals, according to the exclusive view.[4]

For the purposes of the present article, we need not choose between the two views.[5] What is important is to have the disctinction clearly laid out, as it will be relevant in the case of proper names, too, to which I turn now.

3 How names fit into the lexicon and into logic

Before I set out to explain the various ways in which proper names may be incorporated into the general picture outlined in the previous section, I want to look at the data to be accounted for, and will start

---

[4] Regardless of whether one goes inclusive or exclusive in the case of indexicals, there are aspects of lexical meaning that do not reach into semantic content. To take a fairly uncontroversial example, consider the Spanish pronouns 'tu' vs. 'Usted'. It is part of the lexical meaning of the latter that ones uses it to formally address one's interlocutor. But this lexical difference does not get reflected in semantics: from the point of view of semantics, 'tu' and 'Usted' are interchangeable. The difference may play a useful role in communication: consider a speaker who has two interlocutors, only one of whom he addresses formally; whether he uses the formal or the informal pronoun, he will express the same content; yet the choice of pronoun will help decide at whom to evaluate this content for a truth value.

[5] On a personal note, I used to defend the inclusive view (Stojanovic 2008), but am now more attracted to the exclusive view. I first used the terminology 'inclusive' vs. 'exclusive' in Stojanovic (2009), where I viewed both views as being 'equally plausible'.

precisely with the question of whether it makes any sense to talk of *lexical* knowledge when it comes to proper names. The plausibility, for instance, of the descriptivist and, in particular, the metalinguistic view, is going to turn upon one's answer to this question.

At a first glance, one might think that it is just obvious that names lack lexical meaning. For instance, the mere fact that one does not find in any dictionary an entry such as 'Tareq' suggests that this is not a word endowed with any lexical meaning – for, after all, that is precisely what dictionaries are there for, to tell us what the words of a given language mean. But, even if the right answer to our question may well be that proper names have no lexical meaning at all, the answer is not as obvious as one might have thought. It has been suggested by several philosophers (e.g. J. Katz) that there is a notion of lexical meaning that you may plausibly associate with proper names. The idea, as I see it, is that the mere fact that some string of symbols or sounds is a *name* endows this name with the meaning that can be approximated with the description 'whoever bears this name'. So, the lexical meaning of any name N would be obtained by means of the following schema:

The Metalinguistic Thesis:

The lexical meaning of N is 'the bearer of N'.

In the next section, some refinements to the thesis will be made, but for the time being, what matters is that one can plausibly hold that proper names *do* have lexical meanings, albeit all generated using a single schema.

There is yet another way of answering the question whether names have meanings, namely, that some names do, and some don't. For example, 'Tareq' and other 'ordinary' proper names don't, but there are names such that a person who ignores their meaning would not really count as a competent speaker of English. For example, the names of the twelve months in the calendar ('January', etc.), the names of the days in the week ('Sunday', etc.), names such as 'Earth', 'Sun', 'Moon', the names of the eight planets, the names of the continents ('Africa', 'Asia'...), and so on. All these names are excellent candidates for being names knowledge of whose meaning is constitutive of the knowledge of English. These are proper names, yet a person who does not master them may be plausibly charged of not being a fully competent English speaker. Note also that names like these do get translated from one language to another, just as common nouns do, while a person's name such as 'Tareq Al-Mahoud' might perhaps be spelled differently in different languages, but it is not subject to translation.

The proposal here shares something with the classical descriptivist view, in that it holds that names (that is, those that are meaningful) may be associated with a non-trivial lexically encoded material, rather than just the quasi-trivial constraint of being the bearer of a given name. But it is also significantly different from the descriptivist view, on the one hand because it holds that the associated lexical meaning does not vary from individual to individual, and on the other, because it does not generalize to all proper names. But one problem with the proposal is, precisely, the question of where to draw the line. For instance, you might think that 'France' is a name that has a lexical meaning, and that speakers are not fully competent in English if they lack the knowledge that France is a country, that the adjective derived from 'France' is 'French', etc. But, by parity of reasoning, the name of any country should then be part of the English lexicon. Yet, if someone has never heard, say, of Oman, and does not know that the derivative adjective is 'Omani', you may find this person uneducated, but it does not seem right to charge such a person with being an incompetent speaker of English! This is a problem, but I do not think that this is a major problem for this proposal: all it needs is to acknowledge that the borderline between names that do have lexical meanings and those that don't is vague (or at least underdetermined).

Let me now turn to a different, though not unrelated, question, namely: what kind of *logical* inferences are licensed by proper names? Consider an utterance of the following sentence:

(10) Sophie is a mathematician.

What can one logically infer from (10) – that is, what can one infer from (10) merely in virtue of what the words in (10) mean and of how they are combined? For instance, here is a fairly uncontroversial case of something that logically follows from (10):

(11) Someone is a mathematician.

And here is a fairly uncontroversial case of something that does not logically follow from (11), even if we grant that (11) cannot be a true utterance unless the following is also true:

(12) The speaker of (10) can speak some English.

But between the two, there are cases in which the answer is not as clear as for (11) or (12). For instance, one may wonder whether the following can be inferred from (10) merely in virtue of what the words in (10) mean:

(13) Someone is called 'Sophie'.

If the answer is 'yes', then that provides a good reason to go with the metalinguistic view, and if the answer is 'no', that provides a good reason for rejecting it. I do not know the right answer to the question whether (13) logically follows from (10) – if there *is* a right answer, to begin with. What I know is that individual constants in First Order Logic (FOL), to which one often 'translates' proper names, do not support the inference from (10) to (13). Furthermore, if you accept the metalinguistic thesis, and if you accept that logical inference is inference in virtue of what the words mean, then you should accept the following as a logical consequence of (10):

(14) There are two individuals, Sophie and the name 'Sophie', and the former is a bearer of the latter.

But, of course, in FOL, a sentence of the form $F(c)$ (where F is a one-place predicate and c an individual constant), does not entail $\exists x \exists y (x \neq y)$.[6]

---

6   $\exists x \exists y (x \neq y)$ follows from (13) on the uncontroversially true assumption that a person's name is distinct from the person so-named. The argument and, more

4 Compatibility with referentialist and descriptivist approaches

As I announced from the outset, my goal in this article is not to defend any particular view of proper names, but rather, to show that several existing views are compatible with the more general picture of semantic content that I have developed elsewhere and simply outlined here.[7] I will also put forward an original – or, at least, less familiar – view, a view that probably fits best into the general picture, but is also too extreme for me to be able to properly argue for it within the span of this article.

Among the existing views, let me start with the mainstream referentialist view, inspired by Kripke and pursued by Donnellan, Kaplan, Salmon, and many others, with which I assume that the reader will be already familiar. I want to show that it is coherent to endorse a referentialist approach to proper names while giving it up in the case of indexicals.

The easiest way to see that the two views, i.e. the referentialist view of names and the non-referentialist view of indexicals that I am proposing, are compatible is by looking at their formal aspects. Recall the truth clause that I have sketched for a pronoun like 'he' on the inclusive view, stated more explicitly below:

$$[\![\text{'He is F'}]\!](i, w, w^*, t, t^*)$$

$$= \begin{cases} \text{True if } i \in [\![\text{'F'}]\!](w, t) \text{ and } i \in [\![\text{'male'}]\!](w^*, t^*), \\ \text{False if } i \notin [\![\text{'F'}]\!](w, t) \text{ and } i \in [\![\text{'male'}]\!](w^*, t^*), \\ \text{undefined otherwise.} \end{cases}$$

This clause can be straightforwardly incorporated into frameworks that use individual constants, whose interpretation is fixed directly

---

generally, the issue of logical inferences licensed by proper names, is discussed at greater length e.g. in Predelli (2009).

7 A view of semantic content similar to mine (at least in certain respects) has been recently defended e.g. in Carston (2008). See also the discussion in Lewis (1980).

by the interpretation function: the interpretation of an individual constant is a mapping from world-time pairs to individuals; presumably, a *constant* mapping (i.e., it assigns the same individual to every world-time pair), which makes the constant a rigid designator. Suppose that you decide to represent a name such as 'Tareq' by such a rigid individual constant – which is tantamount to endorsing the referentialist view for proper names. That is perfectly compatible with accepting the above truth-clause for the pronoun 'he'. As for the exclusive view, the compatibility is completely straightforward.

Now, if you ask me whether I would opt for the referentialist view, I probably would not. Many among the considerations that lend plausibility to my approach to indexicals are at odds with the spirit of the referentialist view of semantic content, even when this one is restricted to proper names. Recall thus that one of my driving motivations was that when I say 'He is a doctor' to communicate to you that Tareq is a doctor, I am referring directly to Tareq and saying of him that he is a doctor, and the condition of being male, lexically encoded in 'he', merely helps you figure out that it is Tareq that I am talking about. Now suppose that, in the same scenario, there are several men around, so the gender constraint is not at all helpful. But if I know that you know that Tareq's name is 'Tareq', then I could just tell you 'Tareq is a doctor'. It would be nice to explain what happens here along more or less the same lines as in the case of what happened when I used the indexical 'he'. We might want to say that here, too, I was directly referring to Tareq, and that my use of his name was merely heuristic, to help my interlocutors realize that I was talking about him.

Let me now turn to the descriptivist approaches, which hold that proper names are lexically meaningful. What I have called 'classical' descriptivism will associate, with any given name N, some general, descriptive and, in general, informative constraints, such as 'the teacher of Alexander the Great' with the name 'Aristotle', or 'the capital of France' with the name 'Paris', and so on. On the other hand, the metalinguistic view will *systematically* associate a certain descriptive constraint with any given name N, namely, the constraint of being a bearer of N, using a single schema, or rule, that captures, once and for all, the lexical knowledge possessed by any speaker who is deemed competent with proper names *qua* lexical category. I take it to be unnecessary to spell out either classical or metalinguistic descriptivism.[8] Rather, let me show that, when properly construed, either version of descriptivism – or, for that matter, a mixed view that combines both – is compatible with my account of semantic content.

Let D_N stand for the descriptive constraint that the descriptivist view under consideration lexically associates with a given name N (in the metalinguistic view, that will simply be the constraint of either being a bearer of or being otherwise appropriately related to the name N). As in the case of indexical pronouns, the constraints lexically encoded in the meaning of the name would primarily play a heuristic role in that they would help the hearer figure out what the speaker is talking about, rather than being part of what the speaker is actually asserting. Recall our distinction from section 2 between the inclusive vs. the exclusive view regarding the semantic contribution of indexicals. The same sort of distinction may be drawn in the case of proper names. Thus, on the assumption that D_N captures the lexical meaning of N, one has the choice between taking D_N to be part of the semantic content associated with a sentence that contains N, or taking it to be something that, while playing a role in communication, only intervenes at a post-semantic stage to basically help the hearer decide with respect to what to evaluate the semantic content associated with the sentence at stake. Leaving the discussion of the exclusive view for the next section, let us take a look at the inclusive view. Consider:

---

8 Classical descriptivism originates with classics such as Frege and Russell, but for a more systematic picture of how the view works, or might work, it may be more fruitful to look at Kripke (1980) – who, to be sure, criticizes the view, but by doing so explores various options that are available to it. For a more recent defense of this sort of descriptivism, see e.g. Stanley (1997). Metalinguistic descriptivism, defended e.g. in Bach (1987) or Katz (1994), still has a fair amount of partisans; for some more recent discussions, see e.g. Geurts (1997), Bach (2002), and Rast (2007: ch. 4). While all of these might be considered relatively strong versions of descriptivism, I also take it that 'referentialist' proposals such as in Recanati (1993) endorse, at the same time, a version of metalinguistic descriptivism, as will become clear shortly.

(15) It is possible that Tareq should not be a bearer of the name 'Tareq'.

(16) It is possible that Paris should not be the capital of France.

In order to account for the truth of (15) and (16), and, more generally, for the behavior of names embedded under intensional operators (as well as under negation), the inclusive view will distinguish the way in which a proper name contributes to semantic content from the way in which a predicate in the verb phrase does. The same move as in the case of indexicals immediately suggests itself:

$[\![\text{'N is F'}]\!](i, w, w^*, t, t^*)$

$= \begin{cases} \text{True if } i \in [\![\text{'F'}]\!](w, t) \text{ and } i \in [\![\text{'D}_\text{N}\text{'}]\!](w^*, t^*), \\ \text{False if } i \notin [\![\text{'F'}]\!](w, t) \text{ and } i \in [\![\text{'D}_\text{N}\text{'}]\!](w^*, t^*), \\ \text{undefined otherwise.} \end{cases}$

As repeatedly emphasized, my aim is not to defend any particular view of names. The problems that the descriptivist views encounter are well-known, although the views outlined in this section are able to succesfully deal with many among those problems. In particular, the so-called Modal Argument does not affect views whose semantics proceeds along the same lines as the truth clause suggested above.

Now, if you ask me whether I would opt for either version of the descriptivist view, I probably would not. Consider first classical descriptivism. One of its advantages is that it can handle Frege's puzzle and explain how it can be informative to tell someone that Hesperus is Phosphorus, that Superman is Clark Kent, that Louise Ciccone is Madonna, that Gordon Sumner is Sting, etc. But when it comes to ordinary proper names, the view is only plausible (to my sense, at least) if the associated description is determined at the level of a single individual (or his or her idiolect) rather than at the level of a shared dialect, let alone a language like English. But then, if different individuals associate different descriptions (or clusters thereof), it becomes very implausible to view such descriptive constraints as being *lexically* encoded. In other words, while I think that this version of descriptivism could reach a fair amount of plausibility when taken as a theory of *cognitive* content, I do not think that it can give us a good theory of *semantic* content, and I am unclear as to what the resulting theory of *communicated* content would look like. A descriptivist theory of semantic content should, it seems to be, be able to associate, with any proper name, some descriptive constraint that may be plausibly viewed as part of, or derived from, the lexicon (including perhaps some encyclopedic knowledge shared by the competent speakers of the language at stake). As suggested in section 3, there may be words of a language that, from a morpho-syntactic point of view, are proper names, yet have a lexically encoded meaning that is descriptive in a non-trivial, informative way. Thus a name like 'Earth' comes arguably closer to a common noun like 'planet' than to a name like 'Tareq' or 'Sophie'; and similarly for the names of other planets or stars, of continents or oceans, etc. But if we leave those aside, then a descriptivist *semantic* view of those other, 'ordinary' proper names, had better be the metalinguistic view.

Does that mean, then, that I would go for the metalinguistic view? Not necessarily. For one thing, my preference for the exclusive view in the case of indexicals leads me to prefer the exclusive view in the case of names as well; hence even if some lexically encoded content should be associated with a proper name, I would want to view it as playing a heuristic role when it comes to evaluating semantic content for a truth value, rather than as properly contributing to semantic content. More importantly, I think that the plausibility of the metalinguistic view hinges to a large extent on what inferences we want to come out logically valid, i.e. valid in virtue of the syntax and semantics alone of their premises and conclusion. Recall the following inferences from section 3:

(17) Sophie is a mathematician. Therefore, someone bears the name 'Sophie'.

(18) Sophie is a mathematician. Therefore, there are (at least) two individuals who stand in the bearing-of relation.

I would be reluctant to view these as logically valid inferences. To the extent that they might still sound good, I would account for this at the level of pragmatics, just as I would do so for the fact that on the basis of observing that a Spanish speaker has used the formal pronoun 'Usted', one can correctly infer that the speaker has addressed her interlocutor formally. If we accept that these are pragmatic inferences, rather than logical inferences whose truth is warranted by semantics, we are drifting even further away from the metalinguistic (inclusive) view of proper names.

5   The pragmatic view

The pragmatic view is the view that proper names do not contribute anything to semantic content – rather, they are merely pragmatic devices, like pointing gestures, that help the hearer figure out to whom the speaker is referring. It may look as a fairly radical view, but if one thinks of direct reference along the lines that I have sketched in the beginning of the article, namely, as, first and foremost, the act of referring directly, done by a speaker in the course of a conversational exchange, and if, furthermore, one is attracted by a Millian conception of proper names, on which they are like tags for objects and people, then one has every reason to find the pragmatic view very plausible.

There are, however, two ways of arriving at the pragmatic view of names:

The Stronger View:

> All there is to semantic content is the lexically encoded content. Proper names are not associated with any lexically encoded content. As a consequence, proper names make no contribution to semantic content.

The Weaker View:

> All there is to semantic content is the lexically encoded content, but crucially, not all lexically encoded content reaches into

semantic content.[9] Although proper names can be associated with lexically encoded constraints, the latter are precisely of the sort that do not reach into semantic content and only intervene at a post-semantic stage, at which content is evaluated for a truth value. As a consequence, proper names, while lexically meaningful, make no contribution to semantic content.

While the weaker view results from combining the exclusive view of indexicals with some version of descriptivism regarding the lexical meaning of names, the idea on which the stronger view relies is that names are merely pragmatic devices, devoid of lexical meaning, and simply used by the speaker to help her interlocutors figure out to whom or what she is referring. For example, if I use the name 'Tareq', that will help you figure out that I am referring to Tareq – of course, only if you, too, are competent with this pragmatic device, that is, if, in the context at stake, we share the name 'Tareq' as a tag for the same person. Now, one might find it worrisome that language might contain elements that are merely pragmatic devices without any semantic import. But proper names would not be alone in that respect. Consider exclamatives: expressions like 'ouch', 'wow', etc. are also part of the language, yet we do not expect them to have any semantics. Similarly, adverbs like 'frankly', as in 'Frankly, she is brilliant', are often seen as devoid of semantic content. Of course, with proper names the situation might be more subtle. For one thing, names are used in the formation of sentences and often occupy the same positions as, for example, quantifier phrases and other semantically interpreted expressions. One might then worry whether stripping proper names of any semantics is incompatible with compositional semantics.

Without being able to address the question of what the syntax/semantic interface would look like on this view, let me stress that to the extent that the exclusive view of indexicals works, so

---

9 As pointed out earlier, I take this to be an independently plausible assumption: e.g. the case of the lexically encoded information that the Spanish pronoun 'Usted' is a formal pronoun, or the difference between 'dad' and 'father', which I take to be semantically equivalent yet lexically different, prove the point forcefully.

does the pragmatic view of proper names: in either case, we have something in the syntax that then evaporates in the semantics. To be sure, there remains the question of what the semantic system will do when you give it as input a sentence that contains a name. One could clean up the sentence of all pragmatic devices before feeding it into the semantic system (which is, presumably, what one would do with exclamatives like 'ouch'), or else, leave them in the input but teach the semantic system to ignore such inputs. Still, if we ask ourselves what a possible truth clause for a sentence containing a name, e.g. 'Tareq', might look like on this view, here is what immediately springs to mind:

$$[\![\text{'Tareq is F'}]\!](i, w, w^*, t, t^*) = \text{True iff Tareq} \in [\![\text{'F'}]\!](w, t)$$

While this will look perfectly intelligible, I want to stress that the proposed truth clause is not innocent: it short-circuits the passage through the structure of interpretation. The truth clause roughly tells you, if you come across the name 'Tareq', to go and get directly that very individual, viz. Tareq himself, and check if *he* belongs to the interpretation of 'F' (relative to *w* and *t*). Note that what this entails is that for every name in the object-language, there must be a corresponding name in the meta-language; without this, it would be impossible to even write down the proposed truth clause.

A better way of extracting a truth clause for sentences involving names from the pragmatic view is, I believe, to take the proposal quite to the letter: proper names make no contribution to semantics. This gives us the following clause (for any proper name '*N*'):

$$[\![\text{'N is F'}]\!](i, w, w^*, t, t^*) = \text{True iff } i \in [\![\text{'F'}]\!](w, t)$$

In other words, the semantic content associated with '*N* is *F*' is the very same as that associated with '*F*' itself. And this, in turn, captures the idea that just as when I say 'He is a doctor', the constraint of being male might help you, though need not, in deciding to take Tareq (rather than, say, Aysha) to be the individual to whom I am ascribing the property of being a doctor, when I say 'Tareq is a doctor', previous uses of the name 'Tareq' for a certain individual of which you are aware might help you, though need not, in deciding to take Tareq (rather than, say, Khaled) to be the one of whom I am speaking. In either case, reference to Tareq is achieved directly by me (*qua* speaker) and is supported by various contextual factors provided by the setting of our conversational exchange. The pronoun or the name are just one or another among the various devices on which I happen to rely in my act of referring, but they contribute nothing to semantic content.*

References

Bach, K. (1987). *Thought and reference*. Oxford; New York: Oxford University Press.

—— (2002). Giorgione was so-called because of his name. *Philosophical Perspectives, 16*, 73–103.

Carston, R. (2008). Linguistic communication and the semantics/pragmatics distinction. *Synthese, 165*, 321–345.

Geurts, B. (1997). Good news about the description theory of names. *Journal of Semantics, 14*, 319–348.

Glezakos, S. (2009). Public proper names, idiolectal identifying descriptions. *Linguistics and Philosophy, 32*, 317–326.

---

* I would like to thank Luca Baptista and Erich Rast for their kind invitation to contribute to the present volume, and for discussion on these and related topics over several years. I would also like to thank my audience at the Semantic Content Workshop (organized by Max Kölbel in Barcelona earlier this year), where I presented some ideas about reference, semantic content, and indexicals. I am particularly thankful to Genoveva Marti and to Stefano Predelli for having pressed me on the issue of proper names, thereby giving me some incentive to lay down my view in greater detail. Being aware that proper names are such a widely discussed topic, I would also like to apologize to all those who have discussed it in ways that are relevant to the proposal that I have presented and of whose discussions I was not aware. Finally, let me acknowledge partial funding from the European Research Council under the European Community's Seventh Framework Programme (FP7/2007-2013), grant agreements n° 229 441–CCC and n° 238 128, the MICINN, Spanish Government, under the CONSOLIDER INGENIO 2010 Program, grant CSD2009-0056, as well as the Agence Nationale de la Recherche, grant n° ANR-08-JCJC-0069-01.

Kaplan, D. (1977). Demonstratives: an essay on the semantics, logic, metaphysics, and epistemology of demonstratives and other indexicals. In Almog, J., Perry, J. & Wettstein, H. (Eds.) (1989). *Themes from Kaplan*, (pp. 481–563). Oxford: Oxford University Press.

Katz, J. (1994). Names without bearers. *Philosophical Review, 103*, 1–39.

Kripke, S. (1980). *Naming and necessity*. Cambridge, MA: Harvard University Press.

Lewis, D. (1980). Index, context and content. In Kanger, S. & Ohman, S. (Eds.). *Philosophy and Grammar*, (pp. 78–100). Dordrecht: Reidel.

Marti, G. (1995). The essence of genuine reference. *Journal of Philosophical Logic, 24*, 275–289.

Perry, J. (1997). Reflexivity, indexicality and names. In Künne, W., Anduschus, M. & Newen, A. (Eds.). *Direct reference, indexicality and propositional attitudes*. Stanford: CSLI Publications.

—— (2001). *Reference and reflexivity*. Stanford: CSLI Publications.

Predelli, S. (2009). Socrates and 'Socrates'. *American Philosophical Quarterly, 46*, 203–212.

Rast, E. (2007). *Reference and indexicality*. Berlin: Logos Verlag.

Recanati, F. (1993). *Direct reference*. Oxford: Blackwell.

Stanley, Jason (1997). Names and rigid designation. In Hale, B. & Wright, C. (Eds.). *A companion to the philosophy of language*, (pp. 555–585). Oxford: Blackwell.

Stojanovic, I. (2005). *A different story about indexicals*. Amsterdam: ILLC Research Reports PP 2005-05.

—— (2007). Talking about taste: disagreement, implicit arguments, and relative truth. *Linguistics and Philosophy, 30*, 691–706.

—— (2008). *What is said: an inquiry into reference, meaning, and content*. Saarbrücken: VDM Verlag.

—— (2009). Semantic content. *Manuscrito, 32*, 123–152.

— 7 —

Kepa Korta & John Perry

Intentions to Refer

> If something happened along the route and you had to leave your children with Bob Dole or Bill Clinton, I think you would probably leave them with Bob Dole.
> Bob Dole, April 15, 1996, campaigning for President[1]

> I am not at all sure that I'd want to leave my children with someone who talks about himself in the third person.
> Ellen Goodman, April 15, 1996, in the *Boston Globe*[2]

1 Introduction

If language is action (Austin 1961; Grice 1967), referring to things is not something that words do, but something that people do by uttering words. According to this pragmatic view, then, a theory of reference should be grounded on an account of our acts of referring; that is, the part of communicative acts that consists in referring to individual things. In our view, referential plans involve a structure of beliefs about an object the speaker intends to talk about and of Gricean intentions to achieve various effects on the listener, in virtue of the listener's recogntion of them. Among these, we distinguish the

---

1 According to a column by Ellen Goodman in the *Boston Globe* for April 18, 1996.
2 *Op. cit.*

grammatical, directing, target, path and auxiliary intentions, and call our analysis the GDTPA structure of referential plans. In this article we develop the motives for the theory, explain how it works, and apply it to a number of examples. Communicative acts are explained in terms of the speaker's intentions or, better said, in terms of the speaker's communicative plan: a structure of her goals, beliefs and intentions that motivates her communicative behavior. As parts of communicative acts, referential acts are subject to the same sort of analysis.

In this article, we will argue that referential intentions are a complex type of Gricean intention. Referential acts exploit a speaker's cognitive fix on an object and aim to induce a hearer's to have a cognitive fix on that object appropriate to the speaker's communicative goals. The GDTPA structure of referential plans (Korta & Perry forthcoming) offers an account of the paradigmatic use of names, indexicals, demonstratives and (some uses) of definite descriptions as referential devices. In section 2, we present a brief historical summary of the semantic view of reference, in which we argue that there is a change in what is taken as the paradigmatic referential expression, going from proper names and definite descriptions to indexicals and demonstratives. In section 3, we introduce two of our basic theoretical tools: roles and cognitive fixes, before explaining, in section 4, how we understand the pragmatics of reference within a Gricean picture of language and communication. In section 5 we explain in some detail what we call the 'GDTPA structure' of referential plans, giving various examples of paradigmatic uses of referential expressions. In section 6, we draw some conclusions. An immediate consequence of the present picture is that understanding reference is not a matter of just identifying the object the speaker is referring to but identifying it in the manner intended, that is, with the target cognitive fix, that the speaker intends for the listener to have. Another consequence of the picture of language as action is that utterances, qua acts, have a variety of contents relative to different things that can be taken as given.

2 From descriptions and names to indexicals: a paradigm shift in the philosophy of language

Singular reference has been intensely studied by philosophers during the twentieth century, and lively interest in the topic continues. The inquiry is usually regarded as a matter of semantics, the theory of meaning and truth. The key question is usually taken to be what contribution referring expressions make to the truth-conditions of the statements of which they are a part. The issue of how they fit into the speaker's plan to convey information, generate implicatures, and perform speech acts has not been center-stage. The topic of reference has been dominated, since the beginning of the last century at least, by two paradigms, naming and describing. Due mostly to the work of Gottlob Frege (1892) and Bertrand Russell (1905), there was a sort of consensus throughout the first half of the twentieth century. Definite descriptions refer by describing objects; ordinary proper names refer by abbreviating or being associated with descriptions. The consensus began to fall apart in the 50's and 60's, and a set of ideas Howard Wettstein (1991) dubbed 'The New Theory of Reference' became widely accepted. Donnellan (1966, 1970, 1974), for example, argued that definite descriptions can be used to refer, that when they are so used they can refer to objects that do not fit the description, and that proper names do not need a backing of descriptions to pick out the object they refer to. Donnellan thought that both descriptions and names are used to make 'statements' that are individuated by the particular objects they are about, so the same statements could have been made by other means that referred to the same objects in much different ways. Donnellan emphasized the role of the speaker's intentions in securing reference, but did not develop much structure for dealing with those intentions.

David Kaplan's work on indexicals and demonstratives added a third paradigm to the mix. In his monograph *Demonstratives* (1989), he demonstrated that the techniques of formal logic, and in particular ideas from modal and intensional logic, could be applied to indexicals with illuminating results. Kaplan's work reinforced rejection of the thesis that reference required a backing of descriptions to pick out the object referred to, without relying on intuitions about proper names of the sort to which Donnellan and Kripke had appealed.

We think Kaplan's investigation of indexicals, and his concept of character, suggest a new paradigm for thinking about singular reference. They suggest the importance of what we call 'utterance-relative roles'. Our version of Kaplan's character rule for 'I', for instance, is a generalization that quantifies over utterances: An English utterance of the word 'I' refers to the speaker of that very utterance, that is, the person who plays the role 'speaker of' relative to the utterance. The role provides an identifying condition for the referent, but one that is utterance-bound, which is not what classical description theorists had in mind. And even though an utterance of 'I' refers rather than describes, no tag-like direct connection between the expression and the referent is involved. In the case of indexicals, utterance-relative roles are the key to understanding how things work. We think that utterance-relative roles are an important part of the story in all cases of reference. This is not to say that all kinds of singular terms are indexicals. It is rather to say that something comes out very clearly in the case of indexicals, that is also very important, if more difficult to ferret out, in the cases of names, pronouns, and descriptions. Finding this sort of inspiration in Kaplan's work requires a bit of re-interpretation. Kaplan (1989) said he was not providing a theory of utterances, but a theory of 'sentences-in-context'. Utterances do not appear at all in his formal theory. But they often are mentioned in the informal remarks that motivate the theory, and it's clear that the contextual elements of agent, location, time and world, and the fundamental stipulation that the agent be in the location at the time in the world, are suggested by the utterance-relative roles of speaker, location, time and world, and the fact that the speaker of an utterance is in the location of the utterance at the time of the utterance. When he turns to developing a formal theory, Kaplan sets utterances aside because they don't fit well with his goal of developing the logic of indexicals. For one thing, utterances take time, so the premises of a spoken argument won't all occur at the same time, but for the purposes of logic we want them to occur all in the same context. For another, Kaplan wants to consider the content of context-sentence pairs in which no utterance of the sentence by the agent at the time occurs – hence the agent is not dubbed 'the speaker'. From the point of view of pragmatics, however, utterances do not get in the way; they are central to the project. Gricean intentions are intentions to bring about changes in the hearer; they are intentions to produce concrete utterances, in order to have effects on the hearer. The meanings and contents of the concrete utterance contribute to the effect. At the heart of the conversational transaction is the hearer perceiving a concrete token or event, and reasoning about its cause, that is, about the intentions that led to its production. Properties of meaning and content are relevant to intention discovery, but so are many other properties, like being aware that the speaker is attempting to amuse by telling a philosophical joke rather than pronounce a serious and profound philosophical claim.

The concept of a pair of a Kaplanian context and sentence type makes intuitive sense if we think of it as a model for an utterance in which a speaker at the time and location of the context makes use of a sentence of that type. Much the same is true of other concepts important in the development of referentialism; by our lights at least, they fit better with a theory of utterances than with a theory of sentences and other formal objects. The intentions to which Donnellan appealed in his referential-attributive distinction, are intentions that lead to particular acts of using expressions. The causal and historical chains appealed to in the referentialist account of proper names, are best thought of as connecting acts and earlier events.

In what follows we develop an account of the meaning and use of singular reference within a theory of utterances, based on the concept of utterance-relative roles, and of the pragmatics of singular reference, based on the speaker's need to manage roles to produce the intended effect on his audience. For that purpose, first, we'll introduce a couple of useful basic concepts: roles and cognitive fixes.

3 Basic concepts

Roles

We use the word 'role' a lot in this article. We will talk about utterance-relative roles, speaker-relative roles, epistemic roles, pragmatic roles and so forth. So we should say a little bit about what they are.

Roles are not an addition to a metaphysics that recognizes individuals of various sorts, properties, and relations. Rather they are a way of talking about and organizing information about important relations things have to one another. They provide a way of organizing information that comes natural to humans and is reflected in many ways in language.

Roles are, first of all, important relations. If we ask Elwood, 'what roles do you play in your son's life?', we expect an answer like, 'provider, mentor, friend, disciplinarian'. If he said, 'my bedroom is down the hall from his', we might suspect he was telling us that he played no role worth mentioning in his son's life.

Roles are often significant because they are involved in constraints, the laws, principles, rules, conventions and other regularities that provide the structure within which we perceive and plan. Consider the following constraint:

(1) If an x-ray y of a human arm exhibits pattern ψ, then the person of whose arm y was taken has a broken arm.

The constraint makes the relation between an x-ray and a person, that the former was taken of the latter's arm, something of importance. It means that the x-ray can give us information about the person's arm. And of course (1) is simply one of a family of constraints that x-ray technologists learn, telling what kinds of break x-rays mean, for various bones, and much else. Within the practice of using x-rays in medicine, the relation of being the person of whom an x-ray was taken is critical. Similarly with being the speaker-of, in the realm of utterances. In these cases we generalize across roles; it is the health of the patient – that is, the person the x-ray was taken of – that is disclosed by the x-ray. It is the state of mind of the speaker – that is, the speaker of the utterances – that is disclosed by its linguistic properties.

A list of key roles can provide a schema for characterizing salient facts about an object. Sometimes when we are dealing with a lot of facts about numerous inter-related objects, one object will take center stage for a period of time, during which we focus on which objects stand in various relations to it, or, as we say, play various roles relative to it. Elwood is interviewing Angus, asking him a series of one-word questions: Father? Mother? Birthplace? Year of Birth? Angus can give one-word answers or one-phrase answers, specifying the objects that stand in those relations to him, or, as we say, play those roles in his life. Angus could start his answers with words like, 'My father is...', and 'My birthplace is...', but he really needn't mention himself at all. His place in the facts he is using language to state doesn't have to be indicated linguistically, because it is built into the situation. Angus's system of representation is asymmetrical; the objects that play the key relations to him get named, but he makes it into the propositions he asserts just by his role in the conversation.

As Elwood records the information he may also use an asymmetrical system of representation. Angus's name is written in on the top of a card, perhaps, on which words for the various important roles Elwood is to query him about are printed; Elwood fills them in, in response to Angus's answers. For another example, think of a party invitation. The invitation as a whole represents the party; on the invitation the objects (broadly speaking) that fill various roles relative to the party are linguistically identified: time-of, place-of, hosts-of, purpose-of, and so forth.

Handling relational information with roles is useful when one object is the focus of attention and thus a participant in all the relational facts being discussed, and where due to the situation, the way information is being obtained, communicated, or used, there is no need to re-identify him or her or it. During Angus's interview, he is the one Elwood is asking about. We know that all the information given on an invitation is for the same party, the party the invitation is an invitation for.

A particularly important example of organizing information by roles is our ordinary way of perceiving the world in those uncomplicated cases where neither communication, long-term memory, nor long-term intentions are involved; we'll call this 'the natural stance'. Here the perceiver/agent is the fixed object, the 'index'. We look out on the world and see objects to the left, to the right, above and below; we hear things to the left and to the right, near at hand and in the distance; we feel the heft of things we hold in our right or left hands, and the taste of things in our mouth.

Often the occupants of different roles are known to be the same, in virtue of the common index and the architecture of the situation. The stuff I put in my mouth is the stuff I taste in my mouth; the things I hold in front of me are the things I see in front of me. The car I slow by stepping on the brakes is the same one I steer by turning the wheel, and the same one I gather information about by looking through the windshield.[3]

Cognitive fixes

Humans are blessed with a rich variety of perceptual abilities, which allow them to find out things about objects that stand in certain relations to them; that is, play certain roles in their lives. I can find out the color and shape of the object I am looking at; I can discover the hardness and weight of the object I hold in my hand, and so forth. Such objects, we will say, play direct epistemic roles in our lives; that is, they are related to us, on a given occasion, in such a way that we can perceive them to have various properties.

Often the objects that play direct epistemic roles in our lives are also ones that play direct pragmatic roles in our lives. You see an apple; it looks like it is ripe, but perhaps it is overripe and mushy; you pick it up, and squeeze it a little to make sure it is firm; you put it in your mouth and bite off a piece and chew it; you taste it, and on the basis of what it tastes like, go ahead and swallow it or spit it out.

In thinking about this we find a concept and a term from Howard Wettstein useful: 'cognitive fix'. One's cognitive fix on an object is

---

[3] The article is co-authored, hence there really is no referent for 'I.' However, we find the first-person singular too effective for presenting examples to give it up.

how one thinks of it, in a broad sense of 'thinking'. We like the phrase because it is rather vague, and not tied, like, say, 'mode of presentation' to a particular theory. Still, we will gradually develop a theory of cognitive fixes, and tie Wettstein's term to our own theory. We think of cognitive fixes on an object as involving epistemic roles, pragmatic roles, or both. Cognitive fixes may be perceptual, in which case they will be expressed naturally with demonstrative phrases: 'that man', 'this computer'. They may involve the roles the objects play in conversation, in which case they will be expressed naturally with the appropriate indexicals: 'I', 'you'. Often a mere name seems to do the trick, both in thinking and speaking; we call these nominal cognitive fixes. Sometimes we think of things in terms of uniquely identifying conditions; we have a descriptive cognitive fix, and descriptions may be the appropriate expressions to use. We think of singular terms as devices for providing hearers with cognitive fixes on objects, that are appropriate for the communicative aims of the speaker.

Here the apple plays a number of roles in your life: the thing you see, the thing in front of you that you can pick up by moving in a certain way; the thing in your hands; the thing in your mouth; the thing providing certain taste sensations, and so forth. All of these roles are linked; that is, one thing plays all of them. The job of the agent's buffer is to keep track of all these linkages. But there may also be nested roles to keep track of. The apple may be the very one that your office-mate took out of her lunch bag before stepping away for a moment; by eating the apple, you will have an effect on her, perhaps making her angry. And perhaps she has the boss's ear, so the apple is the one that by eating you can anger your office-mate, cause bad things to be said about you to your boss, and get yourself fired.

Signs are objects that play a direct epistemic role in one's life, whose perceivable properties are related in reliable ways to the properties of other objects, to which they are related. You see the paw print along the trail; on the basis of the pattern and size of the print, you learn that it was caused by a fox. The fox plays a complex, indirect epistemic role in your life; it is the animal that caused the print you are perceiving, and hence the animal you learn about by examining the print.

Nature provides us with many signs; that is, certain events carry information about other objects (or about themselves at other times) in virtue of the way nature made them and the way the world works. Other objects carry information because of structures created by humans, which harness natural information for various purposes. A certain characteristic twitch at the end of your fishing rod tells you that there is, or may be, a fish on the hook tied to the end of the line that feeds into the rod. A ringing doorbell tells you that someone is on the porch.

In interpreting a sign, one basically asks what the rest of the world must be like, for the object perceived to be as it is, or for the event or state perceived to have occurred. As in the case of the effects of one's acts, one doesn't worry about everything; one has in mind certain structures, certain objects that are or might be related to the object seen, and certain ways the world works. I see a paw print of a certain shape and size; I know that given the way the world works there is some animal that made it, and that given the shape and size it was a fox. Interpreting signs is a manner of inferring what the rest of the world has to be like (or probably is like, or may be like), given various structures and constraints, for the sign to have occurred.

So, typically, the interpretation of a sign involves perceiving an object or event as having certain properties, and inferring from those properties what the rest of the world must be like. Paradigmatically, this means inferring that various other objects related to the sign in certain ways, have or lack various properties.

Now we are well equipped to introduce our view on referential acts, which we think fits well in a Gricean picture of reference.

4 Gricean Reference

Our terminology differs a bit from Grice's. He distinguishes between natural and non-natural meaning. What he calls non-natural meaning involves an agent doing something in order to change the beliefs, or otherwise affect the cognitions, of a hearer, in virtue of the hearer's recognizing the speaker's intention to effect this change. Language use is a case of non-natural meaning, but not the only case.

According to Grice, if we are talking about natural meaning, '*X* means that *S*' entails that *S*. This view of Grice's is connected with the use of 'information' by Dretske and others, including one of the present authors in previous writings, to imply truth (Dretske 1981, Barwise & Perry 1983). We adopt a looser view in this article. (We use 'information' in the way Israel and Perry use 'informational content' (Israel & Perry 1990, 1991)). When a bird can see an unobstructed view of an object, it takes this as a sign that it can fly directly to the object. In the modern world, this leads many birds to their death, as they fly into windows and plate glass doors on the sides of buildings. We regard this as natural meaning; the bird is responding to a natural sign, but one that is not infallible. The importance of this may be mostly terminological; it allows us to use terms like 'natural sign', 'natural meaning' and 'information' rather than circumlocutions. But natural meaning, in our weaker sense, is the natural concept to explain how the interpretation of phenomena as signs plays an important evolutionary role; as long as the tendencies involved in interpreting signs lead to good results in a sufficient proportion of cases, the trait of doing so will propagate.

Interpreting the intentions and other cognitions of other people is a natural, evolved ability of humans. From this point of view, there is nothing non-natural about this ability, and the development of language as an extension of it is also a part of nature. We draw approximately the same line as Grice, but we see it as a line between signs that are intentionally produced to be the signs of intentions, and other signs.

Now consider an example of Herb Clark's (Clark 1992, 1996). A person stands in line at the checkout counter of a grocery store. When his turn comes, he takes a sack of potatoes from his cart and puts them on the counter. The checker will take this as a sign that the shopper wants to purchase the item, and will proceed to ring it up with the expectation of getting paid. This act has at least some of the features of Gricean communication. The shopper wants the clerk to ring up the sack of potatoes. He probably has no great interest in why the clerk does so, but he at least implicitly expects that part of the motivation will be realizing that the shopper wants to buy them. If he doesn't want to buy them, but merely learn the price of the potatoes, he'll have to say something.

It is natural to find a reference-predication structure in this episode, even though no language is involved. The shopper conveys his intention about a certain item, the sack of potatoes. He conveys that he wishes to buy it. If he had held the sack up and asked, 'How much?' he would have conveyed his desire to have the clerk tell him the cost of the item. The act of putting the sack of potatoes on the counter is a primitive act of reference. The fact that he put the sack on the counter shows that the desire he wishes to convey concerns the potatoes; the fact that he placed it on the counter and said nothing, conveys his desire to buy them. Different aspects of the shopper's act convey different aspects of the desire he wishes to convey.

Clark interprets the act of putting the potatoes on the counter as a demonstration. Perhaps cigarettes are not available for the shopper to put in his cart, but displayed behind the checker, who is not supposed to sell them to those under sixteen. The shopper could convey the same information about a pack of cigarettes that he did about the sack of potatoes by pointing to it. Or he could say, 'That pack of Camels, please.'

The examples have a common structure. The shopper has a desire about a certain item, to purchase it. He wants to convey to the clerk which item it is he wants to purchase. He does so by bringing it about that the item plays certain roles in the clerk's life. That is, he draws the clerk's attention to the item, in such a way that the clerk will realize it is the item the shopper wishes to buy, and will have a cognitive fix on the item that enables him to take the desired action towards the item: to ring it up. The act of reference is the act of getting the referent to play a certain role in the hearer's life, in such a way that the hearer realizes that it is the object that the shopper desires to buy, and has a cognitive fix on the item that permits him to do what the shopper wants him to do with it.

Now suppose that you are eating dinner with a group of people, and you want the salt, which you can't reach. You say to the person next to you, who can reach the shaker,

(2)   I'd like some salt, please.

Here you are conveying to your hearer that a certain person would like the salt. The predicate 'like some salt' conveys what the person, to whom you refer, would like. The word 'I' conveys which person that is, but it does more than that. By producing your utterance, so that it is heard, you provide the hearer a succession of cognitive fixes on the referent, that is, the person of whom wanting the salt is being predicated. It is (i) the person who the speaker is referring to. Your choice of 'I' indicates that that person is (ii) the speaker of the utterance. In this particular situation, the hearer can see who the speaker is: (iii) the person next to him. This puts him in a position to carry out the implicit request, and pass you the salt. Here again your intent is to identify the subject, the person who wants the salt, for the hearer in such a way that the hearer can fulfill your goal in speaking, and pass you the salt.

Suppose now that it is not you who wants the salt, but the woman sitting across from you and your hearer; she is looking at the salt shaker, but is too shy to say anything. You say,

(3)   She'd like the salt,

with a glance across the table. Perhaps you nudge the hearer, so that he will turn towards you, and follow your eye gaze and subtle nod towards the woman. Again, you have a referential plan. You want to convey the belief that a certain person wants the salt. The speaker will understand your sentence, and realize that the person referred to by the utterance he hears wants the salt. Other things being equal, he will take it that that person is a female. He will follow your eye gaze and realize that the person you are referring to is the person seated across from you, someone he is in a position to pass the salt to.

These cases illustrate one of our basic theses. The pragmatic aspects of singular reference are largely a matter of role-management. We refer to objects in the ways that we do in order to provide our hearers with an apt cognitive fix on the people or things or places we want to convey beliefs or other attitudes about, that is, one enables them to take whatever further actions we would like them to carry out with respect to this object.

Suppose now the woman across from you is the movie star Julia Roberts. You say,

(4)   Julia Roberts would like the salt.

Your neighbor hears the utterance, and has an initial fix on the person of whom wanting the salt is predicated: (i) the person the speaker of the utterance I hear refers to. He will realize that she is named 'Julia Roberts', a person he already has a notion of, and can think of as: (ii) Julia Roberts. His is a notion that includes a conception of what she looks like. He will look around the table until he recognizes her. He will then have a cognitive fix on the person who needs the salt as: (iii) the person sitting diagonally across from him, and will pass her the salt. Again, your plan to get Julia Roberts the salt involved providing a path the hearer could take, from having a cognitive fix on the salt-deprived person merely as the subject of the utterance he is hearing, to being the person across from him, an apt cognitive fix that enables him to get the salt to her.

Perhaps the person sitting next to you is a true intellectual, who never sees movies except documentaries; he has barely heard of Julia Roberts, and has no idea what she looks like. Then your plan will fail. Your plan puts a certain cognitive burden on the hearer; in order to follow the path you have in mind, he has to have a notion of Julia Roberts sufficiently detailed that he can recognize her. He may come to believe that Julia Roberts wants the salt, but can't go on from there.

Suppose Bob Dole is at the dinner too. Bob Dole, the Republican candidate for President in 1996, has a habit of referring to himself in the third person. He says to the person next to him,

(5)   Bob Dole would like some salt.

This may not work; he isn't as well-known as he once was. If instead he had said 'I'd like the salt', it would have worked. His choice of words puts an unnecessary cognitive burden on the hearer. It also sounds a bit pretentious – this is probably what Ellen Goodman was reacting to in our opening quote. His plan assumes that people will have a rich enough notion of Bob Dole to recognize him, and that's the sort of assumption most ordinary folk won't make, when there is a simpler way of getting the hearer to have the appropriate cognitive fix, by using the first person.

Perhaps it's 1996, and Bob Dole has been talking politics with you, who have been sitting next to him at a dinner party. As he leaves he says, 'I hope you vote for me'. To vote for someone, you have to know his or her name. He is putting the same cognitive burden as you in the case above. If he is cautious, and thinks the dinner conversation has made a good impression on you, he will say 'I hope you vote for Bob Dole'. Or, more likely, he will say, 'I am Bob Dole. I hope you vote for me'.

He clearly adds something to the conversation by saying 'I am Bob Dole' that he wouldn't have added by merely saying 'Bob Dole is Bob Dole', or 'I am I'. He assumes that the hearer has a notion of Bob Dole, rich enough to include the information that Dole is a candidate. He assumes that the hearer has a notion of the person he has been talking to, which includes that he is an intelligent and affable fellow. The effect Dole wishes to achieve is getting these notions merged, so that the hearer has a single notion that include being a candidate named 'Bob Dole', being the person he is talking to, and being affable and intelligent. Dole's remark gives you two cognitive fixes on one person, as the person speaking to you, and as the person you think of as 'Bob Dole'.

Perhaps it hasn't occurred to Bob Dole that he hasn't been recognized, and he simply says 'I hope you vote for me'. Later you tell a friend about this puzzling remark. 'I was talking to a man at dinner. When he left he said he wanted me to vote for him. I wonder what he is running for.' 'That man is running for President', he tells you. 'He is Bob Dole.' Your friend plans that you will recognize that the person he is referring to with 'that man' is the very one whose behavior at dinner motivated your remark. He is building on a fix you already have on the man, in order to get the result that you merge your notion of the man you talked to, with your Bob Dole notion.

These cases all illustrate our basic thesis that reference involves role-management. The thesis has implications for the semantics of the kinds of expressions we use in singular reference: demonstratives and demonstrative phrases, indexicals, personal pronouns, names, and definite descriptions. The meanings of these expressions are what enables utterances of them to have the role-management uses that they do, and the semantics of these expressions must explain how that is.

5 The GDTPA Structure of Referential Plans

In our view, reference involves a complex of Gricean intentions (intentions aimed at being recognized by the hearer) or plans: structures of intentions and beliefs. We distinguish five aspects of such plans, which we call the grammatical, directing, target, path and auxiliary intentions, and refer to the whole as the GDTPA structure of referential plans.

In a paradigm case the speaker S will have a belief, which we'll call the motivating belief, with a certain content; he intends that the hearer H will come to have a belief with the same content, in virtue of recognizing S's intention to have H do so. This intention will be in the service of further intentions S has for H; inferences, or other actions, S wants H to perform, or refrain from performing.

When reference is involved, the motivating belief will be about (at least) one thing X; the belief's content will be a singular proposition about X, to the effect that X meets a certain condition. As part of instilling the belief in H, S intends to get H to think about X, to have a cognitive fix on X, and recognize S's intention to have H believe that X meets the condition. S will intend for H to think about X as the object that plays a role in H's own life, the target role, one that is suited to S's further intentions for H's actions and inferences. S intends to accomplish this by exploiting a role X plays in S's own life, the exploited role, through use of an expression whose meaning suits it for helping to identify this role. The expression will be part of a sentence, which identifies the condition X must meet for the utterance to be true. H will infer from the fact that X plays the exploited role in S's life, that X plays a role in H's own life, and will think of X in a way suited to thinking of objects that play that role.

In such a paradigm case, there will be a singular term E that is part of the sentence S utters, so that S intends to refer to X by uttering E. This intention will be part of a referential plan that involves the means of reference, and the effects of reference. This is a plan about E, X, the hearer H, an exploited role, and a target role, where the content of S's motivating belief for uttering '$F(E)$' is that $C(X)$:

- S believes that the sentence '...E...' predicates C of the object identified by E, and intends to assert of that object that it meets C (the grammatical intention);

- S believes that X plays the exploited role in S's life, and that the meaning of E makes uttering E a way of identifying the object that plays that role, and S intends, by uttering E, to get H to recognize that he intends to identify the object that plays that role (the directing intention);

- S believes that X plays the target role in H's life, and that by thinking of X in that way, and believing that X meets condition C, H will be likely to perform the further inferences and actions S has in mind, and S intends for H to recognize that S intends for him to think of X in that way (the target intention);

- S believes that H can infer from the fact that X plays the exploited role in S's life, that it plays the target role in H's life, and intends that H recognizes that S intends for H to make that inference (the path intention);

We call this the GDTPA structure of paradigm referential plans. It is also useful to note that S may think that by using E to identify X, certain further information will be conveyed to H about X; the intention to convey this information we call the auxiliary intention. We'll explain the GDTPA structure a bit more, and then apply it to a range of examples.

The grammatical intention

When we predicate a property of an object, or a relation between objects, or some more complex condition, in the usual way by uttering a declarative sentence, the various argument roles involved in the condition are grammatically specified. In English this is mainly done by word order; in other languages case markings carry the bulk of this information. The predicate 'kills' expresses a relation between a killer, a thing killed, and a time of the killing. To understand S's utterances of such sentences as 'Ruby killed Oswald' 'Oswald was killed by Ruby' or phrases like 'Ruby's killing of Oswald', 'Oswald's killing by Ruby', 'the fact that Ruby killed Oswald' H needs not only to recognize that it is killing, Ruby and Oswald who are involved in the belief that S wishes to impart, but the roles they play in the killing; the word order combined with the sort of construction used – active or passive – specifies that Ruby is the killer and Oswald the victim. We will take the intention on the speaker's part to convey this information, the grammatical intention, largely for granted in this article, without meaning to suggest it is unimportant, semantically trivial, or pragmatically insignificant.

The directing intention

In order to impart his motivating belief to H in an apt way, S has to refer to X. He might, as in Clark's case of the shopper and the clerk, do so by putting X directly in H's line of vision, without saying anything. Or perhaps X is a person who stumbles out of a bar and falls at the feet of S and H. 'Drunk', S says; there is no need to get H thinking about X, since he no doubt already is. But we'll focus on cases in which S refers, and uses language to do so.

Our thesis is that the meanings of expressions suit them for use in referring to things that play certain epistemic or pragmatic roles in one's life – that is, things on which one has one kind or other of cognitive fix. In choosing his referring expressions, S's goal is not merely to refer to the object his motivating belief is about, but to refer in a way that is apt for bringing about the right sort of understanding on the part of H. And for aiming at that target S exploits his own cognitive fix or fixes on X. S may have choices here, for he may have (or think he has) different cognitive fixes on the same thing. The directing intention is the intention to refer to the object S's motivating belief is about, by using an expression, or some other intention-indicating device, or a combination, that is associated, naturally or conventionally, with some cognitive fix one has on that object one's motivating belief is about. For example, S may use the word 'I' to refer to himself; the word 'I' is suited for that role by its meaning. S may use the word 'that man' to refer to a man he sees; the phrase 'that man' is suited by its meaning for referring to a man with that role in the speaker's life. S may use 'you' to refer to the person he is talking to; the word 'you' is suited by its meaning to refer to that person. These are directing intentions. In each case, S may have further intentions. He may, by using 'you' and referring to the addressee, intend to refer to Elwood Fritchey, and by referring to Elwood Fritchey, intend to refer to the next Dean of the College. Those are not directing intentions.

Directing intentions are determinative. That is, the speaker has referred to whoever or whatever plays the role involved in his directing intention. The further intentions are not determinative. Suppose S thinks he is talking to Elwood Fritchey, but is instead talking to Elwood's twin Christopher. When he says 'you' he has referred to Christopher, not Elwood.

To the question, 'Does intention determine reference?', our theory says 'Yes and No'. Basically, the speaker has authority over which role he exploits. But he does not have authority over who or what actually plays that role; if his beliefs about that are wrong, he may refer to a thing to which he does not intend to refer. When we depart from paradigm cases, and consider ones in which the words chosen are inappropriate for the role the speaker intends to exploit, or when the speaker is misunderstood by careful hearers, things quickly get complicated. Basically, the speaker gets to choose which role he exploits, but then facts take over, and if the speaker's beliefs about those facts are wrong, he may not refer to the thing he intends to; but we won't much look at these complications here.

The target intention

If S is at all adept at using language, he will not intend to get H to have a belief about some object, but will also have at least a vague intention of the type of cognitive fix on that object that H should have, in order to be in a position to have whatever further thoughts and actions S has in mind for him; that is, an apt cognitive fix. This is the target intention. In the case of passing the salt, the target intention is that the hearer think of the person referred to, the one who wants the salt, in some way that will afford passing the salt to that person. In the case of giving someone information about Cicero, say, to use on an exam, one will likely want the cognitive fix to be via the name that will be used to refer to Cicero.

The path intention

Moreover, if S is an adept speaker, he will have in mind some path, some reasoning, that will lead H from realizing what role the referent has in the speaker's life, that is, from grasping the direction intention, to the target intention, that is to the cognitive fix S wants H to have. When I say, 'I'd like the salt', I expect you to realize that the person who wants the salt is the speaker of the utterance you hear, and so the person you see across from you; this is the target cognitive fix, the one that will enable to you pass the salt to the right person.

Examples

S and H are standing on the east side of Canal Street, just south of Adams, in Chicago. Union Station rises on either side of Canal Street, the main part of the station being underground, running under Canal Street, and connecting the parts above ground. S believes that H's train leaves from Union Station. He intends to impart that information to H, with the goal that H will walk into the nearest part of Union Station. He holds this belief via his notion of Union Station, usually detached, but now connected to perception. In this situation, there are (at least) three ways S could refer to Union Station, exploiting three different cognitive fixes he has on it. He could just say

(6)   Your train leaves from Union Station.

But in order to meet S's goal, H would have to recognize which building was Union Station, and S doesn't think he does. He could point to the part of Union Station that rises on the other side of Canal Street, and say,

(7)   Your train leaves from that station.

But that would doubtless lead to H's unnecessarily crossing busy Canal Street. Or S could point to the near part of Union Station, that rises on the east side of Canal Street, a short distance from where S and H are talking. This is clearly the way of referring that is most likely to lead to the effect on H that S wants; that is, to believe of Union Station, thought of as the building he sees on the same side of the street, that it is the place he needs to go to catch his train.

S's directing intention is to refer to the building he sees as he looks east, by using the demonstrative phrase 'that station'. This fixes the referent. This creates the possibility of a failing to refer to the object he intends to refer to, even though intentions fix reference. Suppose S is in error. Things have changed at Union Station. The above-ground part of structure that used to be the eastern wing of Union Station has been converted to a posh prison for Illinois politicians. Union Station is now just the structure west of Canal Street, plus the part under the street. S points to the structure on the east side, and says 'Your train leaves from that station.' In this case, even though S's utterance was motivated by a belief about Union Station, and the primary referential intention was to refer to Union Station, he has not referred to Union Station, but to the Illinois Politicians' Prison.

In the original example, S, an adept speaker, chose the way of referring to Union Station that would most likely lead H to have an apt cognitive fix on the station. Here we have role-transfer; the kind of cognitive fix S intended for H to have was basically the same sort that was involved in S's directing intention, that is, a perceptual fix. That path that S set up for H to follow was short and direct, basically from 'the station S is looking at' to 'the station I am looking at'. S's referential plan, then, is a complex intention to refer to an object, Union Station, in a way that will induce H to recognize S's directing intention, and then following the path to a perceptual cognitive fix on the same building – the target intention.

But paths are not always simple and direct. S tells H,

(8) Mr. Muggs is wanted on the phone – would you tell him?

Perhaps S answered the phone, at a party, and someone asked for Muggs, whom S already knows. He has the sort of cognitive fix on Muggs that one has in such a situation; he isn't seeing or hearing Muggs, just thinking about him in the way one thinks about someone one knows, via a detached notion. But he wants H to have a perceptual fix on Muggs, for this is required to approach him and give him the message. S's plan puts a cognitive burden on H, to know, or be able to find out what Muggs looks like.

Or perhaps S is a Professor in a large class and Muggs is a student, whose name S does not know. Muggs asks him if he can have an extension on his paper, and S agrees. He tells his teaching assistant H, 'Make a note that he gets an extension'. S is assuming the assistant will know the student's name, for this is required to make a useful note. S's plan, in some detail, is:

- H hears my utterance, and parses it;

- H has the fix: the person the speaker of the utterance refers to with 'he';

- H realizes that I, the Professor, am the speaker;

- H has the fix: the person the Professor is referring to with 'he';

- *H* witnessed my conversation with the student, and realizes that he is who I have in mind;

- *H* has the fix: the student the Professor was just talking to;

- *H* is a responsible assistant and knows the names of his students;

- *H* has a fix on the student via the student's name;

- *H* will be in a position to make a useful note.

The pronoun 'he' provides auxiliary information about the referent, that he is a male. It may be misinformation. In this case, the professor may not have realized that the student he was talking to was a female; it's not always easy to tell. Or the professor may be a fossil who thinks that girls should dress like girls and boys like boys; he was very aware that the student was a girl, but signaled his disapproval to the teaching assistant by using the wrong pronoun. Or maybe his native language is Basque, which doesn't have a gendered pronoun system, and he always says 'he' rather than think about which English pronoun to use. In this case, it really doesn't matter. The teaching assistant will know to whom he is referring, and disregard the misinformation.

Sometimes it does matter. Perhaps two students have been making requests of the professor. He tells the teaching assistant, 'Give her an extension, give him an incomplete'. He is counting on the pronouns to distinguish between the two students, and if he gets it wrong, the wrong students may end up with the incomplete and the extension. This additional information, or misinformation as the case may be, does not affect who or what is being referred to, nor is it asserted of the referent. We say it is projected; but we won't have more to say about this here.[4]

---

[4] But see our book *Critical Pragmatics* (forthcoming), specially chapter 8 on descriptions.

6 Conclusion

If we are right, the pragmatic aspects of singular reference are largely a matter of role-management, and, in that sense, indexicals and demonstratives are more illuminating than the traditional paradigms, proper names and definite descriptions.

This doesn't mean that we're giving up the referentialist view on singular reference, according to which the contribution of the subutterance of the singular term to the proposition expressed (or what is said) by the whole utterance is a particular object. We are essentially referentialist to that extent. But we are critical referentialists, because we think that the way that a thing is referred to, and not just the identity of the referent, is required to deal with traditional problems of cognitive significance. Of course if one cannot tell the difference between co-referential terms in one's theory, one will have little hope of explaining the difference that using one term over another might have, and little hope of explaining a speaker's reasons for choosing one rather than the other.

We refer to objects in the ways that we do in order to provide our hearers with an apt cognitive fix on the people or things or places we want to convey beliefs or other attitudes about, that is, one enables them to take whatever further actions we would like them to carry out with respect to this object. We hope that our GDTPA structure of speaker's plan makes clear the complexity of our referential intentions, and the relevance of roles and cognitive fixes in that respect.

Theories in the philosophy of action have long recognized the multi-level structure of action. An agent moves in certain circumstances, and the combination of the nature of the movement, and the nature of the circumstances, produces certain results, given the way the world works. I move my arm in a certain way unthinkingly, and because of the circumstances I'm in, I knock a cup to the floor. By knocking the cup to the floor, I cause it to break. By causing it to break, I make its owner angry. And so forth. The action is naturally viewed as having multiple informational contents, depending of the facts we take as given. In contrast, theories of the content of language and propositional attitudes are usually 'mono-propositional'. That is, there is a single proposition that is thought to capture the content of a belief, desire, or assertion. We contend that utterances, qua acts, also have a plurality of contents, that derive from facts about the speaker's plan, linguistic conventions and the circumstances of utterance, and which of them are taken as given. Our analysis of referential acts is, hopefully, a step towards clarifying how that works.*

References

Austin, J. L. (1961). *How to do things with words.* Oxford: Oxford University Press.

Barwise, J. & Perry, J. (2001). *Situations and attitudes.* Stanford: CSLI Publications. (First edition 1983, Cambridge: MIT Press.)

Clark, H. H. (1992). *Arenas of language use.* Chicago: University of Chicago Press.

—— (1996). *Using language.* Cambridge: Cambridge University Press.

Donnellan, K. (1966). Reference and definite descriptions. *Philosophical Review, LXXV*, 281–304.

—— (1970). Proper names and identifying descriptions. *Synthese, 21*, 335–358.

—— (1974). Speaking of nothing. *Philosophical Review, LXXXIII*, 3–31.

Dretske, F. (2000). *Knowledge and the flow of information.* Stanford: CSLI Publications. (Original edition 1981, Cambridge: Bradford/MIT.)

Frege, G. (1892). Über Sinn und Bedeutung. *Zeitschrift für Philosophische Kritik, NF 100*, 25–30.

Grice, H. P. (1967). Logic and conversation. In Davison, D. & Harman, G. (eds.) (1975). *The Logic of Grammar,* (pp. 64–75). Encino: Dickenson. Also published in Cole, P. & Morgan, J. L. (eds.)

---

* The work of the first author has been partially supported by a grant of the Basque Government (IT323-10) and a grant by the Spanish Ministry of Science and Innovation (FFI2009-08574).

(1975). *Syntax and Semantics 3: Speech Acts,* (pp. 41–58). New York: Academic Press. Reprinted in Grice (1989), (pp. 22–40).

────── (1989). *Studies in the way of words.* Cambridge: Harvard University Press.

Israel, D. & Perry, J. (1990). What is information? In Hanson, P. (ed.) (1990). *Information, language and cognition,* (pp. 1–19). Vancouver: University of British Columbia Press.

────── (1991). Information and architecture. In Barwise, J., Gawron, J. M., Plotkin, G. & Tutiya, S. (eds.) (1991). *Situation theory and its applications, Vol. 2,* (pp. 147–160). Stanford: CSLI Publications.

Korta, K. & Perry, J. (forthcoming). *Critical pragmatics: An inquiry into reference and communication.*

Russell, B. (1905). On denoting. *Mind, 14,* 479–493

Wettstein, H. (1991). *Has semantics rested on a mistake?* Stanford: Stanford University Press.

Brian Ball
What Is Semantic Content?

1 Introduction

Some linguistic expressions are obviously context sensitive: what the word 'I' refers to depends upon who uses it; what 'that' refers to often depends on what the speaker demonstrates. But some have argued that such context sensitivity is much more pervasive: for instance, it is sometimes argued that gradable adjectives such as 'tall' and 'flat' are context sensitive; that 'knows' is; that attitude ascriptions quite generally are; that epistemic modals are; and so on. Others argue that such expressions are not context sensitive, but assessment relative. Others yet argue that (syntactically complete) sentences containing expressions like these fail to semantically express propositions. Still others deny all of these claims. There are accordingly a number of conceptions – and theories – of semantic content present in the philosophical literature.

In this article I articulate a principled taxonomy of positions, categorizing the views of semantic content of Kent Bach (1994, 2005), Emma Borg (2004), Herman Cappelen and Ernie Lepore (2005a, 2005b), Max Kölbel (2002), John MacFarlane (2005), John Perry (1986, 2001), Paul Pietroski (2003, 2005), François Recanati (1993, 2004, 2002), and Jason Stanley (2007). In doing so I identify some key choice points for those interested in answering the title question, What is semantic content? The investigation is not conclusive. Nevertheless it makes clear a number of considerations which count in favour of and against the various positions, and accordingly may serve as a kind of shoppers' guide for those in the market for a theory of semantic content.

2 The Taxonomy

The taxonomy of positions I provide is organized around the answers given to the following five key questions:

1. Is there such a thing as semantic content?

2. Is semantic content syntactically constrained?

3. Must semantic content be truth-evaluable?

4. How much syntax is covert?

5. Must semantic content be propositional?

The first of these questions serves to distinguish Paul Pietroski's semantic content Nihilism from the positions of the other philosophers considered here; for he denies that semantics yields content at all, while the others agree that there is such a thing as semantic content, but disagree regarding its nature.[1]

The second question distinguishes John Perry and François Recanati's Free Enrichment theories, for instance, from the views of the remaining contributors to the debate – for they suggest that semantics is not strictly constrained by syntax.

The third question differentiates Kent Bach's Propositional Radicalism from the positions of his rivals: while others maintain that semantic content must be truth-evaluable, he denies this.

---

[1] With the possible exception of François Recanati – see the exegetical discussion below.

The fourth question sets Jason Stanley's Indexical Contextualism apart from the views of others (and in particular those of Minimalists like Emma Borg, and Herman Cappelen and Ernie Lepore) – he holds that a lot of syntax is covert, while the others maintain that syntax is mostly overt.

The fifth question might appear to be worse than redundant, in the sense of failing to characterize any new position; it might be thought to be a mere repetition of the second. However, I employ the term 'propositional' in this article to mean *truth-evaluable relative only to a possible world*. This appearance is therefore illusory: the fifth question therefore allows us to distinguish the Relativisms of Max Kölbel and John MacFarlane from e.g. Minimalism.

Table 8.1 on page 190 summarizes these considerations. What grounds can be given in support of some answers to the questions in that table over others?

3 First Question

Semantics is thought to be concerned, on the one hand, with linguistic meaning, and on the other, with word-world relations. The term 'semantic content' reflects both of these concerns: for the expression 'semantic' connects with linguistic meaning, and 'content' with intentionality, i.e. word-world relations.

However, Paul Pietroski claims that 'semantics is concerned with "internalist" features of linguistic expressions, rather than truth *per se*. The fact that (an utterance of) a sentence has a certain truth-condition,' he continues, 'is typically an *interaction effect* whose determinants include (i) intrinsic properties of the sentence that we can isolate and theorize about, and (ii) a host of facts less amenable to theorizing, like facts about how "reasonable" speakers would *use* the sentence' (Pietroski 2003: 218, emphasis original). Elsewhere he says, 'one might think about a... monadic predicate... as (*inter alia*) an instruction for creating a monadic concept' (Pietroski 2005: 271) – though presumably the idea is that the *meaning* of such a

Position	Any such thing?	Syntactically Constrained?	Truth-evaluable?	Covert syntax?	Propositional?
Nihilism	No	n/a	n/a	n/a	n/a
Free Enrichment	Yes	No	Yes	Not much	Yes
Minimalism	Yes	Yes	Yes	Not much	Yes
Propositional Radicalism	Yes	Yes	No	Not much	No
Indexical Contextualism	Yes	Yes	Yes	Lots	Yes
Relativism	Yes	Yes	Yes	Not much	No

Table 8.1: A taxonomy of positions concerning the characteristics of semantic content

predicate is such an instruction, and not the expression itself.[2] Such concepts are taken to be mental items which are not world-involving. 'From this perspective,' Pietroski claims, 'semantics is not the study of symbol-to-world relations' (Pietroski 2003: 219). This suggests that Pietroski can be characterized as a Nihilist about semantic content: he thinks there is simply no such thing.

I will not have anything to say by way of assessment of this position; but it will prove useful to have it located in our taxonomy, so that other views may be compared with it.

4 Second Question

Both John Perry and François Recanati seem to allow that semantic content can fail to be syntactically constrained. Perry, for instance, claims that when one uses the sentence 'It is raining',

> ... the place [typically, though not invariably, that in which one utters the sentence] is an *unarticulated constituent* of the proposition expressed by the utterance. It is a constituent, because, since rain occurs at a time in a place, there is no truth-evaluable proposition unless a place is supplied. It is unarticulated because there is no morpheme that designates that place. (Perry 2001: 45)

So it seems Perry thinks that there are aspects of semantic content which are not the semantic values, in context, of any syntactic element of the sentence uttered – in short, semantic content is not syntactically constrained. Similarly, Recanati argues against what he calls the 'linguistic direction principle', according to which a context-dependent aspect of meaning is part of what is said 'only if its contextual determination is triggered by the grammar, that is, if the sentence itself sets up a slot to be contextually filled.' (Recanati 1993: 240) Apparently then, both philosophers allow the 'enrichment' of semantic content in a manner that is 'free' from syntactic constraint.

---

2 Pietroski later suggests that 'an expression of a spoken language may just be a pair of instructions for creating a sound of a certain sort and a concept of a certain sort' (Pietroski 2005: 272).

There is, I think, a quick argument against this view. According to one prominent account, if the semantics-pragmatics distinction is to be upheld, then it must be drawn in terms of the difference between interpreting utterances (certain speech acts), and their objects (sentences): the former kind of interpretation is pragmatic, the latter semantic. If this is right, then we can see that semantic content must be syntactically constrained. For semantic content – as opposed to pragmatic content – is the content of the sentence uttered; and sentences have syntactic features. Indeed, one might think that it is only by virtue of standing in some syntactic relation to a part of the sentence uttered that something counts as part of that sentence and not merely part of the utterance of that sentence.[3] So if semantic content is a feature of sentences then it is syntactically constrained; and if it is a feature of utterances then it need not be. But, given that we want to draw a distinction between semantic and pragmatic content, we can conclude that semantic content is syntactically constrained.

There are, however, three considerations which muddy the waters here: two are exegetical; the third is more substantive. Let's begin with matters of exegesis. Do Perry and Recanati hold the views that I have attributed to them?

It is quite clear, in Perry's case, that he takes utterances, not sentences, to be the bearers of semantic content (as opposed to linguistic meaning). According to Perry, '[u]tterances are intentional acts... [whereas sentence] tokens are traces left by utterances' (Perry 2001: 37). So it is in this sense that Perry is using these terms when he says that '[i]n some kinds of discourse tokens are epistemically basic, but utterances are always semantically basic' (*ibid*: 36); and it is therefore fair to regard him as maintaining that the propositions *semantically* expressed by utterances often contain unarticulated constituents.

Of course, Perry won't accept the premise of the above argument against free enrichment – the claim that semantics concerns the interpretations of sentences, while pragmatics concerns the interpretation

---

3 This, of course, won't do as a reductive account of sentencehood, invoking the notion of a sentence as it does.

of utterances. The result of rejecting this premise, however, is confusion, or at least equivocation, on Perry's part. For Perry allows that in addition to what he calls 'referential content', utterances possess various kinds of 'reflexive content'. He sometimes speaks of the referential content as the 'official' content (Perry 2001: 84), and one way of interpreting this claim is by acknowledging that it alone is semantic content.[4] However, Perry argues against the view that semantics has rested on a mistake – namely that of assuming that it must account for the cognitive significance of (utterances of) sentences – by allowing that varieties of reflexive content can explain differences in cognitive significance between (utterances of) sentences with the same official content; yet this is only a response, rather than a concession, if such reflexive content is also semantic. Thus, the result of abandoning the above characterization of the semantics-pragmatics distinction is indecision regarding, or perhaps indeterminacy of, semantic content: better then to stick to the view that sentences have semantic content, and allow utterances to differ in their cognitive significance.[5]

There is one further complication regarding the exegesis of Perry's view. Perry claims that the example mentioned above – an utterance of the sentence 'It is raining' – is a 'counterexample' to a principle he calls 'homomorphic representation', namely the principle that '[e]ach constituent of the proposition expressed by a statement is designated by a component of the statement' (Perry 1986: 140). However, he later draws a distinction between an assertion's being *about* some item and its *concerning* it (*ibid*: 147), where – crudely – in the former case the item in question is a constituent of the content expressed, and in the latter it is part of the relevant circumstance of evaluation of the content; moreover, Perry is somewhat equivocal about which of these views he accepts. I think ultimately he does commit to the

---

4   In fact, when the notion of official content is introduced it is defined in terms of 'our common-sense concept of content'; but it is not clear that we have such a notion, nor that if we do it ought to be used as the basis for a science of language.
5   Bach (2007) raises similar concerns with Perry's view. Note that Perry *might* be advocating pluralism about content, or a certain sort of relativity thereof: but it is hard to tell *which* view he wants to endorse.

rejection of a syntactic constraint on semantic content;[6] but if not, then his view will constitute a version of Relativism, which will be discussed below.

The exegetical concern in Recanati's case is somewhat different. Recanati, like Perry, is certainly committed to the view that *'speech acts* [as opposed to sentences] are the primary bearers of content' (Recanati 2004: 3, italics original), and I have said that on his view semantic content is not syntactically constrained; yet Recanati speaks not of semantic content, but of 'what is said' – he might therefore deny that what is said is semantic content. Indeed, Recanati speaks of 'truth-conditional pragmatics' (Recanati 1993: 233), and it seems therefore likely that he will insist that *what is said* is a pragmatic notion.

It is important to have conceptual clarity at this stage. In his book *How to Do Things with Words* John Austin endeavoured to 'consider from the ground up how many senses there are in which to say something *is* to do something, or *in* saying something we do something, and even *by* saying something we do something' (Austin 1975: 94, italics original); he thereby initiated the systematic investigation of speech acts. A crude account of Austin's answer to the above question is that there are three kinds of speech act (corresponding to the different italicized expressions in the above quote). He wrote:

> [T]o say something is in the full normal sense to do something – which includes the utterance of certain noises, the utterance of certain words in a certain construction, and the utterance of them with a certain 'meaning' in the favourite philosophical sense of that word, i.e. with a certain sense and a certain reference. The act of 'saying something' in this full normal sense I call, i.e. dub, the performance of a locutionary act. (Austin 1975: 94)

---

6 He says, 'Could we apply this [relativist] analysis to my younger son's remark [that it is raining]? That is, could we interpret it homomorphically, taking it to express a propositional function, and say that it is true, because it concerns Palo Alto? But this would not be an accurate remark about English. Weather discourse in English does not uniformly concern the place the discussants are at.' (Perry 1986: 148) He then goes on to say some things in favour of relativism.

In addition to locutionary acts, Austin also recognized illocutionary acts such as stating and arguing, whose success consists in their being understood, and perlocutionary acts such as convincing, the success of which require some further effects on the audience.

This is important because, as Bach (2005) has stressed, 'saying' might be construed either as a locutionary act – uttering certain words, in a certain construction, with a certain sense and reference – or as an illocutionary act – stating, or asserting. It is clear, however, that Recanati must intend what is said to be the content of a locutionary act; for he insists that we can speak of what is said by, for instance, the antecedent of a conditional (Recanati 1993: 271) – yet this is not the content of any illocutionary act. Indeed, Recanati seems to acknowledge as much when he writes:

> Grice uses 'say' in a strict sense. In that sense whatever is said must be meant. But we can easily define a broader sense for 'say':
>
>> S says that p, in the broad sense iff he either says that p (in the strict sense) or makes as if to say that p (again, in the strict sense of 'say').
>
> I will henceforth use 'say' in that broad sense. (Recanati 2004: 19)

If we take it that meaning something involves performing an action with an illocutionary force, then 'say' in Grice's 'strict' sense is a generic verb for an illocutionary act; this suggests that in Recanati's 'broad' sense it describes a locutionary act.

One concern about this suggestion, however, is that it is not clear that locutionary acts have contents, if these are construed as language independent entities; for Austin (1975: 92–93) described the locutionary act itself in detail not given in the above quote – in particular, he distinguished (a) the phonetic act, (b) the phatic act, and (c) the rhetic act as (individually necessary and jointly sufficient) elements of the locutionary act. It accordingly seems reasonable to maintain that the object of the locutionary act is the interpreted sentence, whereas the object of the illocutionary act is a proposition or thought.[7] To see this, note that two people might perform the same illocutionary act though they used different sentences. By contrast, the object of the phonetic act is a string of phonemes; that of the phatic act – which might better be called a syntactic act – is a syntactic structure, including vocabulary items.[8] The object of the rhetic act, and therefore of the locutionary act, it seems, is therefore the syntactically parsed, semantically interpreted sentence.

Nevertheless, I think we can say that the content that p is the content of a given locutionary act A, if in performing that the speaker produced a sentence s, meaning – that is, not necessarily asserting, but expressing – by it that p. (Thus, just as one can perform different illocutionary acts with the same content – asserting, or demanding, for instance – so too, according to this suggestion, one can perform different locutionary acts with the same content.) So the view that what is said is the content of a locutionary act seems ultimately intelligible.

Using the above distinctions and clarifications we can now articulate the following conjectures concerning the relations between our central notions: (i) semantic content is locutionary content; and (ii) locutionary content is illocutionary content (in cases of literal speech). Given his account of locutionary saying cited above, it should be clear that Recanati endorses the second of these conjectures; the question before us now is whether he endorses the first.

On the one hand, I think we should endorse the conjecture that semantic content is locutionary content: for it is not clear to me that there is any need for two kinds of content here rather than one. Yet, on the other hand, I think Recanati should not identify semantic and locutionary content: for given his view of the latter as freely enriched, by identifying the two he would also be committed to the claim that semantic content is not syntactically constrained – and by the quick argument above this is not a conclusion we should accept.

---

7 I am here relaxing the suggestion that propositions must be evaluable only relative to a possible world: the point is that illocutionary acts have as objects certain entities which are independent of their linguistic clothing.

8 That is, what Predelli (2005) calls a 'clause' – see below.

If Recanati were to deny the hypothesis under consideration – which he may do – then it is unclear to me how he thinks of semantic content: perhaps he accepts Pietroski's Nihilism - though it seems that his 'quasi-contextualism' can acknowledge the intelligibility of a notion of semantic content distinct from locutionary content (Recanati 2004: 86). Of course, Recanati will regard any such notion as picking out a gerrymandered, rather than natural kind, as he suggests it has no psychological reality in the process of communication (*ibid*: 96).

Nevertheless, there is some evidence that Recanati does accept the identification of semantic content with locutionary content. In a response to Jason Stanley's (2000) binding argument, which aims to establish that there are no unarticulated constituents, Recanati (2002: 339–342) has suggested that there is a level of mental representation distinct from LF, or logical form, which he calls 'SR' or 'semantic representation'. This level contains representational elements which are not triggered by the syntax of the sentence, i.e. unarticulated representational constituents. It seems that the content of this representation is the locutionary content of the utterance in response to which the SR is generated; but it also seems natural to suppose that the content of a 'semantic representation' is semantic content. If so, then my characterization of Recanati's view of semantic content as involving unarticulated constituents is accurate, and the objection above applies.

Let's turn now to the substantive worry concerning the quick argument given in favour of the claim that semantic content is syntactically constrained. There are some linguists and cognitive scientists who think that it is not the noises themselves, which are produced by speakers, but rather mental representations of them that literally have syntactic structure. If so, then it will prove very difficult to determine whether any such mental representation is a representation of a sentence or of an utterance of a sentence (including, e.g. speaker intentions as a proper part). Consider, for instance, Recanati's SR discussed above: it is syntactically structured, but is it a representation of a sentence or of an utterance? An inability to decide this issue threatens to undermine the above argument, and opens up the possibility that Free Enrichment theories of semantic content such as Perry's and Recanati's are correct after all.

Before responding to this worry, let me try to spell it out in more detail. Many Chomskyan linguists have been impressed by the facts that (i) two spoken tokens of the same sentence may differ wildly from one another in terms of their acoustic properties, and (ii) syntactically important boundaries and distinctions are not marked acoustically. They have concluded that these acoustic objects – the sounds – do not have syntactic features independently of our intentional relations to them: crudely, we merely hear (and otherwise think about) them *as* syntactically structured instead.

There are perhaps two ways of filling out this suggestion. According to the first, there are mental representations with the *content* that such and such sound has such and such syntactic features – that it is comprised, for instance, of sub-sounds, one of which is a noun, another of which is a verb, and so on. According to the second, by contrast, there are mental representations whose *objects* are the sounds in question – they are representations *of* those sounds – and which *have* the syntactic features in question.

I am not sure which of these proposals is more plausible – or even if they ultimately differ. The first is perhaps more intuitive: isn't it just what is meant by the representation of a sound *as* syntactically structured? The second on the other hand has the distinctive merit that it provides an explanation of why any transformations which might occur in the representation of a sentence are sensitive to syntactic form – for this just amounts to the suggestion that they are sensitive to the form of the representation itself! But perhaps the former suggestion can be regarded as a version of the latter – after all, if there is a low level language of thought capable of representing the content that a given sound has a given syntactic structure, then will it not also be the case that there is a high level language of thought which has the syntactic features in question? For simplicity I will consider the objection under discussion from the perspective of the second of the two proposals considered here.

Suppose, then, that there is a mental representation which has a certain syntactic structure in virtue of which it is the representation of something as syntactically structured in that way. What is its object? Is it a representation of the sentence token a given speaker has produced? Or is it instead the representation of an event of which that sentence token is a mere part – the speaker's utterance itself?[9] What could possibly determine this? Without an answer to this question it seems we can't be sure that semantic content is a feature of sentences rather than utterances.

I think that although it may be empirically very difficult to provide evidence in support of one answer to this question rather than the other, there is nevertheless a difference in principle between the two answers – a difference which can be drawn out as follows.

A number of authors have taken the view that the semantic features of a concrete sentence token, or an utterance thereof, can be regarded as stemming from the semantic features of an abstract representation of the event in question.[10] Thus, David Lewis advocated this view explicitly in his 'Language and Languages' (1975); Stefano Predelli (2005) has both defended this view and attributed it to David Kaplan (1989); and Scott Soames (1984) has argued that the founder of modern semantics himself, Alfred Tarski (1956), held this view. In Predelli's terminology, an *utterance u* is *represented* by a pair $\langle c, i \rangle$ whose first member is a *clause* and whose second member is an *index*. Intuitively, the pair $\langle c, i \rangle$ stands in the representation relation to the utterance *u* if and only if the clause *c* encodes the syntactic features of the sentence *s* uttered and the index *i* encodes the semantically relevant features of the context of utterance. According to a slight variation of this proposal, which I prefer, it is the sentence (token) *s* itself which is represented by the pair $\langle c, i \rangle$ in such circumstances.

It is worth noticing, however, that for languages with a transformational grammar, there will be more than one clause, or syntactic structure encoding the relevant features of a given sentence token. Some levels of representation which have been proposed include deep structure, surface structure, and logical form. If this is right, then a sentence token will be represented by a pair, not of a clause and an index, but rather of a sequence of syntactic representations together with an index.

---

9 I assume here, following Davidson (1967), that actions (such as utterances) are just events of a certain sort.
10 I here ignore complications arising from written sentence tokens.

Gilbert Harman (1970) has argued that logical form should be identified with deep structure. By contrast, Robert May (1985) has proposed that logical form should be regarded as a level of linguistic representation distinct from deep structure. One way of interpreting May's suggestion is to regard deep structure as a level of representation involved in the production of speech, while logical form is involved in its interpretation. Thus we have the surface structure, which serves as a representation of the product of the utterance – a certain noise – joined by an earlier member of the representing sequence, a deep structure, as well as a later structure, the logical form. A given sentence token will then be represented by a sequence-index pair just in case some mental representation of the speaker has the deep structure in question, the audience (or perhaps normal hearer) of the token has mental representations in succession, one with the surface structure and one having the syntactic structure of the logical form representation,[11] and the parametric values of the index are those determined by the context.

In this way I believe we can distinguish between a representation of a sentence having a certain structure and a representation of an utterance of that sentence having that structure. In particular, we should be able to distinguish between, on the one hand, someone who thinks, for example, *I haven't eaten breakfast today* but intends to produce the sentence 'I haven't eaten breakfast', and on the other, someone who intends to produce the sentence 'I haven't eaten breakfast today' but drops the word 'today' when the time to pronounce it comes. The latter will involve a deep structure involving the word 'today' whereas the former won't. Accordingly, there will be a distinction between two mental representations with the same syntactic features (such as, for instance, logical form) such that one of them is a representation of a sentence while the other is a representation of the utterance of that sentence. Thus, we should be able to distinguish in principle between the production of a sentence with hidden syntax

---

11 In fact, I suspect this way of approaching the issue will ultimately involve two structures in place of surface structure – one on the production end and one on the perception end.

and the expression of a thought by means of a sentence with less syntax than the thought itself.[12]

This dispels the worry raised against the suggestion that semantic content is a feature of sentences rather than utterances, and is accordingly syntactically constrained; but it also suggests a more general lesson – namely, that production is important to the metaphysical determination of the features, including the semantic features, of a sentence (token). We will return to this theme below.

5   Third Question

The third question involved in my taxonomy of views of semantic content, recall, is whether the semantic content of a sentence must be truth-evaluable.

One reason for taking semantic content to be non-truth-evaluable would be if it were simply the output of a modular interpretive system[13] which did not have access to the information required to generate truth-conditional content. If, in addition, pragmatics is concerned with general purpose interpretive reasoning, then it might seem that semantic content can't serve as the input to pragmatic reasoning – after all, reasons are truth-evaluable! Is this a good reason to think that the notion of semantic content can't bridge the gap between syntax and pragmatics? I don't think so. For if the semantic interpretation module yields a non-truth-evaluable semantic content m when given a sentence s, it doesn't follow that the output of semantics is not an appropriate input to general pragmatic reasoning – for the output of the semantic module might be plausibly regarded as the truth-evaluable content that s means m! This is clearly something one can entertain in one's general purpose reasoning.[14]

---

12 Note that this account assumes that natural languages have transformational grammars. I am unsure how this issue will play out if it turns out that they are better described as having lexical functional grammars (Dalrymple 2001).
13 See Borg (2004) for the suggestion that semantic interpretation is modular.
14 Endorsing this response to the present concern, however, may involve the rejection of the second of the two versions of the view that sounds are only represented as having syntactic structure; in particular, it seems to require that one have

Nevertheless, this discussion of modularity raises the question whether semantic content is metaphysically determined by the facts of speech production or of interpretation. I argue that since interpretation is an epistemic process there is no reason to regard semantic content as metaphysically determined solely by this process. Accordingly, views according to which semantic content often fails to be truth-evaluable will seem unmotivated. Before making this case, however, it will be worth clarifying further what I will be arguing – or, more accurately, what I won't be arguing. To this end it will again be worth getting clear on a few issues.

Many kinds of data are presented in support of various contextualist hypotheses, some of which were mentioned in the introduction; yet I think they can all be classed into three types of (alleged) phenomena. First, there is the assignment of values to items which are syntactically, even if not phonetically, present in the sentence uttered. The most obvious cases are the assignment of values to indexical expressions such as 'I', 'he' and 'that'; but also included in this class will be the assignment of values to any variables which occur without phonetic marking (if such there be). Borrowing a term (though not a concept[15]) from Recanati (2004: 7–10), I call this phenomenon 'saturation'.

The next phenomenon is that which, following Bach (1994: 126–133) I call 'completion'. Bach draws attention to pairs of expressions which are near synonyms, but whose syntactic properties differ. Thus,

---

a mental representation whose content is *that* a certain sentence has a certain syntactic structure and a certain meaning.

15 Recanati's account of saturation is related to, but different from, the one proposed here. He says, 'Saturation is the process whereby the meaning of a sentence is completed and made propositional through the contextual assignment of semantic values to the constituents of the sentence whose interpretation is context-dependent' (Recanati 2004: 7). This account assumes that the next phenomenon I will discuss (completion) is to count as saturation. Moreover, Recanati's preferred account of this latter phenomenon seems to involve the interpretation of the overt expression – say, 'noticed' – by an *ad hoc* concept, such as – in our example – *noticed that he is playing the piano*. This does not involve the assignment of a value to an indexical expression or variable, so doesn't count as saturation on my account.

it seems 'finished' and 'completed' are (nearly) synonymous; yet 'Al has finished' is a perfectly grammatical sentence, while 'Al has completed' is not. Bach concludes that, although it is syntactically unexceptionable, the sentence 'Al has finished' stands in need of semantic completion.

Finally, there is the phenomenon that Bach (1994: 133–140) calls 'expansion': this is when semantic material is added to a sentence which is already semantically complete, in the sense that it is already truth-evaluable. Thus, for instance, Bach suggests that a speaker might use 'I've eaten breakfast' to mean that he or she has eaten breakfast on the day in question; yet the sentence can be literally used to mean that the speaker has eaten breakfast at some time in the past – a claim which can itself be evaluated as true or false.

Note that although completion and expansion are defined to be mutually exclusive, it is an open question whether these phenomena are also cases of saturation – Stanley (2007), for instance, argues that they are. Moreover, there is room for disagreement over how to classify specific cases: if someone utters 'He is tall', meaning that he is tall for a 12-year-old boy, is this a case of completion or expansion? The answer will depend upon whether it is possible for someone to be tall *simpliciter*.

Now, Bach gives two kinds of argument in favour of his propositional radicalism. The first concerns completion phenomena. The thought is that if someone says, 'Al has finished' or 'Tipper is ready' then one needs to know what Al is alleged to have finished doing, or what Tipper is claimed to be ready to do, if one is to be able, even in principle, to assign a truth-value to the sentence uttered. I will not be concerned with such reasons for abandoning truth-evaluability here.[16]

Bach's second reason for denying that sentences uttered have truth-evaluable semantic contents derives from considerations surrounding saturation, and in particular the thought that the assignment

---

16 I suspect the correct treatment of these cases depends upon issues of syntax; however, one might hope to assimilate these cases to that of e.g. gradable adjectives discussed below.

of referents to certain context-sensitive expressions such as demonstratives is not a semantic matter. Since truth depends on reference, this gives us grounds for thinking that truth conditions are not a feature of semantic contents. Bach (2005) claims that '[d]emonstratives and most indexicals do not refer as a function of context' (*ibid*: 39); unlike the pure indexicals 'I' and 'today', he says, 'they suffer from a character deficiency'. He writes, 'The communicative context (context broadly construed) enables the audience to determine (in the sense of ascertain) what [the speaker] is referring to [when using such expressions], but it does not literally determine (in the sense of constitute) the reference' (*ibid*). The idea then, is that a token of a sentence such as 'He is happy' or 'That is red' does not have a truth-evaluable semantic content, since the context in which it is uttered merely helps the speaker to correctly identify who is claimed to be happy, or what is said to be red; it does not, together with the linguistic meaning of the impure indexical in question, fix this as a matter of fact. I find this claim implausible; and it is this reason for denying truth-evaluability which I wish to dispute.

All indexicals, I claim, pure or impure, must be grouped together. So if there are considerations, perhaps due to modularity, which tell against counting the reference of an impure indexical as semantically determined, then they tell equally against counting the reference of a pure indexical as so determined. Fortunately such considerations are not compelling, and we can therefore count the reference of overt expressions as semantically determined.

I spoke earlier of a modification of Predelli's (2005) suggestion, according to which we can regard sentence tokens as represented by abstract pairs, the second member of which is an index – that is, an *n*-tuple of parameters determined by features of the context of utterance of the sentence. Now, if we think of the context itself as the situation in which the sentence token is produced, then it seems clear that *this* suffices to determine the reference of any given indexical, whether pure or impure – for the referents of such expressions are determined by the linguistic meaning of the expression along with the speaker's intentions – both of which are aspects of the situation which is the context. But then, why should there not be a parameter of the *index* which encodes this fact? That is, why should the index not include, as one of its members, the relevant demonstratum? Yet if the index – Bach's 'narrow context' – includes a demonstratum parameter (or a sequence thereof, to deal with cases in which multiple demonstratives are used) then demonstratives and other impure indexicals are no different from pure indexicals: both have a reference relative to an index.

One might be concerned that the semantic module of the mind will have no access to information concerning who or what is referred to by a given impure indexical. For clearly, general epistemic resources of the hearer will be called into play in order to ascertain which object is demonstrated when a given speaker uses the word 'that'. But then, the argument goes, if semantic content is the result of modular processing alone, the reference of such a word cannot be one of its semantic features.

This argument has its merits. But I think it proves too much – certainly too much for Bach's purposes. For just as it is clear that general epistemic resources are required on a hearer's part to ascertain what object is demonstrated when a speaker uses the word 'that', so too general epistemic resources are required to ascertain who the speaker is. Clearly the semantic module doesn't do that! (Imagine a lost postcard case: a reader whose semantic module is perfectly intact can't figure out who sent it – nor, therefore, can such a hearer ascertain who the referent of a token of 'I' occurring on it is.) If these considerations are correct, then if semantic content is metaphysically determined solely by the modular process of interpretation, the semantic content of a token of 'I' cannot be the person who produced it. That is, the semantic content of a token of 'I am F' produced by a cannot be the externalist content that a is F; rather, it must be the internalist content that *the speaker is F*.[17] Bach's propositional radicalism is unstable – considerations which support it lead to semantic internalism, and the concomitant Pietroskian semantic content Nihilism.

We can, however, avoid semantic internalism and content Nihilism by denying that semantic properties are metaphysically determined

---

17 Here 'the speaker' is used attributively.

by the process of interpretation alone. It is a perfectly objective fact that a given speaker used a given token of 'I' – and it is this which determines (metaphysically) that that token of 'I' refers to that person. A fact such as this is semantic – even if some non-linguistic cognitive resources must be deployed if one is to come to know it. Sometimes one must know some non-semantic facts in order to ascertain the semantic facts. But this applies equally to pure and impure indexicals: for it is an objective fact that a given speaker intended to refer to a certain object o when using the demonstrative 'that', even if it is one which requires general epistemic resources to recognize. In this way we can resist semantic internalism and content Nihilism; but on this basis we can equally rule out Propositional Radicalism – unless, of course, there are reasons to endorse it due to completion phenomena.[18]

---

[18] Borg (2004: chapter 3) takes a slightly different approach. On her view, semantic features are determined by the process of interpretation, but this process is not epistemically constrained. Thus, when we hear a sentence containing an indexical, we construct a mental representation, or singular concept, whose denotation is the relevant item. (This process, Borg claims, is modular.) The resulting mental representation is directly referential, but nevertheless has a character, which helps the hearer (using non-modular processes) to integrate the singular concept with other mental representations, thereby rendering it useful to the hearer at the personal level. Accordingly, the contents of expressions like 'I' or 'that' are external-world objects, though at a personal level the hearer may not be in a position to identify the objects in question. Borg's view is, I think, an intelligible one without obvious flaws; though it is one which is subject to empirical fortunes. For instance, it can be compared to one which, inspired by Pietroski's semantic internalism, regards the interpretation process as involving instructions to construct concepts. When one hears an indexical expression, on this view one forms the (sub-personal) intention to construct a singular concept, in accordance with certain rules for integration with further information provided by the character of the expression. The view differs from Borg's in that, while on Borg's view one interprets an expression e if one successfully constructs a singular concept α which one may then integrate with, say, a perceptual singular concept A in accordance with the character of the expression e whose interpretation generates α, on this alternative account one interprets e by following the instruction to generate a singular concept in accordance with the character of e. One may fail to do this if one cannot, say, form a perceptual concept associated in the appropriate way with the expression. Basically, the interpretation of e is successful if A is generated, not if α is (though 'understanding' might be said

6 Fourth and Fifth Questions

I take the fourth question – the question of how much covert syntax there is – to be largely empirical; which is not to say that it isn't theoretical! But without strong evidential backing and thorough consideration of the intricacies of syntactic theory it will prove hard to determine which answer to this question is correct. So I will not engage in this debate directly.

Nevertheless, it might be thought that the issue which divides Indexical Contextualists from Minimalists could be approached via the fifth question. For the Indexical Contextualist might argue that sentences without much covert syntax would not have propositional content – they would not be evaluable only relative to a possible world. If so, then if semantic content must be propositional (as both the Indexical Contextualist and the Minimalist agree it must), this would count against the Minimalist.

I argue, however, that without an account of what possible worlds are it will prove difficult to make the charge of non-propositionality stick. Moreover, it will be hard to see why non-propositional contents shouldn't be truth-evaluable.

Consider the case of a word like 'tall' – though something similar could be said about other controversial terms such as 'empty', 'flat', 'knows', 'might', 'right', 'delicious', 'beautiful' or even 'true'. According to some the word 'tall' is context-sensitive. Thus, they claim, we might say truly of a man who is 6'2", 'He is tall', if we have in mind to compare him to the population of men at large; but we might say truly 'He is not tall' if we are concerned with how effective a volleyball player he will be for his national team. Thus, the truth conditions of any given token of 'He is tall' are not that the indicated person is tall *simpliciter*, but rather that the indicated individual is tall *relative to R*, where *R* is some comparison class – say, men in general, or male volleyball players in international competition.

---

to occur anyway). This alternative approach appears to have less commitment vis-a-vis the language of thought hypothesis than does Borg's (it requires just one singular concept, where Borg's requires two); though I confess I don't know what empirical evidence would decide the issue from an epistemological point of view.

Minimalists Cappelen & Lepore (2005a, 2005b) respond to the charge that the truth conditions of 'He is tall' can't be simply that the indicated individual is tall *simpliciter* since it is unclear what it is to be tall *simpliciter*. They argue that a semantic theory needn't provide an analysis of each word in the language; so they don't need to say what it is to be tall *simpliciter*.

I think the Cappelen and Lepore response can be made plausible as follows. A token of 'He is tall' is true at a possible world w, they claim, just in case the indicated individual is tall at w. But what is a possible world? Few of us are willing to countenance non-actual Lewisian possible worlds – mereologically maximal concrete objects which stand in no spatio-temporal relation to us (Lewis 2001). But if we think of worlds instead as something like maximally consistent sets of propositions – or perhaps sets of interpreted sentences – then there is no reason why we should not allow that 'He is tall' is true relative to a world w just in case w contains a proposition or sentence to the effect that the indicated individual is tall. If this is right, then minimal semantic contents are propositional after all.

Perhaps someone will object that my proposal is really relativist in character, not minimalist. Relativism is the view that semantic content must be evaluated relative to a parameter beyond just a possible world[19] – in the case under consideration, a comparison class must also be included in the circumstance of evaluation; perhaps to deal with other cases the relativist would add other parameters as well. But I am simply building the comparison class into the possible world; that is, the objector contends, I am saying that a sentence is true relative to a world and a comparison class – but that my worlds implicitly contain comparison classes. Thus the semantic contents I envision are not minimal propositions – for they are not propositions at all.

---

19 This is how Max Kölbel (2002) characterizes the view; and although John MacFarlane (2005) does not give this account of what relativism consists in, preferring to characterize a semantics as relativist only if it relativizes sentence truth to a context of assessment as well as a context of utterance, his view is ultimately covered by the account given in the main text – see Cappelen and Hawthorne (2009: chapter 1) and my (forthcoming).

My response is that this thought is basically correct – though it is expressed in contentious language. The point I wish to stress is that all parties effectively agree that a token of 'He is tall' is true only relative to a comparison class – but they insist that the comparison class enters into the determination of a truth value in a different way. Yet I can see no semantically tractable difference between the three proposals.[20] There is, of course, a syntactic difference – the Indexical Contextualist maintains that the sentence under discussion contains covert syntax. Recall, however, that we were hoping to find independent semantic evidence which would suggest that we ought to pursue the Indexical Contextualist's hypothesis. My suggestion is that there isn't any evidence of this kind – if we are to make the case for Indexical Contextualism as opposed to Minimalism or Relativism, we will have to do so on purely syntactic grounds.

7 Conclusion

If these considerations are correct, Indexical Contextualism, Minimalism, and Relativism are left as live options concerning the nature of semantic content. What will decide between them is an independent syntactic investigation which I have not been willing to undertake here. But some progress has been made – Free Enrichment theories of semantic content have been ruled out; and it has been argued that if there are no successful arguments from completion phenomena in support of Propositional Radicalism, then the view collapses to an internalist, semantic content Nihilism.[*]

---

20 On Predelli's (2005) account, clause-index pairs are assigned t-distributions, which are assignments of truth-values at 'points' of evaluation. This leaves room for a range of possibilities concerning the nature of those points. My argument here is effectively exploiting this indeterminacy.

* This article benefitted from comments at the CLLC conference in Lisbon. Thanks in particular to Kent Bach, Emma Borg, and François Recanati.

References

Austin, J. L. (1975). *How to do things with words,* (2nd ed.). Oxford: Clarendon Press.

Bach, K. (1994). Conversational impliciture. *Mind & Language, 9,* 124–161.

―――― (2005). Context ex machina. In Szabó, Z. G. (Ed.). *Semantics vs pragmatics.* Oxford: Clarendon Press.

―――― (2007). Reflections on *Reference and Reflexivity.* In O'Rourke, M. and Washington, C. (Eds.). *Situating semantics: Essays on the philosophy of John Perry.* Cambridge, MA: MIT Press.

Ball, B. (forthcoming). Review of Cappelen and Hawthorne's *Relativism and monadic truth. Logical Analysis and the History of Philosophy.*

Borg, E. (2004). *Minimal semantics.* Oxford: Clarendon Press.

Cappelen, H. & Hawthorne, J. (2009). *Relativism and monadic truth.* Oxford: Oxford University Press.

Cappelen, H. & Lepore, E. (2005a). *Insensitive semantics: A defense of semantic minimalism and speech act pluralism.* Oxford: Blackwell.

―――― (2005b). Radical and moderate pragmatics: does meaning determine truth-conditions? In Szabó, Z. G. (Ed.). *Semantics vs pragmatics.* Oxford: Clarendon Press.

Dalrymple, M. (2001). *Lexical functional grammar.* London: Academic Press.

Davidson, D. (1967). The logical form of action sentences. In Rescher, N. (Ed.). *The logic of decision and action.* Pittsburgh: University of Pittsburgh Press.

Harman, G. (1970). Deep structure as logical form. *Synthese, 21,* 275–297.

Kaplan, D. (1989). Demonstratives: An essay on the semantics, logic, metaphysics, and epistemology of demonstratives. In Almog, J., Perry, J. & Wettstein, H. (Eds.). *Themes from Kaplan.* Oxford: Oxford University Press.

Kölbel, M. (2002). *Truth without objectivity.* London: Routledge.

Lewis, D. (1975). Languages and language. *Minnesota Studies in the Philosophy of Science, VII,* 3–35.

―― (2001). *On the plurality of worlds*. Oxford: Blackwell.
Macfarlane, J. (2005). Making sense of relative truth. *Proceedings of the Aristotelian Society, 105*, 305–323.
May, R. (1985). *Logical form: Its structure and derivation*. London: MIT Press.
Perry, J. (1986). Thought without representation. *Proceedings of the Aristotelian Society, Supplementary Volume, 60*, 137–151.
―― (2001): *Reference and reflexivity*. Stanford: CSLI Publications.
Pietroski, P. (2003). The character of natural language semantics. In Barber, A. (Ed.): *Epistemology of language*. Oxford: Oxford University Press.
―― (2005). Meaning before truth. In Preyer, G. & Peter, G. (Eds.). *Contextualism in philosophy: knowledge, meaning, and truth*. Oxford: Clarendon Press.
Predelli, S. (2005). *Contexts: meaning, truth, and the use of language*. Oxford: Clarendon Press.
Recanati, F. (1993). *Direct reference: from language to thought*. Oxford: Blackwell.
―― (2002). Unarticulated constituents. *Linguistics and Philosophy, 25*, 299–345.
―― (2004). *Literal meaning*. Cambridge: Cambridge University Press.
Soames, S. (1984). What is a theory of truth? *The Journal of Philosophy, 81*, 411–429.
Stanley, J. (2000). Context and logical form. *Linguistics and Philosophy, 23*, 391–434.
――n(2007). *Language in context: Selected essays*. Oxford: Clarendon Press.
Tarski, A. (1956). *Logic, semantics, metamathematics*. Oxford: Clarendon Press.

― 9 ―

Sandy Berkovski
Some Remarks on Mthat

1 Introduction

In this article I want to draw attention to a number of problems in Josef Stern's account of metaphorical representation. Their common root, I am going to argue, lies in Stern's attempt to integrate Stalnaker's notion of context into Kaplan's semantic theory. Let me then begin by rehearsing some very familiar features of Kaplan's and Stalnaker's accounts.

Kaplan's target is to provide a semantic account of indexical expressions. Included here are pure indexicals that do not require acts of demonstration, such as 'I', 'now', and possibly 'here'. For the ease of exposition it is better to focus on indexical sentences, i.e. sentences containing one or more indexicals. Now Kaplan claims that the content of such sentences – what they say – varies from one context to another. In one context the sentence

(1)   I am hot.

says that Roger Federer is hot. In another context it says that Barack Obama is hot. The variation of contents is not random. Every time BO utters (1) its content is that BO is hot, and analogously for Federer. What ensures the stability is the purely lexical meaning of 'I'. Kaplan calls it 'character'.

Further, content will yield the semantic value of a sentence depending on the state of the world, or on what Kaplan calls 'the circumstance of evaluation'. If circumstances are such that BO is hot, then the semantic value of (1) is TRUE.

A tiny bit of a formal apparatus allows us to summarise the view as follows. Character is a function from contexts to contents. Its argument is a context, and its value a certain content. Contents, in turn, are functions from circumstances of evaluation to semantic values. In the case of sentences semantic values will be TRUE and FALSE, while in the case of singular terms semantic values will be the individuals referred to. The content of indexical sentences changes with contexts, so their character is represented by a variable function, whereas the character of non-indexical sentences is a constant function.

Circumstances of evaluation are arrays of parameters such as world, agent, place, and time: $\langle w, x, p, t \rangle$. Contexts are represented by a similar structure, but with an added restriction that the agent x is present at the place p at the time t in the world w. Notably the parameters in the array are not parameters of an utterance. We can assign content and truth value to the sentence (1) even if no one ever uttered it (compare the sentence 'I am silent'). Nevertheless we can instead identify them with parameters of possible utterances.

Enter Stalnaker. Like Kaplan's, his theory is supposed to describe the dependence of contents on contexts. But the setting is entirely different. We examine the contents of actual utterances and we place virtually no limits on how a particular utterance token, a speech act, is interpreted by the addressee. By occupying himself with utterance tokens, Stalnaker envisages a situation where the addressee of my utterance (call him 'Jacob') interprets his sensory experience as an act of assertion. Such an interpretation is an integral part of a successful assignment of semantic values to the particular assertion, i.e. of Jacob's presuppositions. It has several components. In the first place, it must contain some sort of a behavioural theory allowing Jacob to identify the opening of my mouth as an act of assertion, rather than as an act of clearing my throat. Secondly, Jacob should have a lexical theory associating the sequence of noises emanating from my mouth with linguistic items. When I utter a statement – say, 'Snow is white'

– Jacob's lexical theory should tell him I utter it in English, rather than in some obscure Chinese dialect vocally indistinguishable from English.

So we consider concrete utterance tokens, and for every such utterance token different addressees of the utterance along with the utterer himself may form different pragmatic presuppositions. These latter are nothing but propositions assumed by the speaker, who can either seriously believe in them, assume them 'for the sake of argument', or perhaps pretend to believe in them. Similarly to Kaplan's account, there is a two-step procedure in place: from contexts we get to propositions which themselves are functions from possible worlds to semantic values.

2 The Cross-Breeding Ploy

As Stalnaker himself emphasised on several occasions, for all their superficial similarities the two theories are very different. First, they are different in their goals. Whereas Kaplan intends to provide a semantic theory of a fragment of language, Stalnaker's aim is to provide a model of conversation. Kaplan identifies properties of sentences (utterance types), while Stalnaker deals with utterances (utterance tokens). Second, there is an asymmetry in the explanatory order. On Kaplan's view, indexical sentences have their content by virtue of their character. But utterances have their propositional concepts (formally analogous to characters) by virtue of their semantic contents.

Nevertheless there is one aspect in which Stalnaker's account might be seen as a generalisation of Kaplan's, and this is the notion of context. What if we wanted to create a semantic theory of context-sensitive expressions other than indexicals? And what if we did not have natural elements of context arrays such as time and place? There might be a straightforward solution. We may plug the agent's presuppositions directly into the arrays of Kaplanian contexts. The ploy is to cross-breed the two approaches. We inherit the methodology and semantic machinery from Kaplan. We are looking for a *semantic* theory for a class of expressions other than indexicals. Our goal is not to understand the dynamics of conversation involving that new class of expressions, but to have a theory assigning, in a given context, semantic contents and semantic values to those expressions. Unfortunately, in contrast to indexicals, there is no readily available contextual elements. We need a broader notion of context which we can inherit from Stalnaker. Contexts will contain the speakers' presuppositions.

One might think that cross-breeding was already done by none other than Kaplan himself in the account of demonstratives (as opposed to pure indexicals). Suppose you point at the picture of Carnap and say, 'The picture shows one of the greatest philosophers of the 20th century.' This is what you actually say in English. However, according to Kaplan, given the fact of demonstration your utterance must be assigned a special logical form containing the operator 'dthat[·]':[1]

(2) Dthat['the picture'] shows one of the greatest philosophers of the 20th century.

The argument of 'dthat[·]' is an act of demonstration, or a definite description (in its demonstrative use), or generally a singular term. The point of its introduction is in rigidifying its operand: for every context c and for every expression ϕ, an occurrence of 'dthat[ϕ]' in c rigidly designates the individual denoted by ϕ in c (and it designates no one if there is no such unique individual). To simplify, suppose ϕ is a definite description. Then there is the following consequence.[2] 'Dthat[ϕ]' takes an expression whose character is constant and yields an expression whose character is no longer constant: it delivers different contents in different contexts. Along the way it also converts

---

[1] There is a marked ambiguity in Kaplan (1978) regarding the syntax and semantics of 'dthat'. In one use it is an operator, but in another it is a directly referential singular term. The ambiguity is addressed in Kaplan (1989b: 579-82). Since for Stern's purposes the operator interpretation is the only relevant one, we can ignore the singular term interpretation.

[2] Kaplan also argues for the 'isomorphism' between the semantics of demonstrations and descriptions, since we can associate character with each act of demonstration. See Kaplan (1989a: 525-27).

the content of the embedded description into part of the character of the resulting dthat-expression.

At a minimum we have enlarged the previously pristine context arrays suitable for pure indexicals with acts of demonstration. But more is coming. What if my demonstration act is indistinct? I am on a visit to an art gallery standing in front of *Annunciation*. I say:

> Dthis[waving my hand] is a typical Fra Filippo.

But right next to *Annunciation* there hangs *Repentant Magdalene* by Caravaggio. My demonstration may be inconclusive to determine the content of my utterance, or it may even be that I inadvertently pointed at Caravaggio's piece. In such cases Kaplan believes the directing intention is an essential part of the context. Since I meant to refer to *Annunciation*, that is what the demonstrative designates.

Yet Kaplan cannot quite make up his mind on the matter. In Kaplan (1978) there is a well-known discussion of the Carnap/Agnew case. Suppose Carnap's picture hangs on the wall behind me. I utter (2) while pointing at the wall behind me, fully intending to make a claim about Carnap's picture. Unbeknownst to me, Carnap's picture was replaced by Spiro Agnew's picture. Then, says Kaplan:

> I think it would simply be wrong to argue an 'ambiguity' in the demonstration, so great that it can be bent to my intended demonstratum. I have said of a picture of Spiro Agnew that it pictures one of the greatest philosophers of the twentieth century. (Kaplan 1978: 687)

When the demonstration is clear, then it should override any intention I might have. But he continues:

> Still, it would perhaps be equally wrong not to pursue the notion of the intended demonstratum. ... There are situations where the demonstration is sufficiently ill-structured in itself so that we would regularly take account of the intended demonstratum as, *within limits*, a legitimate disambiguating or vagueness removing device. (*ibid*)

By the time of 'Afterthoughts' Kaplan's view has drifted decisively towards emphasising the role of 'directing intentions' in the context. There he treats the Carnap/Agnew case as 'rather complex, atypical'.[3]

How significant is Kaplan's move, and how is it related to the Ploy? I think the answer to these questions brings us to the centre of the debate between contextualists and their opponents and will ultimately help us assess Stern's theory. But let me pick up some details of that theory before returning to deal with the Ploy.

3 Metaphor and context

According to Stern, metaphorical sentences are both truth-apt and context-sensitive. We deploy Kaplan's formal machinery with the following modification: contexts will include speakers' presuppositions. At the surface level, Stern represents metaphorical expressions with the operator 'Mthat[·]' acting on a literal expression ϕ. So, analogous to indexicals (and demonstratives), the character of 'Mthat[ϕ]' is not constant: it yields different metaphorical contents for different contexts. We have:

Definition. For every context c and every expression ϕ, an occurrence of 'Mthat[ϕ]' in '···Mthat[ϕ]···' in c expresses a set of properties P presupposed to be associated with ϕ in c.

For example, consider the sentence:

(3) Juliet is the sun.

To interpret this sentence we must follow several steps. We must recognise the presence of the metaphorical expression 'is the sun'. We must assign it a variable character using the operator 'Mthat[·]'. Analogously to (2), (3) gets transformed into:

(4) Juliet Mthat['is the sun'].

What permits the transformation on each occasion of the utterance is our recognition of the context. A pagan worshipper can utter the

---
3 See Kaplan (1989: 582).

English sentence (3) while purporting to name the sun god (compare 'Helios is the sun'). In this case the transformation does not go through. If Romeo utters the same sentence, it should. The facts about the utterer, his beliefs, and so forth all belong to a context. Yet this is a presemantic role of the context.[4] It allows us to assign conventional linguistic meanings to the strings of shapes and noises. Due to the same presemantic context the interlocutor realises that, e.g., (3) is uttered in English, or that someone is saying something, rather than just clearing his throat.

It is a central claim of Stern's that the Mthat-transformation is done at this presemantic level. The logical form of the utterance of (3) is given by (4). Or alternatively, the character of that utterance is given by (4). Using the type/token distinction, we can also say that the utterance-token of (3), given the facts of the presemantic context, instantiates the utterance-type (4).

The implications are significant. Stern rejects the view on which there is a literal meaning encoded in (3) subsequently to be transformed into metaphorical meaning. There is no place, then, for the thesis that (the vast majority of) metaphorical statements are literally false, but metaphorically true (or false). The metaphorical locution enters too early for us to be able to talk intelligibly of literally false/true statements. The literal meaning is encoded directly by (4), but, like the case of demonstratives, it cannot be assigned a truth value unless we supply a semantic context.

That semantic context is provided by metaphorically relevant presuppositions of the speaker. When we have a locution '...Mthat[ϕ]...', the speaker will have identified certain properties metaphorically associated (m-associated) with the expression ϕ. His beliefs about those m-associated properties will constitute the set of presuppositions for the given metaphorical sentence. How exactly m-presuppositions are selected is governed by pragmatic rules *à la* Grice.[5] But there is a detail specific to metaphors. The set of presuppositions will divide into two subsets. One contains those presuppositions that generate

---

4 See Perry (1998).
5 See Stern (2000: 128, 135-39).

each and every m-associated property of ϕ. Thus the expression 'is the sun' may presumably have m-associated properties 'is bright', 'is extremely hot', 'is old', 'is life-giving', 'is magnificent', and so forth. Not all of them are appropriate to ascribe to Juliet if the utterer is Romeo. Stern then postulates a second set of presuppositions that would serve to filter the properties appropriate in the given context. So while 'is life-giving' would be appropriate in the context of Romeo talking about Juliet, 'is old' would not be so.

4 Contextualism, minimalism, literalism

To get a better perspective on Stern's account, it is useful to locate it in the current debate between contextualists and their opponents. The usual outline of that debate goes something like this. *Contextualists* claim that only speech acts, as opposed to sentences, should be ascribed semantic (truth-conditional) content.[6] Now such ascriptions will be necessarily contextual: the same sentence can be used in speech acts with varying contexts and produce different contents. The idea of a context is a Gricean one. It is constituted by the speaker's intentions, along with the clues instrumental for guessing these intentions.

Their opponents disagree. *Minimalists* claim that genuine context-dependent expressions are far and few. Among them are indexicals and demonstratives, along with a (very) limited number of other expressions. A sentence containing no such expressions will have the 'minimal' propositional content shared by every utterance of that sentence. Particular utterances may possess other propositional contents. And such contents do vary across contexts. Their study is naturally relegated to pragmatics.[7]

Other theorists, while no friends of contextualism, reject the idea of minimal propositions. One strategy here is to find counterexamples where the alleged minimal proposition is never asserted (as in Stanley's 'Every bottle is in the fridge.'). These theorists join hands

---

6 See e.g. Recanati (2004: 83).
7 See Cappelen & Lepore (2005).

with contextualists in regarding minimal propositions as somewhat mythological, having at the very least no explanatory value and being theoretically idle.

Literalists (whose chief representative I will take to be Jason Stanley) are in agreement with minimalists regarding the unique role of the narrow class of genuine context-sensitive expressions such as indexicals and demonstratives.[8] But they are equally in agreement with contextualists on the claim of widespread semantic – as opposed to pragmatic – context-dependence. The way literalists oppose contextualist sentiments is by offering a different mechanism governing the context-sensitive production of semantic contents and the assignment of semantic values. When the sentence contains no elements from the narrow class of context-sensitive expressions, and when, on the other hand, we observe its semantic context-sensitivity, we must find a covert element in its logical form responsible for producing that context-sensitivity. So the context of course plays a major role in the explanation of context-sensitivity, but it is only one factor, the other key factor being the 'real' logical form of the sentence.

Where does Stern's account fit in this debate? Minimalism is not an option. The minimal proposition associated with the English sentence (3) is the proposition of identity between Juliet and the sun. While there may be contexts in which the utterance of (3) is made and where this proposition is asserted, in metaphorical contexts this proposition, according to Stern, is never asserted. A minimalist about metaphors is likely to fall back on the Davidsonian view on which metaphorical utterances, however useful and fascinating, would have literal propositions as their semantic contents and would, therefore, be almost always false.

Stern's view belongs in the literalist camp. Metaphorical contents are necessarily context-sensitive, but the semantic content is determined not only by the context, but also by the hidden element of the 'Mthat[·]' operator. That operator is not available at the level of the phonetic structure of an utterance. It should be recovered by the speakers (or rather, hearers and readers) at the pre-semantic stage of

---

8   For a concise statement of literalism see Stanley (2000: 398–401).

utterance interpretation. The outcome of this interpretation would be the correct logical form of the utterance in question.

A question arises whether the literalist has any independent argument against the contextualist analysis of metaphors. Stern has recently discussed this issue at length.[9] One option available to the contextualist is to treat metaphors by analogy with sentences such as 'Rome is covered in snow.' The correct pragmatic interpretation of that sentence may involve the process of loosening: under reasonable assumptions, the utterance should be understood as 'Many parts of Rome are partially covered in snow.' Other pragmatic processes would include semantic transfer and free enrichment, but loosening seems especially well adapted to metaphorical analysis and has been the favourite candidate of Recanati and the Relevance Theorists. Stern's complaint centres on the perceived lack of analogy between the literal/loose contrast and the literal/metaphorical contrast. I think the complaint is well-taken. In the typical cases of loose talk we have the speakers 'roughly' or approximately expressing in words the content they intended to express. But in typical metaphorical utterances there is no approximation involved. It is plain false that Juliet is 'almost' the sun. There is no simple qualifier to insert for converting the literal into the metaphorical. For a serious discussion I refer the reader to Stern's careful examination and criticism of this strategy.

The second contextualist option is to treat metaphorical contents as a class of secondary meanings dependent on primary meanings. The metaphorical content will be inferred, in some way, from an antecedent literal meaning of the utterance. The analogy here is with conversational implicature. A colleague asks me to have lunch together. I reply, 'I've just had lunch.' What I imply, among other things, is that I have to decline the invitation. But this is not what I literally said with my words. For the hearer to correctly interpret my utterance, he must first understand what I literally said, and then, aided by the context, derive the implied content. On Recanati's view, conversational implicatures always involve such two-stage interpretative procedures. But metaphors, Recanati also believes, must involve

---

9   See Stern (2006: 245-61).

a different procedure.[10] The hearers do not have to go through multiple stages. Their interpretation is 'immediate'. When I hear the utterance of (3), I do not first figure out the literal meaning (the identity proposition) and then infer the metaphorical meaning. Rather, the latter is grasped immediately.

Though Recanati provides no support for his conclusion other than citing phenomenological evidence and 'feeling', one should not deny the plausibility of the contrast he wishes to draw with typical instances of conversational implicature. Nevertheless the situation may be different with complex metaphors. Think especially of poetic metaphors. Thus Auden on Yeats:

> Let the Irish vessel lie
> Emptied of its poetry.

There is a metaphor here, but nothing about it is immediate. First, it is not immediately clear that there is a metaphor. And once we realise there is one, it takes some effort to get from the literal level, the one about empty vessels of Irish origin, to the metaphorical level, which is perhaps about Yeats leaving his poetry to posterity. The way to the metaphorical interpretation clearly goes through my reflection on the literal meaning of Auden's English sentence. So there must be here some form of functional determination of the metaphorical by the literal. Unfortunately, the contextualist lacks the resources to describe that determination.

The contextualist may have another move though. Granted there is no immediacy (or 'transparency', in Recanati's jargon), wouldn't this inferential procedure taking us from the literal to the metaphorical be quite dissimilar to the conversational implicature interpretation? Stern thinks that the contextualist can avail himself of a rather neat argument. The two-stage process alleged by Recanati to characterise conversational implicature involves the assignment of a semantic value to the literal content of the utterance and the subsequent assignment of a semantic value to the metaphor. But there is no assignment of semantic values to the literal content of Auden's metaphor, since

---

10 See Recanati (2004: 74-8).

there may be no truth-conditional literal content there. Within the truth-conditional semantic framework, the meaning of an utterance will have to be determined by the truth conditions of that utterance. Or to put it differently: the speaker must know the truth-conditions of U in order for him to understand U. Now there is no sensible truth condition attached to something like the literal utterance of Auden's sentence. When would a vessel (what kind of vessel?) of Irish origin be empty of its (vessel's!) poetry? Similarly there is no condition in which Juliet is a massive star. But if so, there can be no two semantic stages in the interpretation of metaphorical utterances.

The argument, I think, is neat, but fallacious. The contextualist will begin by rejecting the truth-conditional semantics. It is precisely because we cannot figure out the truth conditions of English sentences that the project of truth-conditional semantics has to be abandoned. It may be replaced by the project of truth-conditional theory of speech acts. In that theory, the lexical meanings of individual words will be only one of the factors in the assignment of truth-conditional contents to speech acts. So the initial demand that we must have semantic understanding of sentences is, from the contextualist perspective, entirely misplaced.

All this might not matter in the end. Suppose the contextualist wished to maintain the conversational implicature analogy. Then he must recognise some form of a two-stage (or multi-stage) interpretative procedure. But the Spartan menu of pragmatic processes in that procedure would again yield the same implausible option of loosening. And therefore, Stern's ultimate conclusion will be re-affirmed: contextualists recognise the dependence of the metaphorical on the literal, but they have no adequate theoretical resources to explain this dependence.

5 Another way to format the debate

The critical comments I want to make in the remainder of this article have a shared theme: Stern has not provided us with a semantic *theory* of metaphor. To understand why, we have first to note how the methodological assumptions underlying his view are fundamentally opposed to Kaplan's.

It is clear that contextualists and their opponents disagree on many specific issues. They have different stances on the role of truth-conditional semantics, on compositionality, the nature of truth-bearers, the place of context in the determination of semantic value, and so forth. Each of these issues is interesting and significant. But they may obscure a more general divide in this debate. There is, on the one hand, a belief that linguistic practices are systematic, that there is a possibility of a theory that would explain and predict linguistic phenomena. The parameters of the solution are well-known. Laying down the rules of formation, of inference, and of denotation for a given vocabulary we can predict what the semantic content of the utterance-in-L would be. Given facts about the world, we can further predict the semantic value of that utterance. Deviations from such theoretical predictions, while recognised, will be treated on a par with deviations of concrete physical environment from the predictions yielded by theoretical physics (say, mechanics). There are two basic premises in this approach: that linguistic behaviour is essentially regular, and that it is not beyond human capacity to grasp these linguistic regularities.

Thus Kaplan's theory of (pure) indexicals is entrenched within this theoretical framework. Contents of indexical sentences depend on contexts, and thus are very unlike mathematical or pure scientific contents. But no matter: since that dependence is regular, we are still able to describe it. I can perfectly well predict what the content of your tomorrow's utterance of 'Today is hot' will be. Given facts about the weather, I can perfectly well predict its truth-value too. I can similarly explain, with the most satisfying generality, the difference between the content of your utterance of 'Today is hot' when made today, and the utterance of the same sentence made tomorrow.

We can label this first methodological (or meta-theoretic) approach 'neo-positivist', without reading too much into this term. It is very clear, I think, that minimalists are neo-positivists. Their approach is expected to safeguard the predictive power of semantic theory. No matter what perverse pragmatic purpose a concrete utterance of a sentence S could achieve, the semantic content of S is always subject to a compositional calculation.

By contrast, contextualists are committed to another view of linguistic behaviour, which I label 'neo-sceptical'. We may believe that there is little, if any, regularity in the meanings conveyed by linguistic utterances. Or at the very least we may believe that linguistic behaviour is chaotic: even if there is no conclusive reason to deny the regularity, it is too complex to be grasped by our theoretical capacities. The consequence is the same: it is not possible to create a semantic theory that would predict the meanings of particular utterances. So the utterance of the *English* sentence 'Today is hot' might, on occasions, convey the proposition $\langle 1/1/2000, \text{hot} \rangle$, but it might also convey the proposition $\langle 1/1/2000, \text{cold} \rangle$. And there will be no principled way to segregate the 'correct' contents associated with the given utterance. It is, I think, because of the same methodology that the proponents of the neo-sceptical view should also find it natural to insist on utterances as truth-bearers, as opposed to sentences. The prospects of a systematic semantic theory for sentences in L seem incomparably better than the prospects of the semantics of utterances. And even if such a theory would work for only a subclass of natural language sentences (say, those of a simple subject-predicate form), that would testify to sufficient regularity in a large fragment of linguistic practices.

Note also that, although the neo-sceptical view rejects the possibility of prediction, it does not necessarily reject the possibility of explanation. After the fact it is possible to see why the utterance had the content it actually had. Other chaotic phenomena, such as weather or stock markets, have the same feature: the persistent failure of prediction cohabits with the similarly persistent attempts at explanation. Linguistic practices have got to be intelligible, since otherwise genuine communication won't be possible.

The idea that semantic contents essentially depend on the speaker's presuppositions fits well the neo-sceptical framework. The concrete intentions of the concrete speakers, while not random, are too complex for us to discover any stable regularity in them. In different circumstances the same sentence can perform different tasks depending on the purposes the speakers want to achieve with their speech acts. There is generally no fixed rule connecting sentences with those speech-act purposes. So a theory able to generate predictions is impossible. What is possible nevertheless is a 'typology' of cases. People share enough physiology, background, moral character, and so forth to detect similarities in their linguistic action. The observer can therefore develop a skill of interpretation, and can also identify certain structural elements in that interpretation. The pragmatic processes attributed to the speakers are the result of this *practical* ability to get on with the interpretation.

To return once more to Kaplan, the theory of (complex) demonstratives is originally conceived, I think, in the neo-positivist mould. There is a context enriched with demonstrations, but the production of content is perfectly predictable and verifiable. We look at the demonstration, we examine its direction, we compute the content. But as Kaplan was quick to realise, we are in for trouble when demonstrations are too imprecise to pick out, e.g., an object in the group of other relevantly similar objects. The theory of directing intentions developed in the 'Afterthoughts' was supposed to offer a fix: such intentions will override any imprecise demonstrations. When my imprecise gesture fails to pick out the object, my intention was meant to do the job of determining the reference of the demonstrative. However, when the gesture is entirely off target, we have a wrong result. I am offered to have either pork or beef. I have a strong preference for the pork, but I clearly gesture at the beef and say 'I'd have this.' It seems that I said that I would have the beef, despite my prior intention to have the pork, but Kaplan's theory predicts otherwise.[11]

Presumably Kaplan sensed the looming trouble when he declared the Carnap/Agnew case of a rupture between intention and demonstration 'atypical'. Perhaps he wished to limit his theory to simpler cases. Or perhaps other fixes can be offered on Kaplan's behalf. But there is a feeling that as soon as we allow richer contexts into our theory, we are on the way to the neo-sceptical approach. We may grant that contents are functionally determined by contexts, but we also are

---

11 See Reimer (1992).

aware of the extreme unmanageable complexity of that determination. In the end we are left with a picture of how this determination occurs, but not with a workable theory answering the neo-positivist demands.

Now we can understand the residual problem of the Cross-Breeding Ploy with which we began. The goal of a theory of pure indexicals is to have an effective procedure of computing semantic contents and to have a clear rule exhibiting the functional determination of contents by contexts. But given the contexts construed as the speaker's presuppositions, we get neither such a procedure, nor a particular function showing the context-content determination.

6 Triviality threats

I have not said where we should put literalists in the neo-positivist/neo-sceptical divide. On the one hand, literalists believe in the possibility of a substantive semantic theory able to yield effective predictions. This would put them in the neo-positivist camp. On the other hand, I doubt they can carry out their own semantic programme. But I hesitate to make a claim of such generality. Literalists deal with specific fragments of discourse, and so any assessment of their programme must be piecemeal. The claim I make here is about Stern's literalist account. It is as follows: despite Stern's neo-positivist commitments, he has not provided us with a neo-positivist theory of metaphor.

Consider first the relation between the speaker's m-presuppositions and metaphorical contents. The purpose of 'Mthat[·]' is to allow us to get from the literal meaning of the metaphorical expression to its semantic metaphorical content. Then, if I am given the metaphorical utterance:

(5) Mthat['My days'] are Mthat['in the yellow leaf'],

my m-associated presuppositions may include statements about Byron writing near the end of his life and correspondingly the belief (or make-belief) that he anticipated his death, was bitter, had no appetite for life, and so forth. All this I bundle into my interpretation of the two metaphorical expressions involved. But then the content of (5) is in effect already contained in the context. So the character supposedly charged with producing contents is an identity function. Its argument is the same as its value. And then, it would seem, the semantic account of metaphorical interpretation is trivialised. (Notice here too that no such triviality is present in the theory of pure indexicals.)

In response Stern argues that the semantic account has a non-trivial role. It tells us that content depends solely on m-associated presuppositions (presumably in addition to its character). But the point of the response is not clear. What are m-associated presuppositions? They are those that are relevant for the interpretation of the metaphorical utterance. I may have a presupposition that Byron was an aristocrat, yet it does not contribute to the content of (5). On the other hand, my rudimentary botanical knowledge and my presuppositions about certain other facts of Byron's biography are relevant to the grasp of the content of that utterance. How I select relevant presuppositions the semantic theory does not tell me, since this is a pragmatic affair. All it tells me is: select whatever relevant presuppositions there are. I think, therefore, that we haven't got a theory. We have a methodological proposal about the role of context in metaphorical interpretation.[12]

We can go further. Here is a stronger claim: Stern's account cannot distinguish well between metaphorical interpretation and other kinds of interpretation. Consider the following randomly chosen sentence:

(6) Fayu bands and modern states represent opposite extremes along the spectrum of human societies.

It is rather ordinary and non-metaphorical (doubts may persist about the occurrence of 'spectrum'). Faced with (6), you are probably going to ask the utterer: ' "Spectrum" – what spectrum? "Extremes" – what

---

[12] Brian Ball pointed out to me at the conference that a theory should have not only a descriptive role, but also a normative role. Stern's clearly has such a role. That's fair enough. But I should believe that a theory which has a normative role alone is not really a theory. It is rather an announcement of a research programme.

do you mean exactly? in what sense? Tell us more.' An obvious way to interpret the content of this utterance is to learn more about the presuppositions of the speaker. Such presuppositions must be relevant to interpreting the occurrences of 'extremes' and 'spectrum'. And our approach may well be literalist. We may hold those occurrences primarily responsible for triggering the contextual determination, though they themselves have no semantic content.

The story told about the semantic mechanism of metaphors will be paraphrased into the story of the interpretation of (6). The interpretative procedures applied to (6) and to a metaphorical sentence such as (5) will in essence be identical. To sharpen this a bit, we may ask: how should we individuate 'Mthat[·]'? Recall the definition of 'Mthat[·]':

Definition. For every context c and every expression ϕ, an occurrence of 'Mthat[ϕ]' in '···Mthat[ϕ]···' in c expresses a set of properties P presupposed to be associated with ϕ in c.

The problem is that there could be a range of context-sensitive expressions whose semantics would mirror the semantics of putative metaphors. An interesting case, I think, would be the class of expressions used to describe emotions. Examples will include binary predicates 'x loves y', 'x hates y', 'x despises y', or 'x admires y'. They have their conventional meanings to be looked up in the dictionary. But in every utterance of these expressions, unless we know what the background assumptions of the speaker are, no semantic content can plausibly be assigned to them. For each such expression we could then define a semantic operator working analogously to 'Mthat[·]'. For consider:

Definition. For every context c and every expression ϕ, an occurrence of 'Ethat[ϕ]' in '···Ethat[ϕ]···' in c expresses a set of properties P presupposed to be e-associated with ϕ in c.

The operator 'Ethat[·]' takes as its operand an emotion expression, such as the predicates above, and produces different properties 'emotionally' associated (e-associated) by the speaker with that expression on the given occasion. When the speaker says, 'Obama loves hamburgers', the set of properties associated with the love predicate will include the properties 'x enjoys the taste of y', 'x regularly eats y', and perhaps some other. When the speaker says, 'Romeo loves Juliet', there will be quite a different set of properties e-associated with the same predicate.

There are key similarities between Stern's Mthat-theory and the just described Ethat-theory. (i) There is no semantic content generated by the bare sentence such as 'Romeo loves Juliet.' (ii) Semantic content is generated by the covert contextual operator acting on the character of the given expression (e.g. the predicate 'x loves y'). That is: so far as character constrains the use of the contextual operator, both theories will be classified as literalist. (iii) The context is constituted by the speaker's relevant presuppositions.

When we look closer at the two definitions, similarities look increasingly like identity. The only difference is that in one case we have m-associated properties, while in another we have e-associated properties. But neither theory anyway is supposed to tell us what those properties are. They are identified by pragmatics. So we might just as well drop the explicit mention of 'm-associated' and 'e-associated'. We could simply have properties 'relevantly' associated by the speaker. And then the operators 'Mthat[·]' and 'Ethat[·]' will merge into one.

Now, what I have claimed may be no more than this: emotional expressions should be given a literalist treatment. The definition of 'Ethat[·]' was a way to express this claim. I have not shown you what the semantics of emotional expressions would be, though I may have shown what it could not be – e.g., it could not be minimalist. And this, I think, is what Stern has achieved in his treatment of metaphors. Consider the following analogy:

Solar eclipse. Suppose I am telling you that celestial bodies obey causal mechanical laws. This is not a trivial statement, so far as it rules out, for instance, that celestial bodies obey the will of Zeus. Then you ask me to use these laws to predict when the next solar eclipse will occur. I reply that this cannot be done. I do not know what these laws are. Perhaps even I *cannot* know what they are, since they may be too complex for me to describe. But with regard to the eclipse I can say two things: (i) its occurrence will be governed by those laws, (ii) I can still predict it more or less well based on many earlier observations and different relevant facts currently known to me, such as the mutual position of the Sun, the Earth, and other planets. That is, I have some limited piece of theoretical knowledge, but not a theory of celestial mechanics. And that piece of knowledge I cannot use in practice. For all practical purposes I am using the sort of craft equally available to the people of a different theoretical persuasion.

The Mthat-theory delivers a very similar result. It gives us a nominally non-trivial piece of theoretical knowledge about metaphors. It is non-trivial so far as it rules out other accounts of metaphors, such as minimalism. When, however, it comes to showing how the semantic mechanism works it offers little help. Moreover, when we want to know what metaphorical content was expressed on the given occasion, the Mthat-theory tells us to look up the relevant presuppositions of the speaker. But this is in essence what the contextualist account would tell us, too. Of course one might keep insisting on the minute differences between the semantic mechanism postulated by one theory and the pragmatic mechanism postulated by another. But like in the solar eclipse story, this reminder should be irrelevant in any actual grasp of the metaphorical content. The art of interpretation envisaged by the Mthat-theory runs parallel to the kind of interpretation endorsed by contextualism. As long as I know the speaker's (relevant) presupposition, my interpretation of his metaphor should go through on either view.

This convergence between contextualism and the Mthat-view should be evident in the introduction of filtering presuppositions mentioned in §3. The correct interpretation of a metaphor depends on the ability to separate properties 'commonly' m-associated with the given item (say, a referent of the general or singular term) from the properties pertinent on the particular occasion. We are not given any rule for this filtering procedure. We are rather expected to follow our good linguistic sense. And this strikes me as a typical neo-sceptical contextualist stance. There can be no rules for understanding linguistic behaviour, but there is plenty of skill to learn that will give you a decent understanding on each particular occasion.

7 Conclusion

Let me summarise the discussion in terms of the topic with which we began. Stern's attempt of cross-breeding Kaplan's theory of pure indexicals with Stalnaker's notion of content did not yield a semantic theory answering the requirements of neo-positivism. Using speakers' presuppositions as contexts precludes (at least in the case of metaphors, or at all events, in Stern's account thereof) the possibility of giving universal rules and procedures that would form such a theory. Kaplan may have himself initiated that cross-breeding in the later theory of demonstratives, with very mixed results – even though its application was restricted to a very narrow fragment of discourse.

Now, since Stern's theory provides no actual semantic mechanism of the context-content determination, any concrete metaphorical interpretation necessarily falls back on some form of pragmatic skill of interpreting the speaker's presuppositions. But this skill is reminiscent of the contextualist approach. In the end, therefore, Stern's literalist view in its practical employment becomes indistinguishable from the rival contextualist view which has incompatible theoretical assumptions. In terms of the division suggested in §5 one could say that Stern's literalist assumptions put him in the neo-positivist camp, whereas his reliance on Stalnakerian contexts pushes him into the neo-sceptical camp.

References

Almog, J., Perry, J., & Wettstein, H. K. (Eds.) (1989). *Themes from Kaplan*. Oxford; New York: Oxford University Press.

Cappelen, H. & Lepore, E. (2005). *Insensitive semantics*. Blackwell.

Kaplan, D. (1978). Dthat. In Ludlow, P. (Ed.). *Readings in the philosophy of language*. MIT Press.

────── (1989a). Afterthoughts. In Almog, J., Perry, J., & Wettstein, H. K. (Eds.). *Themes from Kaplan*, (pp. 565–614). Oxford; New York: Oxford University Press.

―― (1989b). Demonstratives. In Almog, J., Perry, J., & Wettstein, H. K. (Eds.). *Themes from Kaplan*, (pp. 481–564). Oxford; New York: Oxford University Press.

Perry, J. (1998). Indexicals, contexts and unarticulated constituents. In *Proceedings of the 1995 CSLI-Amsterdam Logic, Language and Computation Conference*. Stanford: CSLI Publications.

Recanati, F. (2004). *Literal meaning*. Cambridge: Cambridge University Press.

Reimer, M. (1992). Demonstrating with descriptions. *Philosophy and Phenomenological Research, 52*(4), 877–893.

Stanley, J. (2000). Context and logical form. *Linguistics and Philosophy, 23*, 391–434.

Stern, J. J. (2000). *Metaphor in context*. MIT Press.

―― (2006). Metaphor, literal, literalism. *Mind & Language, 21*(3), 243–279.

— 10 —

Teresa Marques

Truth and the Ambiguity of Negation

1 Introduction

The concept of negation is intertwined with the most fundamental principles that appear to govern the notions of truth and falsehood. We need negation to express conditions for falsehood, or at least of untruth; moreover, whether the principle of bivalence holds or has genuine counterexamples depends on what truth and falsity require, and thus also on what negation is.

Semantic paradoxes like the liar, but also other cases, from presupposition failure to borderline cases of vagueness, seem to offer putative counterexamples to bivalence. But how is a putative counterexample to be described? Prima facie, a counterexample to bivalence is an item (of the relevant sort) that is neither true nor false. We need negation to express that something is a counterexample to the principle as much as we need negation to explain when something is not true, or when something is false. However, as a simple argument purports to show – we will refer to it as 'the Incompatibility Argument' –, the assumption that the very same principles for truth and falsehood are correct taken together with the assumption that there are counterexamples to bivalence leads to a contradiction.

Many believe that the principles for truth and falsehood are essential for what truth is. The idea that the schemas are essentially correct can be understood in different ways. Each of these ways requires different commitments to the role the schemas are to play. One may just hold (i) that the truth-schemas are extensionally correct, and that all their instances must be true,[1] or (ii) one can add that the schemas are not only extensionally correct, but also that they display something essential about truth, for instance that the meaning of 'true' is conveyed in instances of the schemas, or that grasping the concept of truth requires assenting to all their instances. Finally, (iii) one may maintain all of the above and furthermore add that there is nothing else to say about truth. Deflationists, in particular, will hold precisely that the meaning of 'true' is fully given (or implicitly defined) in instances of (some version of) the schemas, and that no further facts about truth are to be uncovered.

Significantly, some of the cases that seem to provide counterexamples to bivalence, in particular paradoxes like the liar, seem also to provide counterexamples to the weakest claim above, namely that all instances of the truth-schemas are correct (and a fortiori to the remaining stronger claims (ii)-(iii)). Given the centrality of negation in the principle of bivalence and in truth and falsity conditions, a tempting strategy to avoid the incompatibility argument is to hold that negation is semantically ambiguous.

This article has one aim, to reject the claim that negation is semantically ambiguous. The first section presents the putative incompatibility between gaps and the truth-schema; the second section presents the motivation for the ambiguity thesis; the third section summarizes arguments against the claim that natural language negation is semantically ambiguous; and the fourth section indicates the problems of an introduction of two distinct negation operators in natural language.

---

[1] One may defend this view by holding that truth-schemas play a central role in semantic theories, while holding a different view about truth, say, defending a substantial account of truth as correspondence, or defending that truth is primitive and indefinable.

2 The incompatibility

A recognized problem for the claim that all instances of the truth-schema must be correct is that an instantiation of the truth-schema with a liar sentence offers an apparent counterexample to the claim. We can settle for simple disquotational schemas. Let 'S' stand for a sentence; if 'S' contains no context-dependent terms, we can just disquote it and use 'S' itself to state what it says. Thus simplified, truth and falsity schemas can be formulated as:

(T) 'S' is true iff S.

(F) 'S' is false iff not S.

Let β be our liar sentence:

(β) β is not true.

If β instantiates T, we obtain:

'β is not true' is true iff β is not true.

Replacing 'β is not true' by its name, we can infer that

β is true iff β is not true.

Since a biconditional is true if both its left- and right-hand sides have the same value, this biconditional cannot be true, and β gives hence a counterexample to the claim that all instances of disquotational schemas for truth are correct.

A related, more general, difficulty for the claim that all instances of truth-schemas are correct is what Beall (2002) calls The Incompatibility Argument (cf. Beall 2002: 301): If a sentence 'S' is gappy, i.e., if 'S' is neither true nor false, it follows, given the schemas, that it is not the case that S and that it is not the case that not S, i.e., not S and not not S, which is a contradiction. Hence it seems that the supposition of gaps is incoherent, if it is assumed that all instances of the disquotational schemas are correct. In either case, the schemas appear to be incompatible with the liar and with gaps, generally.[2]

A further problem that gappy sentences (or sentences that are neither true nor false) pose to the T-schema is the following: if a sentence is neither true nor false, that is, if it is undetermined or gappy, then it is not true, i.e., it is false that "'S' is true" when 'S' is undetermined. And if it is false that "'S' is true" when 'S' is neither true nor false, then the disquotational schema, 'S' is true iff S', has false instances. This a point that is made, for instance, by Dummett:

> A popular account of the meaning of 'true', also deriving from Frege, is that 'it is true that P' has the same sense as the sentence P. If, as Frege thought, there exist sentences which express propositions but are neither true nor false, then this explanation appears incorrect. Suppose that P contains a singular term which has a sense but no reference: then, according to Frege, P expresses a proposition which has no truth-value. This proposition is therefore not true, and hence the statement 'It is true that P' will be false. P will therefore not have the same sense as 'it is true that P', since the latter is false while the former is not. (Dummett 1959: 4–5).

How can the truth-schemas be rescued? A hypothesis is, in the first place, to discern two senses of negation. Perhaps two meanings of 'not' can be defined and introduced in the language (Beall's stance is that each negation can be introduced and learned with inference rules, Beall 2002: 303), or perhaps 'not' is anyway ambiguous in English (in the next two sections each alternative is evaluated). For clarity of exposition, we can distinguish the two alleged readings of 'not' adopting Tappenden's (1999) designations for the duo, internal and external. (Other names for the duo are weak and strong, choice and exclusion. Here 'internal' and 'external' does not point towards structural ambiguities such as the different scope readings obtained when negation interacts with other operators, which of course exist). We can, also for clarity, use $\sim$ for internal and $\neg$ for external negation.

---

[2] A form of the same argument is notoriously advanced by Williamson 1992 and 1994 against the supposition of gaps, in general, and more particularly against gaps generated by vagueness.

Truth and the Ambiguity of Negation

The two meanings are often distinguished with the aid of truth-tables, where '*' stands for gappy or undefined:

A	$\sim A$	$\neg A$
T	F	F
F	T	T
*	*	T

If negation is semantically ambiguous between these two readings, Beall's suggestion for evading the Incompatibility Argument becomes clear; the argument is invalid because it commits a fallacy of equivocation, conflating internal and external negation. Once the two meanings of negation are disentangled, the argument is no longer a problem for the truth-schemas. The argument is to be now understood in this way. From:

$\neg$ ('S' is true) and $\neg$ ('S' is false)

it follows that

$\neg S$ and $\neg \sim S$.

This is not a contradiction.

In the second place, we may recognize that there is a sense in which "'S' is true'" is not true (is false) if 'S' is gappy; we may call this sense strong truth. But the sense of 'true' captured in the truth-schema is weak truth, according to which the equivalence thesis holds. The truth-schema can be rescued since 'S' and "'S' is true" are both acceptable, rejectable or undecided in the same circumstances. The biconditional in the schema must be taken as true when both sides are true, both false, or both neither.

Strong truth can be derived from weak truth, which may be done via the two negations, internal and external. The strong sense of 'true' ($true_s$) may be defined thus:

'S' is $true_s$ iff $\sim \neg S$.

The appeal to strong truth, as opposed to truth, to accommodate the sense in which a truth-predication is false when the predicated sentence is gappy or undefined, depends essentially on the correctness of the account of the duo of negations, internal and external. With the duo of negations and the distinction between truth and strong truth in place, the disquotational truth-schema can be rescued, as well as the intuition that a gappy sentence is not true. The incompatibility can, it seems, be dispelled.

With respect to the liar sentence at hand, it can be held that it now provides a true instance of the disquotational schema, if it is itself a gappy sentence. If 'true' in β is weak truth and if 'not' is $\sim$, then an instance of T with β permits inferring only that 'β is true iff β is not true' which will itself be a gappy sentence. Beall still manifests the worry, in any case, that with 'strong negation one faces the problem of strengthened Liar-like paradox' (Beall 2002: 304). (We will return to this later).

The hypothesis of the semantic ambiguity of negation offers, then, an attractive possibility for handling paradoxical cases, for rescuing the disquotational truth-schema, and for disarming the Incompatibility Argument. As the proposed solution relies essentially on the semantic ambiguity of negation, the ambiguity thesis needs to be sufficiently well motivated, otherwise the proposal is, although convenient, ad hoc.

3 The motivation for the duo of negations

The appeal to the ambiguity of negation is relatively popular. Wolfgang Künne (2005), for instance, tries to rescue the coherency of the truth- and falsity-schemas and the existence of gaps precisely by drawing the distinction between internal and external negation (*ibid*: 41)[3], although the way he attempts to motivate the distinction is not the most felicitous, since he illustrates the apparent true readings of external negation with what he takes to be 'non-significant sentences', as in 'adverbs don't hibernate' (whether or not category mistakes

---

3 As do Pelletier & Stainton (2003).

are non-significant is independently disputable, but not our concern here). Künne's distinction between internal and external negation is meant to capture the internal reading where negation attaches to a verb phrase, or perhaps to a predicate directly. Falsity is to be defined as truth of the internal negation. External negation is in turn expressible as 'it is not true that...'/ 'it is not the case that...', where the sentence embedded under negation may lack sense, as in the example considered by Künne, 'adverbs hibernate'.

However, there are clear cases of external readings of negation in Künne's sense (precisely when negation takes wide scope over the whole sentence, for instance because the negated sentence contains other operators with narrower scope) where we want to say, against Künne, that the truth of the negation is tantamount to the falsity of the unnegated sentence, for instance in 'it is not the case/true that everything is made of water'. Moreover, there should be clear examples of the distinction between internal and external negation that do not depend on some felicitous uses of negated non-significant sentences. After all, the point of having a lexically distinct negation operator must be, in the context of this debate, that sometimes the negation of a significant sentence (that could have been truth-valued) not only yields another significant sentence, but also one with a truth-value. It seems implausible to introduce an operator that produces sense from non-sense. Furthermore, felicitous uses of negated non-significant sentences, if they exist, can probably be subsumed under the distinct general phenomenon of metalinguistic negation (Horn 2001), a pragmatic process where some aspect of a previous utterance is corrected, as in 'he didn't flaunt Grice's maxims, he flouted them'. And it should be clear that metalinguistic negation is of no avail to rescue the joint consistency of gaps and the truth-schemas, where gaps are assumed to be significant and possibly evaluable sentences.[4]

This does not mean there is no motivation for the ambiguity thesis. Historically there is, and Horn (2001, for instance ch. 2) covers it in

---

4 Arguing that this is so is beyond the scope of this article, since here I am only concerned with the semantic ambiguity of negation, and not with pragmatic processes by which some aspect of an utterance, independent of the literally asserted content (if any), is objected to.

detail. Three types of case have motivated the ambiguity of negation during the last century. Initially, the ambiguity between external and internal readings was indeed seen as structural, as noted by Russell, in cases like:

(1)   a. The king of France is not bald – the king of France does not exist.

      b. The king of France is not bald – he has long dark hair.

In (a), the negation of 'the king of France is bald' is meant to be external, or to take wide scope, whereas in (b) it is meant to be internal, or to take narrow scope, but this is explained by the claim that in 'the king of France is not bald' there are two operators interacting, the negation operator and the definite article, which is treated as a quantificational operator.[5]

Now, it seems that the same distinction can be drawn in sentences containing proper names instead of descriptions, as in 'Santa Claus is not coming for Christmas':

(2)   a. Santa Claus is not coming for Christmas – Santa Claus does not exist.

      b. Santa Claus is not coming for Christmas – you were a naughty boy this year.

Russell would have held that proper names function like abbreviated descriptions, and hence allow for the same scope ambiguities, with a wide and a narrow scope reading. However, there are good (semantic and modal) arguments not to treat proper names like descriptions, but rather as genuine singular terms (Kripke 1980). Given this, it is arguable that proper names are insensitive to scope distinctions in (at least) extensional contexts, in particular, in the context of negated

---

5 Clearly, 'internal' and 'external' here do not mean the same as what the truth table above means to capture; it merely describes whether negation takes narrow or wide scope. On the Russellian analysis, both disambiguations are truth-valued, in (a) the negated sentence is true and in (b) the negated sentence is false.

sentences (cf. Neale 1990).[6] So, the scope ambiguity of negation seems to be unjustified in simple sentences with proper names.

Other authors, like Strawson (1950), take a Fregean line, and regard the existence clause as a presupposition of a (use of a) sentence with a singular term, rather than part of the content of the sentence, or of its truth-conditions. If the existence presupposition fails, then the utterance of the sentence containing the singular term is neither true nor false. The presupposition is, for Strawson, a condition for either a sentence or its negation being successfully used in making an assertion or statement. Yet, it is unclear whether Strawson accepted presupposition cancelling readings of negations as in the (a) sentences above.

Presuppositionalists after Strawson, however, allowed for ambiguous readings of the negation of sentences like 'the King of France is bald' or 'Santa Claus is coming for Christmas'. The idea is that there is a marked reading, captured in the (a) sentences, which is true even if the presupposition fails, and an unmarked natural reading, captured in the (b) sentences, which is truth-valueless when the presupposition fails. The first marked and unnatural reading is taken to be the presupposition-cancelling one.

The existence of marked, presupposition-cancelling readings, as well as the unmarked or natural uses of negation, is claimed to occur in further cases not involving reference failure, as in:

(3) a. John didn't stop *smoking* – he never smoked in his life.

   b. John didn't stop smoking – he smokes more than ever.

---

6 Nevertheless, some authors still believe that there are scope differences in negated sentences with proper names, for instance Sainsbury (2005: 71). Undoubtedly, there are semantic models where there are scope differences in the negation of a simple sentence with a singular term. The question, however, is what should lead us to accept that such models capture how natural language negation interacts with proper names. After all, the modal argument against descriptivism depends on the fact that proper names are insensitive to scope differences even in modal contexts. A very strong case would have to be made in favour of the claim that in one extensional context, as that of negation, proper names are not scope insensitive.

(4) a. I don't regret going to *the* dinner – it was cancelled in the last minute.

b. I don't regret going to the dinner – I am happy I went.

Internal negation is argued to be the more natural one, and to reveal a general feature of presuppositions, namely that they are preserved under embeddings (not only under negation, but also in conditionals, disjunctions, etc.). If one accepts that presupposition failure entails that a sentence is neither true nor false, and at the same time accepts that there are marked true readings, one has arrived at the motivation to distinguish between internal and external negation, as captured in the truth table above.

Finally, category mistakes have also motivated the ambiguity thesis. To use Künne's example, 'adverbs don't hibernate' can be argued to have a reading that is neither true nor false – where negation is internal – and a true external reading, as in 'neither adverbs hibernate nor they don't'.

Different formal multivalued systems were developed in the past century (for instance Kleene 1938, 1952; Smiley 1962; Herzberger 1970) that are compatible with a distinction between the two negation operators, one presupposition preserving and a presupposition cancelling (internal/weak and external/strong negation.) [7]

The two negations can be applied to further problematic cases. Take vagueness first, with an example from Tappenden 1999.[8] Suppose you have to sort out colour samples. In one bin you are to put samples that look red to you. In another bin you are to put samples that do not look red to you. Moreover, if there are samples that you cannot distinguish between the ones that look red and the ones that

---

[7] For a summary, cf. Horn (2001: 122-132).
[8] The motivation for the ambiguity thesis is also discussed by Tappenden (1999: 214). Tappenden offers a comprehensive discussion of the topic. Although I agree with much of his criticism against the thesis of the semantic ambiguity of negation, I have reasons to disagree with his account of how negation semantically functions and his support of the pragmatic ambiguity of negation. The discussion of pragmatic side of the issue is, as mentioned before, beyond the scope of this article.

do not look red, you are to put them on a separate shelf. Cases like the sorting of samples that look red from the rest gives rise to two ways in which we can deny that a sample looks red. We place a sample in the bin with non-red things, asserting 'this samples does not look red'. We can also say 'this sample does not look red' by placing it neither with the things that look red nor with the things that don't look red, because it looks indistinguishable from either. In one case, 'this does not look red' seems as incorrect to assert as 'this looks red'. In the other case, 'this does not look red' seems correct to assert whenever 'this looks red' does not seem to be correct to assert.

The semantic ambiguity of 'not' may also be applied to the liar paradox. Consider again the simplest form of the Strengthened Liar mentioned earlier:

(β) β is not true.

If we think that β must be neither true nor false, then β is not true. Since 'β is not true' is β itself, it follows that β is after all true, and we land back in the paradox. We may adapt Tappenden's point here:

> Clearly (β) has something wrong with it – it cannot be correctly asserted... [and it is wrong to assert (β)] because the facts are not as (β) says they are. But how is this to be conveyed? The suggestion that (β) is neither true nor false attempts to convey what is wrong with (β), but can we say this without falling back into the liar cycle? (Tappenden 1999: 264)

The inclination to deny the liar, accompanied by the unwillingness to land back in paradox, can lead one to make use of the two readings for 'not'. So, consider the result of applying the duo of negations to β; β says it is not true. But if there are, in general, two ways to read negated sentences, one in which 'β is not true' can be as incorrectly asserted as 'β is true' and another in which 'β is not true' is correctly asserted whenever 'β is true' is incorrectly asserted, then β could be said to be not true without thereby asserting β itself.

4 Against the semantic ambiguity of negation

Although the idea that negation is semantically ambiguous seems reasonably motivated, and would be useful if true, it faces considerable obstacles. This section summarizes some reasons why natural language negation is not lexically ambiguous.

Consider (3a) and (3b), 'John didn't stop smoking – he never started' and 'John didn't stop smoking – he smokes more than ever'. Although cases of this sort have been taken to motivate the ambiguity of negation, several studies have indicated that natural language is not semantically ambiguous – in particular, that negation is not lexically ambiguous.

In the first place, the claim of the semantic ambiguity of negation should pass a Kripkean test (Kripke 1977).[9] The test is not a proof, but it should be taken as giving strong evidence for or against any semantic ambiguity claim. Here is the test: if 'not' were lexically ambiguous in English, then there should be a natural language in which the two meanings are expressed by distinct expressions. For instance, if 'not' allowed for the semantic ambiguity marked in the truth-tables for internal and external negation, we would expect this difference to come out in translations of, say, 'this is not red' into other languages. But this is not the case, even in cases where it is more plausible to claim the existence of an ambiguity, for instance in the difference that comes out between marked and unmarked readings of negated sentences carrying presuppositions.

As noted by Horn (2001: 366), Tappenden (1999: 270), and argued by Gazdar (1979: 65–66), among others,[10] no natural language has two negation operators corresponding to the external and internal readings given earlier that offer a disambiguation of 'John didn't stop smoking'. In fact, translations of such sentences like this into

---

9 For more on ambiguity tests and the difference between semantic ambiguity and multiple understandings of particular sentences for other reasons (vagueness, unspecifity, indeterminacy, etc.) based on identity-of-sense tests, cf. Zwicky & Sadock (1975). Negation also fails these tests, although I will not cover the details here.
10 For instance, Alwood (1972), Atlas (1977) or Kempson (1977).

other languages are as likely to allow a presupposition cancelling as well a presupposition preserving reading. If the explanation for both readings rested in the existence of a lexical ambiguity, then it would be expected that it should be revealed if negation passed the Kripkean test. In particular, it would be expected that a translation of 'John didn't stop smoking' into Portuguese – 'O João não deixou de fumar' – would disambiguate between the two readings. But this is precisely what does not happen. The sentence carries the same presupposition, and raises the same issue, as the original sentence in English does. If the Kripkean test had been passed, a phenomenon analogous to that verified in (5) below (which translates into Portuguese either as (b) or as (c)) would occur:

(5)   a. John sat at the board on the bank.

       b. O João sentou-se na tábua na margem do rio.

       c. O João ocupou uma posição na direcção do banco.

So, negation fails the Kripkean test for semantic ambiguity.[11]

In the second place, as Horn (2001: 365) remarks, although internal and external readings are meant to be captured in the difference between 'it's not true/the case that the John stopped smoking' and 'John didn't stop smoking', the fact is that either form allows a presupposition cancelling and a presupposition preserving reading. So, it is not clear that the phrases 'it is not true that'/ 'it is not the case that' capture the desired external reading of negation.

These results indicate that natural language negation is not semantically ambiguous. This could be a defect of natural languages – there should be, it may be claimed, two distinct uses for negation corresponding to the specified internal and external negations, and a theorist is free to introduce two such distinct operators. If a distinction between the internal and the external reading of negation

---

11 Gazdar (1979) uses examples like these to make the same point. Gazdar draws further considerations against the claim of the ambiguity of negation (Gazdar 1979: 65-66). Cf. also Tappenden (1999: 270), with a similar claim against the semantic ambiguity of negation.

makes the truth-schema compatible with truth-value gaps, and is moreover useful to reject particular uses of sentences, for instance some paradoxical or vague ones, then this in itself is sufficient to introduce (perhaps, as Beall suggests, via the respective inference rules) the two distinct negation operators. The next section argues that this move is unjustified: it simply reproduces new versions of the problematic cases.

5 Resilient Problems

The duo of negations could be useful to handle the Incompatibility Argument if there were any evidence that such a semantic ambiguity exists. But there is, instead, evidence to the contrary. Yet, it may be argued two meanings of negation can be defined and introduced in our language. This requires that there be some independent reasons in support of the introduction – that the duo of negations can cope with semantic paradoxes, for instance. The remaining cases – semantic paradoxes like the liar, or borderline vague utterances – are part of the problem the duo of negations is meant to cope with. Unless the ambiguity thesis is successful in coping with these cases, there is no justification to introduce the two negation operators.

Once we have internal and external negation, and weak and strong truth, a liar sentence like:

(β) β is not true.

can be read in four ways:

(β_1) $\sim$ (β_1 is true)
(β_2) $\neg$ (β_2 is true)
(β_3) $\neg$ (β_3 is true$_s$)
(β_4) $\sim$ (β_4 is true$_s$)

We may suppose that if the negation in β is internal – and we have β_1 – then we can reject β_1 by saying: $\neg \sim$ (β_1 is true). Yet, β_2 is a stronger liar than β_1:

(β_2) ¬ (β_2 is true)

'¬ (β_2 is true)' is true if β_2 is either gappy or false, and false when β_2 is true. But since '¬ (β_2 is true)' is β_2 itself, we have landed back in paradox. So, the ambiguity of negation does nothing to prevent the resilient strengthened liar. Likewise paradoxical are β_3 and β_4, because 'true$_s$' is defined with weak and strong negation: 'S' is true$_s$ iff $\sim \neg S$. The result is that strong truth, unlike weak truth, is a well-defined predicate: each sentence is either true$_s$ or not true$_s$. It is easily verifiable that β_3 is a further form of the liar paradox: a sentence that says of itself that it is not strongly true. The same happens with β_4. The ambiguity of negation is here of no help – there is no further negation operator that would allow for the correct non-paradoxical denial of β_2, β_3 or β_4. Since the alleged recognition of the distinction between two meanings of 'not' is at best used to discard one of the readings of the strengthened liar, β_1, and is useless against the other readings, the introduction of a duo of negations to cope with the liar is here unjustified. Beall's fears of a new strengthened liar were well grounded.

Similar worries arise for the success of the duo of negations in rescuing the truth-schemas. A liar sentence seems to be a counterexample to T. The semantic ambiguity of negation would have been useful only if the negation operator in a liar sentence were internal negation, and if the relevant notion of truth were weak truth. In that case, the instance of schema T with the liar is true, even though both sides of the biconditional "'β is not true' is true iff β is not true" are gappy. But since there are several other strengthened liar sentences in the vicinity, the question arises as to whether these offer false (or, at least, untrue) instances of the truth-schema.

Recall that the weakest thesis on the role the truth-schema plays that is considered in the beginning of this article is that all instances of the schema are correct – i.e, true. Inserting any sentence in the place of S in the schema must yield a true equivalence. But a sentence like:

(β) β is not true.

can now be read in four different ways. So, consider all the alternatives β_1 to β_4. Unsurprisingly, the only of these sentences that provides a true instance of the T-schema is β_1, that is formulated with weak truth and weak (internal) negation:

(T$_1$) '$\sim$ (β_1 is true)' is true iff $\sim$ (β_1 is true).

which entails:

β_1 is true iff $\sim$ (β_1 is true),

which again will not be false if β_1 is gappy, as the proposed solution intends. All other instances of T, namely:

(T$_2$) '$\neg$ (β_2 is true)' is true iff $\neg$ (β_2 is true)
(entailing: β_2 is true iff $\neg$ (β_2 is true)),

(T$_3$) '$\neg$ (β_3 is true$_s$)' is true iff $\neg$ (β_3 is true$_s$)
(entailing: β_3 is true iff $\neg$ (β_3 is true$_s$)),

(T$_4$) '$\sim$ (β_4 is true$_s$)' is true iff $\sim$ (β_4 is true$_s$)
(entailing: β_4 is true iff $\sim$ (β_4 is true$_s$)),

are false, as can be easily verified.

So, the duo of negations cannot save the truth-schema from the liar paradox. Even if there were an ambiguity of 'not' in English, it would not save the truth-schemas, since the existence of several negations just results in the existence of several forms of the liar. Moreover, if the introduction of a distinct meaning of 'not' generates a different version of the same paradox, then handling the liar and rescuing the truth-schema from paradox does not justify the introduction of two semantically distinct negation operators.

Now, can the duo of negations help handling vague cases? Suppose that we have a similar task of sorting out colour samples as was described earlier. We have to sort out those that look red to us, and all the remaining samples. The question is: does the existence of a negation operator, that allows us to truly assert that a given sample is either red or not, help us in any way in deciding whether a given sample (about which we are undecided) should go with the red things or not? The question posed is 'Does this look red?' You are to answer 'yes' or 'no', bearing in mind that when you say 'no' you are separating that sample from all the remaining red samples. The expected outcome of this task is, it seems, that there will be a good number of coloured samples about which you are less than certain of what the answer should be. And, if that is right, the usefulness of a further operator that allows a sharp division between red things and all the rest should be reconsidered. One is not in a better position to discriminate red samples, say, from all others by having a use for negation that in principle permits truly making the discrimination.

The use that is left for two negation operators is their application to disarm the Incompatibility Argument. But we cannot introduce the duo of negations to show that the argument commits a fallacy of equivocation. The burden of proof – establishing that there is indeed some ambiguity of negation, or that distinguishing two readings is well justified – rests with the ambiguist. It is ad hoc to claim that there is such an ambiguity in the absence of independently grounded reasons. So, the argument cannot commit a fallacy that rests on an ambiguity that does not exist, as all evidence indicates, and that is ill justified, as we have just argued. As Burge (1979) puts it, concerning the liar:

> Now one might appeal to the restrictions on the truth-schema, which all gap theorists appeal to, to treat the 'ordinary' paradoxes (and pathologies like 'this is true'), and a hierarchy of negations (and of material conditionals!) to deal with the strengthened versions. But such an approach, though technically feasible, promises little philosophical illumination. The semantical paradoxes are remarkable in their similarity. The Strengthened Liar does not appear to have sources fundamentally different from those of the ordinary Liar. What is wrong with the proposed account is that it gives no insight into the general phenomenon of semantical pathology and offers instead a hodgepodge of makeshift and merely technical remedies. A theory of semantical paradox should focus on semantical notions. (Burge 1979: 177)

It seems that the thesis of the ambiguity of negation – in the absence of independent justification – gives no insight into the general phenomena at stake and offers a merely technical remedy.

The question of whether or not there are counterexamples to bivalence, and whether the truth-schema can be rescued, must depend on other issues, for instance, on whether paradoxical sentences can instantiate the schemas in the first place (are they sentences that say that something is the case? This is disputed by Laurence Goldstein 2000, 2001), or on whether there is some pragmatic form to reject given troublesome sentences that is not tantamount to negating them (this is defended by Parsons 1984, Richard 2008, Smiley 1996, and Tappenden 1999, for instance).[12] The issue remains open, furthermore, as to whether the very assumption that every instance of the truth-schema is correct should be dropped.*

References

Allwood, J. (1972). Negation and the strength of presuppositions. In Dahl, Ö. (Ed.). *Logic, pragmatics and grammar*, (pp. 11–57). University of Göteborg Department of Linguistics.

Atlas, J. D. (1977). Negation, ambiguity and presupposition. *Linguistics and Philosophy, 1*, 321–36.

Beall, J. C. (2002). Deflationism and gaps: untying 'not's in the debate. *Analysis, 62*, 299–304.

Burge, T. (1979). Semantical paradox. *Journal of Philosophy, 76*, 169–198.

Dummett, M. (1959). Truth. In Dummet, M. *Truth and other enigmas*, (pp. 1–28). London: Duckworth.

---

[12] The question of whether negation is pragmatically ambiguous, perhaps signalling a distinct speech act of denial, as these authors hold, or some distinct pragmatic process, is the subject of another article.

* I am grateful for the support of the research projects C-project: Truth, Semantic Confusion and Embodiment, Code: HUM 2006-08236/FISO (C-CONSOLIDER) and PERSP – Philosophy of Perspectival Thoughts and Facts, CSD2009-00056 from the Spanish Ministry of Education and Science.

Frege, G. (1892). On sense and reference. In Richard, M. (Ed.) (2003). *Meaning,* (pp. 36–56). Oxford: Blackwell.

Gazdar, G. (1979). *Pragmatics: Implicature, presupposition and logical form.* New York: Academic Press.

Goldstein, L. (2000). A unified solution to some paradoxes. *Proceedings of the Aristotelian Society, 100,* 53–74.

——— (2001). Truth-bearers and the liar: A reply to Alan Weir. *Analysis, 61,* 115–126.

Herzberger, H. (1970). Truth and modality in semantically closed languages. In Martin, R. L. (Ed.). *The paradox of the liar,* (pp. 25–46). Reseda, CA: Ridgeview.

Horn, L. (2001). *A natural history of negation,* (reissue ed.) Stanford: CSLI Publications.

Kempson, R. (1977). *Semantic theory.* Cambridge: Cambridge University Press.

Kleene, S. C. (1938). On a denotation for ordinal numbers. *Journal of Symbolic Logic, 3,* 150–55.

——— (1952). *Introduction to metamathematics.* New York: Van Nostrand.

Kripke, S. (1977). Speaker's reference and semantic reference. In French, P., Vehling Jr., T. & Wettstein, H. (Eds.). *Contemporary perspectives in the philosophy of language,* (pp. 6–27). University of Minnesota Press.

——— (1980). *Naming and necessity.* Oxford: Blackwell.

Künne, W. (2005). *Conceptions of truth.* Oxford; New York: Oxford University Press.

Neale, S. (1990). *Descriptions.* Cambridge, MA: MIT Press.

Parsons, T. (1984). Assertion, denial and the liar paradox. *Journal of Philosophical Logic 13*(2), 137–152.

Pelletier, F. & Stainton, R. (2003). On 'The denial of bivalence is absurd'. *Australasian Journal of Philosophy, 81,* 369–382.

Richard, M. (2008). *When truth gives out.* Oxford; New York: Oxford University Press.

Russell, B. (1918-19). Lectures on the philosophy of logical atomism. In Marsh, R. C. (Ed.) (1956). *Bertrand Russell: Logic and Knowledge Essays 1902–1950.* George Allen and Unwin.

Sainsbury, M. (2005). *Reference without referents*. Oxford; New York: Oxford University Press.

Smiley, T. (1960). Sense without denotation. *Analysis, 20*, 125–135.

—— (1996). Rejection. *Analysis, 56*, 1–9.

Strawson, P. F. (1950). On Referring. *Mind, 59*, 320–344.

Tappenden, J. (1999). Negation, denial and language change in philosophical logic. In Gabbay, D. & Wansing, H. (eds.). *What is negation?* (pp. 261–298). Kluwer Academic Press.

Williamson, T. (1992). Vagueness and ignorance. *Proceedings of the Aristotelian Society, Supplementory Vol. 66*, 145–162.

—— (1994). *Vagueness*. London; New York: Routledge.

Zwicky, A & Saddock, J. M. (1975). Ambiguity tests and how to fail them. In Kimball, J. P. (Ed.). *Syntax and semantics 1*, (pp. 1–36). New York: Seminar Press.

Ana Falcato

The Contextualist Fight Against Minimalism

1 How to Obtain a Minimal Proposition

In *Insensitive Semantics* and in several other articles Cappelen & Lepore (2005) defend and define Semantic Minimalism as being supported by the following semantic framework:

(a) It recognizes just a limited number of context sensitive expressions in a natural language such as Portuguese and thus acknowledges a small effect of the context of utterance on the semantic content of the uttered sentence. In this framework, the only recognized context sensitive expressions are those listed and analysed in Kaplan's 'Demonstratives' (1989), that is, the set of indexical expressions Kaplan divides in 'pure indexicals' and 'true demonstratives'.

(b) Because of this limitation in the phenomenon of context-sensitivity in natural languages, semantic minimalists like C&L[1] argue that all semantic context-sensitivity should be grammatically triggered.

---

1 Henceforth I will mention Cappelen and Lepore as 'C&L'.

(c) Beyond fixing the semantic value of indexicals, the context of utterance has no relevant effect on the proposition semantically expressed or on the truth conditions of the uttered sentence. Thus, the semantic content of each utterance u of a sentence S is the proposition that all utterances of S express (keeping stable the semantic values of indexicals).

Moreover,

(d) In Emma Borg's approach to minimalism an even stronger claim is made to the effect that 'every contextual contribution to semantic content must be formally tractable' (Borg 2006: 19).

(e) As a consequence of (d), Borg also restricts the correspondent semantic theory. If we want a semantic theory that provides a general, systematic, and syntax-driven account of sentential content, then we cannot allow any aspect of the context of utterance, which determines its content, to be formally intractable. Under 'formally intractable aspects of the context of an utterance' we should count current speaker's intentions, as they are not considered as semantically relevant.

As we shall see, this semantic approach to the content of an utterance of any sentence picked from a natural language gives us an extremely poor account of the content actually communicated by the sentence uttered.

When we think about the Gricean distinction between sentence meaning and speaker's meaning, we soon reach the conclusion that the latter type of meaning, far from including only the implicated content of an utterance in a particular speech-act, also concerns *what is said* or the proposition actually expressed by such an utterance of one particular sentence-type. Let me illustrate this topic with an example. The English sentence:

(1) I am a woman

has a conventional meaning which, as the meaning of a sentence-type, is not affected by different utterances of that sentence on different occasions of speaking. The context-independent meaning of the sentence-type mentioned in (1), however, contrasts with the multitude of possible context-dependent propositions expressed by different utterances of this sentence in different contexts. Thus if I now utter (1), this utterance expresses the proposition that *I* (the speaker of (1)) am (at the moment of my speaking) a woman. But if my sister Mary happens to utter that same sentence-type at a different time, her utterance will express the different proposition that *she* is a woman by the time of her utterance, even though the linguistic (or literal) meaning remains the same across both contexts of use.

So far, I have only illustrated those features of context-sensitivity that are so obvious as to obtain consensus and rule-theoretical treatment on the part of philosophers and linguists. We are still, more or less, within the scope of the unproblematic point (c), well accepted by the semantic minimalist.

But we have already started departing from minimalism once we have pointed out that, although the most remarkable feature of a sentence-type is the context-independent character of its conventional meaning, in general this conventional meaning falls short of being propositional – even in minimal terms – and thus, truth-evaluable. To sum up: we have pointed out that what is said by each utterance of a sentence *S* does not correspond to the conventional meaning of *S*.

Up to now, I have been following the clues of a contextualist approach to the content of utterances, which states that – in contrast to Semantic Minimalism – what is said or the proposition actually expressed by an utterance *u* of a given sentence *S* results from fleshing out the conventional meaning of the sentence-type (considered as no more than a 'propositional schema') so as to make it propositional. In the light of this approach, the propositions that an interpreter can arrive at through the contextual enrichment of the conventional meaning of a propositional schema are constrained by the schema which serves as input to the propositionality process. This is the reason why the sentence-type 'I am a woman' can express a multitude of propositions in different utterances by different speakers, but this set of propositions ought to be compatible with the semantic potential of the sentence, and so it cannot be used to express the proposition that twenty butterflies are around my desk (because this proposition cannot be paired with the semantic potential of the sentence-type).

The minimalist framework stresses the close connection between the conventional meaning of a sentence-type and what is said by particular tokens of the former. Together sentence-meaning and what is said (by an utterance u of a sentence S), obtained as soon as you ascribe particular values to indexicals and demonstratives in u, deliver the literal meaning or the *minimal proposition* expressed by u, quite detached from the correspondent speaker-meaning.

2 Brands of Frege's Context Principle

Let's go back to Frege for a short while. In the Introduction to *The Foundations of Arithmetic* Frege (1884) stated three fundamental principles, a sort of axioms for the subsequent investigation on the logical foundations of arithmetical statements. Along with the Principle of the Separation between logical and psychological contents and the Principle of the Distinction between Concepts and Objects, we have the well-known *Context Principle*. The Context Principle is usually regarded as one of Frege's most important achievements and has been endorsed by subsequent philosophers from the early Wittgenstein onwards. As formulated in the Introduction to *The Foundations of Arithmetic*, it runs as follows:

> The meaning of a word must be asked for in the context of a proposition, not in isolation. (Frege 1997: 90)

It is my aim to argue that, in a multitude of different theses and approaches, contextualism about the meaning of sentences in a natural language descends from a fight against this principle. According to Frege, questions of interpretation always precede the fixation of the meaning or content of a proposition expressed by some sentence.

When a thinker grasps the thought expressed by some sentence, and does so following the compositional rules that deliver the meaning of the whole sentence on the basis of the meaning of its parts, she is thereby leaving aside the possibility of interpreting or modulating in one way or another the senses of the component words or phrases. A given thought is the sense of a given sentence and is quite independent from interpretation processes concerning the senses of its parts. Frege's Context Principle is just a semantic rule. Any thinker that follows it can fix the sense of any meaningful sentence.

This same principle lies at the basis both of compositional theories of meaning for natural languages and of truth-conditional semantics (because the conditions under which some sentence can be true are fixed by the semantic properties ascribed to its components). Although labelled 'Context Principle', Frege's Principle concerns only the whole of a sentence, meaning that the particular senses of its components are contextualized within the same sentence, being irrelevant the circumstances under which the sentence is uttered.

Semantic minimalism is heir to this principle, for according to its main proposal no contextual influences are allowed to affect the truth-conditional content of an utterance unless the sentence itself demands it.

Different as they may be, all contextualist approaches to the meaning of uttered sentences in a natural language challenge this principle. This is so because the *context* at issue in semantic contextualism is not the 'inner context' that bounds the parts of a sentence, but different contexts in which the same sentence is or may be uttered.

Basically, what is at stake within contextualism is how the external context of an utterance can affect the meaning of component parts of the uttered sentence and, thereby, its whole meaning, delivering different truth-conditions for different utterances of the same sentence-type. In particular, two utterances of the same sentence might vary in content as a result of differences between their respective contexts that do not map onto any indexical elements in the sentence, and that much is at odds with Frege's 'Proposition Internal Context'.

3 Pragmatic Processes and Availability of Content

Henceforth my aim is to deal with a battle inside the Contextualist camp itself. The main disagreement concerns what I will call the 'Propositionality Constraint'.

In section 1 I have sketched the main features of one contextualist proposal concerning the interpretation of uttered sentences in a natural language, according to which the conventional meaning of a sentence-type proves itself insufficient to deliver a full-fledged proposition, being considered as no more than a *propositional schema*. Taking 'saying' and 'what is said' as pragmatic notions – which have to do with what the speaker means and/or with what the hearer understands –, the proponents of such a theoretical framework argue that, in order to obtain the content actually expressed by an utterance, one must contextually enrich the propositional schema until we obtain what is said. Philosophers arguing for this type of contextualist interpretation of utterances, such as François Recanati, provide a set of pragmatic processes that bridge the 'meaning-gap' between the propositional schema and what is said.

Let us consider some well-known examples of sentences discussed both by contextualists and anti-contextualists:

(2)   I have had breakfast.

(3)   You are not going to die.

(4)   John has had enough.

Besides using the semantic rule that points out the speaker of (2) as the referent of the indexical term 'I' and the tense rule that defines the time of uttering (2) as the correspondent evaluable time index, reaching thus the goal of *saturation*, a competent English speaker feels as if some interpretative data are missing in the minimal proposition (arguably) expressed by an utterance of (2) to the effect that the speaker has had breakfast before having uttered (2). Taking that minimal proposition as a truth-evaluable item, an utterance of (2) would be true even if the speaker had breakfast thirty years ago and never since. This is clearly not what the speaker means if, answering the question 'Are you hungry?' she replies: 'No, I have had breakfast'. She thereby means something more specific, namely that she has had breakfast *on that very day*, the day including that particular utterance of the sentence provided in (2). This aspect of the speaker-meaning, however, has to be construed as external to the conventional meaning of the sentence-type plus the indexical resolution. The time span indicated by 'on that very day' results from a non-minimal and optional pragmatic process of free enrichment.

On Recanati's account, free enrichment, jointly with semantic transfer and loosening are considered optional primary pragmatic processes with regard to what I have labelled the 'Propositionality Constraint'. This is so because the minimal interpretation of (2) to the effect that the speaker's life was not entirely breakfastless; of (3) to the effect that the addressee is not going to die *tout court* (as if she were immortal) or of (4) to the effect that John has had enough of something or other, are supposed to be sufficient to make any utterance of those three sentences propositional or to make them express a complete thought.

But is this correct? What turns a propositional schema into a 'complete thought', whether minimal or non-minimal?

I have already stated that, according to Recanati's contextualist proposal, the content or what is said by an utterance of a sentence *S* includes *both* the conventional meaning of *S* and contextual factors of some particular occasion where *S* is uttered. This is the reason why, in Recanati's framework, the Propositionality Constraint concerns only the subpersonal level of the literal meaning of an uttered sentence.

Including contextual relevant factors, what is said has a non-minimal character and should be consciously available to the participants in the speech situation at issue. What is meant by the requirement of 'conscious availability'? Perhaps we should depart from one of the sentences stated above or add a more flagrant example. Let us take the following sentence:

(5)   Ludwig has five dogs.

According to a formalist or literalist approach, the proposition literally expressed by an utterance of (5) is the proposition that Ludwig has at least five dogs, that is, no less than five, but possibly more. If we think about (5) as part of the antecedent of a counterfactual conditional, as in:

(6) If Ludwig had five dogs, he could benefit from a discount in veterinary appointments.

we can imagine some contexts where the minimal content arguably expressed by an utterance of (5) would correspond to what the speaker actually means. Nevertheless, in the majority of imaginable contexts someone who utters (5) will mean that Ludwig has exactly five dogs, neither more nor less. In most of the circumstances in which we can imagine (5) being uttered, this last non-minimal proposition (to the effect that Ludwig has *exactly* five dogs) is the only one that a competent speaker of English will be conscious of having expressed. In particular, she will be unaware of having expressed the minimal content that Ludwig has at least five dogs.

The same principle holds to a non-enriched interpretation of an utterance of (3). In the sequence of a cut, the minimal content of (3) would not be relevant to the communicative process involving speaker and hearer. Clearly, no reasonable speaker or interpreter would thereby be aware of having said that the addressee is not going to die *tout court* – as if she were immortal.

In such a contextualist framework, this is the reason why the role of minimal propositions within communicative exchanges is hard to find out. A minimalist analysis of each of the mentioned sentences would be tempted to consider those enriched aspects in the overall meaning of utterances as conversational implicatures, since they do not belong to the sentence-meaning of the correspondent sentence-type. However, conversational implicatures, as secondary pragmatic processes, do have an *inferential character* and thus take us from the speaker's saying what is said to something else that follows from the fact that she has said what she has said. In implying something by saying something else, the speaker intends the hearer to recognize both contents (the implicature as well as what is said) and the inferential process holding between them. What is said, what is implied and the connection between the former and the latter must be consciously available to the interpreter if the speaker's speech act is to be felicitous.

It is easy to find out that, in examples like (2)-(5), we do not have two consciously available types of contents (the minimal *and* the non-minimal), as the supposed minimal content could be unidentifiable even to the speaker.

The Availability Principle states that what is said must be intuitively accessible to the conversational participants. Once the minimal content of an utterance can be unavailable to speech-act participants, sometimes requiring deduction from the intuitive content of an uttered sentence (just as implicatures do), the *available content* and the minimal content of an utterance u of a sentence S can differ.

From an analytical point of view, a choice between the two is required concerning the content and the truth-conditions of u.

4 The Counterfactual Status of Minimal Propositions and the Challenge from Occasionalism

In *Literal Meaning* (Recanati 2004) we find a diagram defining the boundaries between literalism and contextualism. On the contextualist side, a gradable set of positions are listed, from the weakest to the strongest one.

The main question of the debate between literalism and contextualism concerns the legitimacy of ascribing truth-conditional content to natural-language sentences or to uttered sentences in different speech-acts, respectively. Once we have reached this point, I would like to argue that the *main criterion* to evaluate positions within the contextualist scope itself is the role given to minimal propositions. Recanati (2005) schematizes two different contextualist positions with regard to this criterion:

> From the optional character of modulation,[2] it follows that the minimal proposition, even if it plays no causal-explanatory role, has at least this counterfactual status: it is the proposition which the utterance *would* express if no pragmatic process of modulation took place. To get full-fledged contextualism we must deprive the minimal proposition even of this counterfactual status. While quasi-contextualism considers the minimal proposition as a theoretically useless entity, and denies that it plays any effective role in communication, contextualism goes much further: it denies that the notion even makes sense. Contextualism ascribes to modulation a form of necessity which makes it ineliminable. *Without contextual modulation, no proposition could be expressed.* In this framework, the notion of 'minimal proposition' collapses: there is no proposition that is expressed in a purely 'bottom-up' manner.[3] (Recanati, 2005: 179)

In order to go further in the analysis of what effectively counts as a 'full-fledged' contextualist approach to the meaning of sentences from a natural language, I think it is worth to depict the occasionalist argument. In his 'Insensitive Semantics', Travis (2006) stated that his main disagreement with minimalists is about *which properties* we should legitimately ascribe to simple expressions and utterances of a natural language such as English.

Accepting that the main goal of minimalism in assigning properties to sentences in a natural language is to obtain theorems such as:

> (T) The sentence 'The submarine is yellow' (expresses the minimal proposition that *the submarine is yellow* and) is true iff the submarine is yellow,

we should also recognize (T) as identifying what the sentence 'The submarine is yellow' says to be so and which state of affairs should obtain for such a sentence to be true.

---

2 That means in Recanati's jargon the set of optional primary pragmatic processes.
3 This would correspond to the proposition obtained after saturation is accomplished. *Saturation* is the primary pragmatic process of assigning values to indexicals and free variables in the logical form of some uttered sentence.

The occasionalist argument put forward by Travis against the validity of such theorems runs as follows:

1. *The* state of affairs described by all possible utterances of some sentence *S* simply does not exist. Thus a theorem like (T) is unable to state the conditions that the world must satisfy for a sentence such as 'The submarine is yellow' to be true.

2. Travis argues that open sentences in a natural language (e.g. _*is yellow*) are always susceptible to understandings. Therefore, in order to ascribe the predicate _*is yellow* to an object *o* in some utterance *u* – and make a statement about *o* that can express a complete thought and be truth-evaluable – we must specify an understanding for such a predicate in the utterance under analysis.

Following this standpoint, Travis goes on saying that in a theorem such as (T), whether the predicate _*is yellow* in the consequent of the biconditional is used on some particular understanding (of being yellow) or it is not. If the predicate is used on some *particular* understanding (1st scenario), then the necessary and sufficient conditions that must obtain for the sentence to be true consist in assigning to the predicate (and so to the sentence) a property that it does not have. (For the *mentioned* sentence in the left-hand side of the biconditional does not specify any understanding for *being yellow*). But, if the predicate _*is yellow* is *not* used on any particular understanding (2nd scenario), then the biconditional fails to determine any condition under which the sentence could be true.

Why should that be the consequence of the second scenario? Because on the right-hand side of the biconditional (which provides the necessary and sufficient conditions for the mentioned sentence to be true), the whole sentence is *used* (and so is the predicate _*is yellow*). Without ascribing any particular understanding to the predicate, the biconditional just fails the purpose of providing the necessary and sufficient conditions for the sentence to be true. For a speaker to evaluate an object *o* as being yellow or not she must rely on some parameters.

If we accept Travis' premises, we must cope with two desolating possible inferences. Within the scope of the first scenario the biconditional proves false. Within the scope of the second scenario – and in the absence of necessary and sufficient conditions for the sentence to be true –, a theorem such as (T) simply fails to state anything about the corresponding truth conditions.

What we would need in order to turn minimalism into a defensible position and block both scenarios is that things and states of affairs in the world be such a way that we might speak of them without understandings. If this were achievable, then we could reasonably infer theorems which, like (T), ascribe the minimal proposition *P* to some sentence *S*, stating thus the truth conditions of *S*.

The 'occasionalist challenge' to this theoretical method of learning and giving the meaning of sentences from a natural language addresses the *indispensability of understandings* to say something that might be true. If we do not go further than accepting the general compositionality rules for building and analysing the meaning of sentences, we certainly will not be able to say *whether* and *when* a particular submarine we are talking about in a language would count as yellow, and which understanding will turn some particular utterance u_{22} of 'The submarine is yellow' into a true utterance.

It happens that to assign an understanding *x* to the predicate __ *is yellow* in u_{22} blocks the possibility of ascribing to u_{22} (or to any other token of the same sentence) the minimalist favourite semantic property, i.e. the minimal proposition expressed by such an utterance – for minimal propositions, in not specifying understandings to its components, will fall in one of the scenarios described above.

5   Concluding Point: a Paradox

In deepening my own analysis of what I have labelled the 'occasionalist challenge' I found out a sort of paradox underlying Travis's proposal.

The occasionalist is not searching the property that all the yellow objects shall have in common in order to be yellow – as if she were persuaded by some sort of essentialism of properties or as if she were a realist concerning universals. What is being demanded are *more details* as to when an object *o* would count as yellow and, specifically, whether what is said in a particular utterance of an English sentence as 'The submarine is yellow' should be considered true.

What counts as having been said on an occasion of uttering 'The submarine is yellow' does not count on another occasion. Therefore, there is no 'logical space' for the minimal proposition expressed by all possible utterances of this sentence.

All those steps lead to Travis's Paradox:

> It cannot be said of a proposition *P* that it is true unless we specify some understanding for what *P* says to be such-and-such. However, if we assign a particular understanding to what is stated by a sentence *S* which expresses *P*, we cease to have *P* – that is, the proposition arguably assignable to all utterances of *S*. No matter which understanding specifies *P*, *P* no longer is *P*.

And so, to conclude, *P* – the minimal proposition arguably expressed by *S* – should vanish away from the picture.

References

Borg, E. (2007). Minimalism versus contextualism in semantics. In Preyer, G. & Peter, G. (Eds.). *Context sensitivity and semantic minimalism: essays on semantics and pragmatics*. Oxford; New York: Oxford University Press.

Cappelen, H. & Lepore, E. (2005). *Insensitive semantics*. Oxford: Blackwell.

Frege, G. (1884). Introduction to *The foundations of arithmetic*. In Beaney, M. (Ed.) (1997). *The Frege Reader*. Oxford: Blackwell.

Kaplan, D. (1989). Demonstratives: an essay on the semantics, logic, metaphysics, and epistemology of demonstratives. In Almog, J.,

Perry, J. & Wettstein, H. (Eds.). *Themes from Kaplan*. Oxford; New York: Oxford University Press.

Recanati, F. (2004). *Literal meaning*. Cambridge: Cambridge University Press.

—— (2005). Literalism and contextualism. In Preyer, G. & Peter, G. (Eds.). *Contextualism in philosophy: knowledge, meaning and truth*. Oxford; New York: Oxford University Press.

Travis, C. (2006). Insensitive semantics. *Mind & Language, 21*, 39–49.

Salvatore Pistoia-Reda
Some Notes on Game Theory and the Pragmatics of Alternatives

1 Game theory and Gricean pragmatics

Cheap talk

Since the beginning of the Gricean project, game theory and the pragmatics of communication have been felt to be closely tied. Explicit reference to this parallel is found in Lewis (1969), and in more recent works such as Parikh (2000) and Jäger (2008b). Further discussions are found in the collection Benz et. al. (2005). In his contribution to this volume, Stalnaker presents a theoretical justification of the parallel in explaining patterns of real communication. Two aspects are taken as playing a key role in the parallel. The first one involves the Gricean general program on the philosophy of language.[1] According to Grice, any definition of communication has first to make reference to the intentions and beliefs of the speakers involved in communicative situations. This is to say that the conventionalized practice that speakers use in carrying meaning and communicating things, that is, language, has to play no essential role in that definition. Communication is to be defined in terms of its strict function. Language is, in

---

1 See Grice (1989).

some sense, *central* to communication, but keeping things separated can help us, for example, in interpreting cases in which speakers drift away from the literal readings of linguistic messages in order to say, or to implicate, something more than language would strictly allow. The game-theoretical concept of *cheap talk* can go a long way in giving account of this aspect. Before I define what a cheap talk move is, consider that moves that players make in a game can be generally described in terms of their consequences for the game, since the following holds:

> Move in G. Let m and m' be distinct moves of game G; and s be the game resulting from move m in G; and s' be the game resulting from move m' in G. Then, for every next available game of G, $s \neq s'$.

Moves then change the game, and make the subsequent options of the game relevantly dependent on them. A cheap talk move, on the other hand, does not change the game, technically speaking because players' payoffs are not affected by it. Then, any other rational move available before a cheap talk move will be available after it.

> Cheap talk move in G. Let m and m' be distinct cheap talk moves of game G; and s be the game resulting from move m in G; and s' be the game resulting from move m' in G. Then, for every next available game of G, $s = s'$.

This of course gives rise to the problem of credibility of cheap talk speech, but I will not discuss it here.[2] I now turn to the second aspect, which will be of real significance for my analysis, namely strategic considerations.

Strategic considerations and reasoning

Reference to strategic considerations in defining the parallel between game theory and Gricean pragmatics is rather straightforward. As

---

2 The interested reader should refer to Rabin (1990).

it is well-known, one of the main tenets of Grice is that pragmatic inferences arise as a result of a strategic reasoning that takes into considerations others' beliefs and intentions. The definition of *speaker meaning* in terms of recognition of intentions derives from this. As for game theory, consider that games can be defined as sequences of decision problems that involve two or more players. Players involved in a specific game have preferences for possible outcomes of the game, but there is no way to get the preferred outcome without interacting with the other player. Take the following pairs, where outcomes are represented as utilities – the first number stands for the utility of player 1, the second number for the utility of player 2.

a. $(5,0)$ b. $(0,5)$ c. $(2,2)$ d. $(-1,-1)$

Player 1 has a strong preference for the situation described by the pair (a), while player 2 has a strong preference for the situation described by the pair (b). Since situations materialize just in case players perform the correspondent actions, both players will get the preferred outcome just in case the other player plays accordingly. But for pair (a) to materialize player 2 should perform an action that would give him an expected payoff lower than he would get by playing in accordance with the second or the third pair. The same pattern holds for player 1 and pair (b). This is impossible though, since players are assumed to be perfectly rational. The remaining pairs are those in which players perform their actions conditionally. Pair (d) is of course ruled out by similar rationality considerations. As a result, both players will play in accordance with the pair (c), which is the best they can get given the structure of the game.[3] Given this

---

[3] Note though that this is true only in the abstract situation I just depicted. Once we insert further theoretical presuppositions, as it is common in the complete description of games, we can well think of cases in which, for instance, pair (a) is in fact an equilibrium, and predict that players will act accordingly. These considerations would lead the present discussion too far afield. The reader interested in a precise and detailed definition of a game-theoretical solution concept, like that of a Nash-equilibrium or the iterated elimination of dominated strategies, is referred to the locus classicus Osborne & Rubinstein (1994). What matters to me now is to emphasize the role of interactive behavior in games, and

strong interconnection between pragmatics of communication and game-theoretical reasoning, it is rather straightforward then to try a formalization of the latter by means of game-theoretical tools. Let me consider the case of scalar implicatures.

2 Modeling scalar implicatures

A classic account

Scalar implicatures (henceforth: SIs) have been heavily discussed in the recent philosophical and linguistic literature. Different accounts on the computation of SIs have been presented, some of which point towards a reconsideration of the very role of pragmatics in the derivation of linguistic processes. So-called globalist accounts generally assume that the computation of implicatures is tied to speakers' intentions, speech acts, and cooperative behavior. Localist accounts, on the other hand, has contrasted such a position and proposed a view of the computation of implicatures based on a purely grammatical procedure. Although the localist/globalist debate does have some relevance for the present discussion, I will not provide here any argument in favor of neither of the two accounts.

One of the reasons that may explain why there is so much interest around SIs is that people seem so good in deriving them. In every occasion in which the derivation of a SI is called for, we derive it. But more interestingly, we are even able to *freeze* it if the linguistic context makes the derivation infelicitous.[4] The kind of competence SIs require must then be somehow related to fairly systematic principles of linguistic behavior. Consider the following sentences:

(ϕ) Some of the colleagues are coming.

(ϕ') All of the colleagues are coming.

$\hookrightarrow \neg \phi'$: Not all of the colleagues are coming.

I take my example to be an useful one to enhance understanding (even if we should bear in mind that the result it provides is strictly incorrect).

4 See early discussion in Chierchia (2004).

(ψ) Yesterday, I talked to Uli or Benjamin.

(ψ') Yesterday, I talked to both Uli and Benjamin.

$\hookrightarrow \neg\psi'$: Yesterday, I did not talk to both Uli and Benjamin.

In normal circumstances, an utterance of sentences ϕ or ψ will get the hearer to derive the implicatures indicated by the hook arrow. According to a view based on scalarity,[5] this comes from the fact that items like *some, all* and *or, and* are disposed in lexical scales that have some specific properties. In such scales, items are ordered on the basis of their informativity, where this is intended as equivalent to logical entailment. Here are some scales:

- Positive quantifiers: $\langle some, all \rangle$

- Logical connectives: $\langle or, and \rangle$

- Numerals: $\langle 1, 2, 3, \ldots, n \rangle$

- Modals: $\langle possibly, necessarily \rangle$

   Direction of entailment: ←

In a Gricean environment, we assume speakers to be cooperative and maximally informative. Specifically, we assume that they keep to the overarching Principle of Cooperation, further divided into four so-called conversational maxims (quantity, quality, relevance, and manner). In the case of SIs a central role is played by the (first part of the) maxim of quantity, namely: make your contribution as informative as is required (for the current purposes of the exchange). We are then entitled by simple principles of conversation and cooperative behavior to expect speakers to produce the most informative sentence they have evidence for. An utterance of a sentence ω containing a medium scalar term α, will conversationally implicate that the sentence ω', obtained by the replacement of α with the more informative

---

5 See Horn (1972; 1989).

term α' in the scale, does not hold. Importantly then, implicatures come about as a result of a reasoning about alternatives that could have been used. The question of how comes that these alternatives are available to us is left unanswered: scales are somehow given to us.[6] The following is a classical instance of Gricean reasoning.

1. The speaker uttered sentence ϕ: ... α ...

2. It is possible to build a sentence ϕ', such that it is the result of the substitution of α by α' in ϕ, and $\alpha \leftarrow \alpha'$.

3. According to the (first part of the) maxim of quantity, she should have uttered ϕ' if possible.

4. Something must be wrong with ϕ'.

5. Further step: The speaker is well-informed.

6. The speaker must believe that ϕ' is false

Note that no other maxim than that of quantity has been used so far.

Introducing complexity

Recently though, proposals have been made to the effect that reference to the maxim of manner (do not use long and complex messages if simpler ones are also assertable) can help us in understanding something more concerning how alternatives are activated. Unsurprisingly, interesting proposals in this direction come from the game-theoretical side. On the surface of it, this seems to be quite in line with how speakers behave. *In lieu* of intending alternatives as given, the possibility arises to make their understanding *endogenous* to our analysis of SIs. Reasoning with manner follows.

1. The speaker uttered sentence ϕ: ... α ...

---

6 See Gazdar (1979: 58).

2. It is possible to build a sentence ϕ', such that ϕ' is the result of the substitution of α by α' in ϕ, and $\alpha \leftarrow \alpha'$, and α' is not significantly more complex than α (manner).

3. According to the (first part of the) maxim of quantity, she should have uttered ϕ' if possible.

4. Something must be wrong with ϕ'.

5. Further step: The speaker is well-informed.

6. The speaker must believe that ϕ' is false.

Other stronger alternatives to ϕ are in principle available, for example $\phi''{:}\ldots\alpha''\ldots$, where $\alpha'' =$ *some but not all*. In order to convince yourself that *some but not all* is indeed stronger than *some*, consider that the set of worlds in which sentence ϕ'' is actually the case is a subset of the set of worlds in which ϕ holds. However, if we take ϕ'' to be an alternative to ϕ and as a consequence of the utterance of the latter we negate the former, we obtain the following contradictory result.

(ϕ) Some of the colleagues are coming.

(ϕ') All of the colleagues are coming.

(ϕ'') Some but not all of the colleagues are coming.

$\hookrightarrow \neg\phi'$: Not all of the colleagues are coming.

$\hookrightarrow \neg\phi''$: Not some but not all of the colleagues are coming.

Although both ϕ' and ϕ'' seem to be possible alternatives to ϕ, if we negate both simultaneously we get a contradiction that makes the derivation of the empirically attested implicature inexplicable. In the literature, this problem has been labeled 'the Symmetry Problem' and has been explicitly discussed by Irene Heim and Kai von Fintel.[7] It seems that every theory of SIs must provide a solution to such problem.

---

7   See von Fintel & Fox (2002) on this.

What we need then is that some procedure prevents ϕ'' from being an alternative to ϕ. Integration of manner, as it seems, does the right job without using any lexical stipulation (different from scalarity approaches). Let me present now in some more details the structure of a complexity-adversity strategy defined in game-theoretical terms. I will try to keep discussion at a rather informal level, though, so I will refer to the model sketched in Jäger (2008a). The reader interested in formal details should refer to Jäger (2008b).

An instance of reasoning

In formalizing SIs, game theorists provide examples of the following sort. Consider a situation in which two players are involved, call them S for 'sender' and R for 'receiver'. R is planning to host a party. All of his colleagues have been invited. Suppose that at a certain moment, R needs to know whether his friends are going to show up. Suppose further that S, an R's friend, knows the truth and wants to tell it to R. Players can be assumed to be cooperative since both prefer communication to be successful, that is to say that both want R to correctly interpret S's utterance. The game then consists in understanding what is the mental state of S when she utters a scalar sentence. S has the following messages available.

(ϕ_1) Some colleagues are coming.

(ϕ_2) All colleagues are coming.

(ϕ_3) No colleague is coming.

(ϕ_4) Some but not all colleagues are coming.

Crucially, messages differ in degree of complexity. Message ϕ_4 is taken to be the most complex one, while the other messages are taken to be equally complex. This means that a conversational cost function c can be defined such that $c(\phi_1) = c(\phi_2) = c(\phi_3) = x$ with $x = 0$; and $c(\phi_4) = y$ with $y > 0$. The values of x and y must then be subtracted from the expected utilities of players.

Suppose that S finds herself in a situation in which no colleague is coming, then she can safely send message ϕ_3. Suppose she is in a situation in which all colleagues are coming. She can now send message ϕ_1 or message ϕ_2. Since sending the former might lead R to assign some probability to the situation in which some but not all colleagues are coming, S will send message ϕ_2. In a situation in which some but not all colleagues are coming, S can literally send message ϕ_1 or message ϕ_4. From the previous reasoning, R knows that message ϕ_1 would never be used in a situation in which all colleagues are coming. In addition, the utterance of message ϕ_4 would trigger the application of the cost function defined above. In such a situation, then, S will safely send message ϕ_1 and expect R to strengthen its meaning in a *but not all* interpretation. Thus, the SI is born.

3 Discussion

No implicature yet

After a closer look at this line of reasoning, two difficulties become apparent. The first one relates to the very concept of complexity employed in the model, which is intended in a fairly intuitive sense. I will say something more on this below. The second one is of immediate importance for the present analysis. As we saw, the elimination of the more complex alternative comes about as a result of a reasoning. Note that before reasoning applies there is no strong lexical, or structural constraint restricting the set of the possible alternatives. But then according to any weak constraint, there seems to be no reason for excluding a further alternative, namely message ϕ_5: *some and possibly all*, that is one of the two possible readings of ϕ_1 literally realized. The game theorist should be happy with such a move, since the application of the cost function would rule out this new alternative as well. But here comes the problem. Let us go along that reasoning again. In a situation in which no colleague is coming S can still safely send message ϕ_3. In a situation in which some but not all colleagues are coming S can send message ϕ_1 or message ϕ_4. In order to prevent R from giving some probability to the situation in which S believes that some and possibly all friends are coming (S is uncertain), S will send message ϕ_4, no matter is cost. In a situation in which all friends are coming, S can send message ϕ_1 or message ϕ_2. As in the previous case, also in this case S will avoid sending message ϕ_1. As a conclusion of this reasoning, in a situation in which some and possibly all colleagues are coming S will safely send message ϕ_1. The alternative has not been eliminated. Therefore, the strengthening fails to be obtained. There are too many alternatives out there.

Understanding complexity

The other diffculty mentioned has to do with the concept of complexity employed in the model. So far the notion of complexity we have been dealing with can be equated with brevity. The longer the expression is, the more complex it tends to be.[8] Note though that a theory concerned with conversational reasoning and quasi-personal inferences should pay special attention to a sense of complexity related to the effort required to interpret a given message. A computational notion of complexity would then enter the discussion. We might want to define it along the following lines: a message ω is more complex than another message ω' if ω requires more inferential work than ω' to be interepreted. This seems to be uncontroversial. The problem is that this new notion would reverse the previous ordering, and the yield as a result that message ϕ_1 is indeed more complex than message ϕ_4. After all, while the former is open to different possible readings, the latter only requires a decoding process in order to be understood. This does, as is clear, produce interesting consequences for the present analysis. The main one is that the alternative ϕ_4 seems to be ineliminable by means of a reasoning.

Another option to define complexity is to take the structural composition of messages into consideration. The complexity of a certain message (where we take messages to be parse trees) with respect to another message is defined in terms of the nature of the operations needed in order to obtain the former from the latter. One of the most recent attempt to provide such a structural characterization

---

8 Discussion on possible candidates for a length-oriented account can be found, for instance, in Poser (1992).

for the selection of alternatives is found in Katzir (2007). This general framework is further taken up in Fox and Katzir (2009) in which a discussion on the similarity between the selection of alternatives in SIs and in association with focus is provided. Katzir proposes a definition for the set A of structural alternatives to ω based on the relation *no more complex than*.

A message ω' is *no more complex than* ω if we can transform ω in ω' by a finite series of operations such as deletion, contraction, and replacement of constituents of ω with constituents of the same category taken from the lexicon. Formally: $\omega' \lesssim \omega$.

The set of alternatives to ω is then defined as follows:

$$A_{str}(\omega) := \{\omega' : \omega' \lesssim \omega\}$$

It is quite easy to show that with this definition of complexity we get the desired result. Since ϕ_4 is not transformable in ϕ by a finite series of those operations, it cannot be part of the set A of structural alternatives to ϕ_1: $\phi_4 \notin A_{str}(\phi_1)$. *Some but not all* and *some and possibly all* are then ruled out and we are entitled not to consider them as alternatives to *some*. This end result is generalizable. It works well in excluding for example the possible alternative *or but not both* from the set of $A_{str}(or)$ or *exactly n* from the set of structural alternatives to numerals, $A_{str}(n)$. I refer to the article by Katzir for further considerations, especially on the objections of Matsumoto (1995) to structural accounts of alternatives.

It seems quite clear why such a notion of complexity cannot be adopted by an approach such as Jäger's. A rather intuitive way to make this point is to suggest that the difference between structural and conversational principles is one in time of activation (where the term 'time' has to be intended loosely). They function as filters. So, if alternatives are selected via a structural process, the alternatives filtered out during this process will not be available for the conversational reasoning. This seems to be a good point. Note that if we take the Katzir's definition just as a way of ordering alternatives, and put the responsibility of eliminating them into the hands of the conversational reasoning, so to speak, we would get exactly the same problem as Jäger above. The switch from a conversational to a structural account of alternatives is thus promising, even though it will remain sketchy, and seems to be conceptually simple. But it has an important outcome.

4 Towards a new parallel between game theory and the pragmatics of communication

We started out from an account of the game theoretical applications to pragmatics based, among other aspects, on the role of the reasoning in the derivation. We provided an instance of such applications. In the discussion we concluded that conversational reasoning does not lead to the desired result because of the nature of the derivation upon which it has to rely. Even if such arguments do not count as a critique of the parallel itself, one may want to argue that at this point we are indeed forced to abandon the project of intergrating game theory with the study of the pragmatics of communication, at least in the case of implicatures' computation. I do not think we are forced to such a radical conclusion, though. Since according to the former characterization game-theoretical formalizations were related to the ability of speakers to reason in a particular way, we were forced to apply rationality considerations to speakers. Every time a communicative game is going on, speaker and hearer coordinate because rationality dictates so, and every time they adopt a certain conversationally founded strategy. More in accordance with the present standpoint we might want to apply rationality considerations directly to language rather than to speakers. In deriving SIs, we do not take into consideration more complex alternatives because we use language, which is designed to minimize our efforts in derivation. Such a framework is taken up in the recent van Rooij (2004) and dates back to the influential Zipf (1949). An analysis of this point in connection to the case of SIs is still to come in the literature. For reasons whose detailed explanation I leave for future work, such conventionalist approaches could make different predictions with respect to the determinability of equilibria.*

---

* Many thanks to V. A. Cirrito and B. Spector for discussions.

References

Benz, A., Jäger, G., & van Rooij, R. (2005). *Game theory and pragmatics*. Houndmills: Palgrave Macmillan.

Chierchia, G. (2004). Scalar implicatures, polarity phenomena, and the syntax/pragmatics interface. In Belleti, A. (Ed.). *Structures and beyond*, (pp. 39–103). Oxford; New York: Oxford University Press.

von Fintel, K. & Fox, D. (2002). *Classnotes for 24:954: Pragmatics in linguistic theory*. Lecture notes. URL http://hdl.handle.net/1721.1/36355

Fox, D. & Katzir, R. (2009). On the characterization of alternatives. Manuscript. http://web.mit.edu/linguistics/people/faculty/fox/FoxKatzir.pdf

Gazdar, G. (1979). *Pragmatics: Implicature, presupposition and logical form*. New York: Academic Press.

Grice, P. (1989). *Studies in the way of words*. Cambridge, MA: Harvard University Press.

Horn, L. (1972). On the semantics properties of logical operators in English. Doctoral Dissertation. University of California, Los Angeles (UCLA).

────── (1989). *A natural history of negation*. Chicago: University of Chicago Press.

Jäger, G. (2008a). Applications of game theory in linguistics. *Language and Linguistics Compass, 2/3*, 406–421.

────── (2008b). *Game-theoretical pragmatics*. Manuscript. University of Bielefeld. URL http://www2.sfs.uni-tuebingen.de/jaeger/publications/lola2Revision.pdf

Katzir, R. (2007). Structurally-defined alternatives. *Linguistics and Philosophy, 30*(6), 669–690.

Lewis, D. (1969). *Convention: A philosophical study*. Cambridge, MA: Harvard University Press.

Matsumoto, Y. (1995). The conversational condition on Horn scales. *Linguistics and philosophy, 18*(1), 21–60.

Osborne, M. J. & Rubinstein, A. (1994). *A course in game theory*. Cambridge, MA: MIT Press.

Parikh, P. (1991). Communication and strategic inference. *Linguistics and philosophy, 14*(5), 473–514.
—— (2000). Communication, meaning, and interpretation. *Linguistics and philosophy, 23*(2), 185–212.
—— (2001). *The use of language.* Stanford: CSLI Publications.
Poser, W. J. (1992). Blocking of phrasal constructions by lexical items. In Sag, I. & Szabolsci, A. (Eds.). *Lexical matters,* (pp. 111–130). Stanford: CSLI Publications.
Rabin, M. (1990). Communication between rational agents. *Journal of Economic Theory, 51*(1), 144–170.
Stalnaker, R. (2005). Saying and meaning, cheap talk and credibility. In Benz, A., Jäger, G., & van Rooy, R. (Eds.). *Game theory and pragmatics,* (pp. 83–100). Houndmills: Palgrave Macmillan.
van Rooy, R. (2004). Signalling games select Horn strategies. *Linguistics and Philosophy, 27*(4), 493–527.
Zipf, G. (1949). *Human behavior and the principle of least effort.* Reading, MA: Addison-Wesley.

Andrei Moldovan
Can Uses of Language in Thought Provide Linguistic Evidence?

1 Speaks's test

In this article I focus on the argument that Jeff Speaks develops in Speaks (2008). There, Speaks distinguishes between uses of language in conversation and uses of language in thought. Speaks's argument is that a phenomenon that appears both when using language in communication and when using language in thought cannot be explained in Gricean conversational terms. A Gricean account of implicature involves having very complicated beliefs about the audience, which turn out to be extremely bizarre if the speaker is her own and only audience. Therefore, it is extremely implausible that we implicate anything when using language in thought. So, a use of language in thought needs to be explained in some other way. This article is an attempt to clarify the notion of a *use of language in thought,* and ultimately to argue that there are no uses of language that satisfy all the conditions that are needed for Speaks's argument to work.

Although Speaks does not spend much time in clarifying the concept of a use of language in thought, he seems to have in mind uses of language that intuitively belong to the category of talking to oneself, cases where 'there is no audience-directed intention at all' (Schiffer

1972: 76), and solitary uses of language (a characterization suggested to me by François Recanati); these are cases of uttering a sentence, either thinking out loud, or 'silent thinking' (Grice 1989: 112-3), the latter being '"internal" assertions or judgments, conscious voluntary episodic acts performed by "saying in one's heart" or inwardly accepting an aural mental image of a sentence.' (García-Carpintero 2009: 80). The above characterizations of the use of language in thought get at some of its essential features, but should be further developed into an analysis of the concept.[1] I will come back later to the discussion of such a possible analysis.

Speaks argues that a linguistic phenomenon that is present both with uses of language in communication and with uses of language in thought cannot be explained in Gricean conversational terms. The general argument can be reformulated as follows:

1. Consider a phenomenon that is present *both* when using language in thought and when using language in conversation.

2. Given that it is the same phenomenon, a unitary account is needed.

3. It is impossible to implicate anything in thought.

4. Therefore, a Gricean conversational account (which involves implicature) is not acceptable for that phenomenon.

Speaks offers the conclusion of the argument in the form of a principle, which he calls the Communication/Implicature Principle: 'The fact that a sentence S may be used in conversation to communicate (convey, assert) p can be explained as a conversational implicature only if S cannot be used by an agent in thought to judge (think) p.' (Speaks 2008: 113)

---

[1] This concept of use of language in thought is in no obvious way connected to the Language of Thought hypothesis, as developed by Gilbert Harman, Jerry Fodor and others.

He applies this argumentative strategy to quantifier domain restriction. This is the phenomenon of uttering 'Every bottle is empty' and meaning that *every bottle in the apartment is empty*. This phenomenon, Speaks observes, is present both in communication and in thought. I can use the sentence 'Every bottle is empty' to convey in communication that every bottle in the apartment is empty; and I can use the same sentence in thought, to entertain the same proposition. If the phenomenon is present both in thought and in communication, a unitary account is needed. But in thought no implicature can be generated. According to Grice (1989: 25), implicature generation requires that the proposition implicated be derivable, but we cannot make sense of the process of implicature derivation with uses of language in thought. Speaks considers the hypothesis that quantifier domain restriction is to be explained as follows: when I utter 'Every bottle is empty' meaning that *every bottle in the apartment is empty*, I assert that *every (unrestricted) bottle is empty* and I implicate that *every bottle in the apartment is empty*. He then wonders:

> Is it really the case that I manage to use this sentence to say to myself that every bottle in the apartment is empty only because I think that I am capable of working out that the assumption that I believe this is needed to make my utterance to myself consistent with the norms of conversation and, further, think that I know that I am capable of working out that I think this? Even if I could have these strange beliefs on an occasion, it hardly seems that they are required for me to use 'Every bottle is empty' in thought to mean that every bottle in the apartment is empty. (Speaks 2008: 109)[2]

---

2 According to Grice (1989: 31) calculability is a necessary condition for an implicature to be conversational. But Grice is not involved in the project of explaining the psychology of interpreters, as Saul (2002) argues. However, Speaks formulates the argument as if it rested on the implausibility of a certain interpretive strategy. But someone could reply that I may implicate something when I use language in thought even if it is highly implausible that I ever get at the implicature by way of such a derivation. The implausibility of a certain interpretive strategy does not entail non-calculability. But Speaks's point remains valid, because the impossibility of having the kind of intentions that the derivation

Speaks's point is that it is extremely implausible that, when I am the only intended audience, I ever form the complex and bizarre intentions that the derivation of implicatures requires that I have.[3] He concludes that quantifier domain restriction is not to be explained by Gricean pragmatics. The argument does not rule out non-conversational pragmatic accounts of quantifier domain restriction or other linguistic phenomena (Speaks 2008: 109). Kent Bach's notion of *impliciture*, which involves completion and expansion of a propositional radical, or François Recanati's cognitive account of *primary pragmatic processes* involving modulation are just two such possible pragmatic explanations that are explicitly differentiated from implicature generation.

The above argument concerns *symmetric* phenomena, which are present both in thought and in conversation. Speaks suggests a further argument concerning *asymmetric* phenomena, which are present exclusively in communication, and have no counterpart in thought:

1. Consider a phenomenon that is present *exclusively* when using language in conversation, and not when using language in thought.

2. An account of the phenomenon must explain why the phenomenon is not present in thought.

3. It is impossible to implicate anything in thought.

---

scheme requires makes the calculability requirement impossible to fulfill in thought.

3 Another problem that I see for the possibility of implicating anything when talking to oneself is that it is not clear that the Cooperative Principle makes any sense in those cases. And if CP is the reason behind the maxims, these maxims lose their justification in non-conversational settings. One the one hand, CP makes reference to a *conversation*; on the other, even if it makes sense to speak of having a conversation 'with myself', it does not seem to make much sense to ask whether I am *being cooperative* or not when I am doing something on my own. Gunnar Björnsson suggested to me in conversation that there is a sense in which I could be uncooperative even when I act on my own. I may sometimes be 'in two minds', pursuing different aims that pull me in opposite directions, and so I may be acting in ways that obstruct other intentions I may have. However, I perceive this use of 'being cooperative' as rather metaphoric.

4. Therefore, a Gricean conversational account is preferable for that phenomenon.

Asymmetric phenomena not only *can* but also *should* be explained in Gricean terms, given that a conversational account also explains why the phenomenon is asymmetric: conversational phenomena are exploitations of the maxims that govern communication, and which have no counterpart with usage of language in thought. Speaks uses this latter argument with asymmetric cases of uses of language. He considers the famous case of a professor writing a recommendation letter and using 'The student has excellent penmanship' to communicate the proposition that the student is not good at philosophy. But a corresponding use in thought is not possible. In thought, someone can use this sentence in this way only if one has 'already made the judgement, or entertained the thought, that the student is not a very good candidate. The use of "The student has excellent penmanship" cannot itself be a way of making this judgement, or thinking this thought.' (Speaks 2008: 112-3) If this is so, then the phenomenon described is asymmetric, and specific to communication. According to the second of the two arguments presented above, a Gricean explanation is appropriate.

The two arguments taken together form a test for determining whether a conversational account of a certain phenomenon is preferable or, on the contrary, unacceptable. Speaks applies this test not only to quantifier domain restriction, but to referential uses of definite descriptions as well. He claims that they are present with uses of language in communication but not with uses of language in thought. Definite descriptions exhibit an asymmetry in the sense mentioned above, and so, they should be accounted for in Gricean terms. He also considers conversational accounts of Frege's puzzle about proper names, as well as pragmatic accounts of metaphors. His discussion of metaphors is rather complex (see Speaks 2008: 116, fn. 8).

2 A definition of a use of language in thought

I will not discuss here the conclusions that Speaks draws from applying his test to different linguistic phenomena. I will rather focus on the key concept in Speaks's argument, which is that of a use of language in thought. An approximation to a characterization of a use of language in thought can be arrived at following Speaks's characterization of the concept. Thus, a use of language in thought is a case of entertaining a thought or making a judgment that involves the utterance (or, in some way, the production of) a token of a linguistic expression such that:

(i) the subject *means* something by her utterance;

(ii) the subject *does not intend to address any audience* (other than herself);

(iii) the utterance of the expression leads the subject to *make a judgment* or *think a thought*.

The reason for introducing (i) is that Speaks explicitly characterizes uses of language in thought as cases in which speakers mean something by their words.[4] And indeed, when I say to myself, for instance, 'Every bottle is empty', and entertain the thought that every bottle in the apartment is empty, I am not merely uttering words and then interpreting them, but I mean something by the utterance. Condition (iii) is suggested in the following passage: 'Just as certain sorts of acts can only be performed by uses of language in communication, so certain sorts of acts can only be performed by uses of language in thought; *by using a sentence in thought, an agent can make a judgment or think a thought.*' (Speaks 2008: 112, my emphasis) I have changed 'can make a judgment' into 'leads the subject to make a judgment' in (iii), and thus moved away from Speaks's characterization of a use of language in thought. The reason is that, on the one hand, it is important for the purposes of Speaks's test that the use of the expression play a causal role in actually getting the subject to make a judgment, not only that it be possible to have this outcome (whatever this possibility may be). So even if the definition is more restrictive than the one Speaks suggests, it is surely the definition of the kind of

---

4 See the last sentence in the fragment quoted above from (Speaks 2008: 109).

uses of language relevant for his test. On the other hand, the claim that the expression can be used to entertain a thought, as opposed to actually being used that way, seems to be trivially true, given that it does not seem that there is a class of sentential expressions that in principle could not be used to entertain thoughts. Concerning condition (ii), a reason for introducing it is that Speaks characterizes this use in various places as a case of saying something to myself, or talking to myself, or thinking to myself.[5] However, leaving aside any technical sense of 'use of language in thought', it is not clear that (ii) is intuitively a necessary condition for thinking out loud. It seems that one can think out loud in a conversation as well, or at least, that there is some use of language in the vicinity of thinking out loud for which only (i) and (iii) are necessary conditions. That is, conveying something in conversation does not require that the content one wants to convey be in one's mind before one starts talking. This suggests that the distinction that Speaks proposes, between uses of language in thought and uses of language in conversation, should be replaced by two different distinctions: using language in conversation (i.e. addressing an audience) as opposed to solitary uses of language (i.e. where there is no audience); and using language to make a judgment (i.e. a judgment that was not actively entertained previous to the utterance), as opposed to using language to express or convey a thought that one actively entertained previous to the utterance. Nevertheless, for the purpose of Speaks's test it is desirable to focus on episodes where language is used to make judgments, *and* which take place *outside* conversation. Speaks's test relies on intuitions about whether a particular sentence could be used in a particular context to form a particular judgment. Whether a sentence can or cannot be used to make a judgment in a certain context is independent of whether its use for that purpose is part of a conversation or not. So, for the purposes of the test, one can completely ignore uses of language in conversation, and focus only on solitary uses of language. The advantage of focusing on solitary uses is that in conversation we have

---

5 For the latter see (Speaks 2008: 116). For 'saying to myself' see the passage quoted above from (Speaks 2008: 109).

various purposes that we try to achieve by making assertions, and which are not present with solitary uses of language. To give just one example, in thought I may refer to a particular window that I have in mind with 'that window'; but in conversation, if I want the audience to identify a particular window in the environment, I usually need to give more descriptive information, except when that particular window has been referred to before in the conversation or was made salient in some other way. Communicative success depends on the fulfillment of certain conditions that are independent of whether language is used to make judgments or not, and which are specific to the interpretation of utterances.[6] Condition (ii) eliminates all the requirements that are specific to success in conversational settings and selects those uses of language that are only vehicles of getting the subject to entertain a thought outside of conversational settings. So, for methodological reasons, it seems desirable to focus on solitary uses of language, and to add (ii) as a condition on what counts as a use of language in thought in the sense relevant for Speaks's test. However, the argument that I will defend later does not depend on whether (ii) is a condition on uses of language in thought or not.

3 Some cases of use of language in thought

I turn now to a search for cases of uses of language that may intuitively fall under the definition proposed above.[7] The purpose of this is to get a better grasp of what episodes of using language fulfill the three conditions, as opposed to those that are closely related but do not.

---

[6] As Stanley (2005: 140) puts it, 'There are no felicity conditions governing expressions in the language of thought (if such there be).' The same seems to be true for uses of language in thought.

[7] My classification only partially coincides with the ones various authors propose, such as Grice (see his 1989: 113), Schiffer (see his 1972: 76-89), Speaks (see his 2003: 30). This is partly because my attempt is motivated by different concerns than theirs, which is to find and discuss counterexamples to Grice's analysis of meaning.

(a) First, condition (ii) is not fulfilled by cases in which I am *de facto* the only audience, although I intend to talk to an audience different from myself. Thus, I may hallucinate that there is an audience different from myself that I am addressing; or, I may be simply mistaken in believing that there is one, given that I have not noticed that the phone connection was lost, or that the audience has left the room; or, simply, the audience is present physically, but not listening at all, being completely absent-minded. These cases are not relevant for Speaks's test because in all these cases I can implicate that *q* by saying that *p*, although no one is present (or no one present is an audience), because having the intentions that the derivation of the implicature requires does not depend on the actual existence of an audience, only on my *belief* that there is an audience that I take to be cooperative.

(b) Cases of *writing in a diary* (and similar ones) with the purpose of reading it later myself (and no one else) fail on condition (ii). The audience that I am addressing is myself, but not my *present* self. Grice puts such cases under the heading '[u]tterances for which the utterer thinks there may (now or later) be an audience.' (Grice 1989: 113) The case is similar in a relevant respect to a conversation, as the reader does not have privileged access to the writer's intentions, and so the reader sometimes needs to discover these intentions in an indirect way, making use of the details of the context and of background knowledge that the reader has about the writer. The writer may exploit this common knowledge to implicate certain things.[8]

---

8 I consequently also disagree with Speaks (2003) when he claims that diary entries are a counterexample to Grice's analysis of meaning precisely because, he claims, I cannot have the complex intentions that the analysis requires: 'Are we to say that by writing something in my diary I intend to bring about a certain belief in myself by recognition of this (my own) intention? I already know that I have the relevant belief.' (Speaks 2003: 30) But in writing in a diary I may be writing for my future self, and of course, I know that in the future I will not have privileged access to my present intentions. That may be the reason, after all, why I am writing the diary. Class notes and shopping lists are similar in this respect.

(c) Cases of *imagining* or *pretending* that I am in a conversational setting, although I am not, are cases in which (ii) is not fulfilled. Grice thinks of them as '[u]tterances which the utterer knows not to be addressed to any actual audience, but which the utterer pretends to address to some particular person or type of person' (Grice 1989: 113). Schiffer imagines a sadistic lieutenant who, while alone, takes delight in saying aloud 'Private Goodfellow, run your bayonet through your abdomen and look sharp about it!' (Schiffer 1972: 78) He would not do it in the presence of Goodfellow, because the private might just obey the order, but enjoys imagining the scene. Cases of talking to my invisible friend, talking to pets, to the babies, or to the dead, are also forms of *pretending* that, or of *acting as if*, there is an audience different from myself. These cases do not fulfill condition (ii) because, although there is no audience other than myself, I am acting *as if* there was such an audience. My actions can only be made sense of if I am assumed to be pretending to talk to someone. I am, in a sense, addressing an imagined audience, to which I may try even to implicate something.

(d) Cases which Grice explicitly considers different from the above are those where 'verbal thoughts merely pass through my head as distinct from being "framed" by me' (Grice 1989: 113). With respect to them, Grice writes that it is inappropriate to say that the subject has *meant* something by producing those words. These cases do not fulfill condition (i), and are clearly not the kind of uses we are looking for. Indeed, when I dream of meeting Quine and listening to what he says, or of reading from a book a sentence, or when a line from a poem comes to my mind involuntarily, that is not the result of an intention to use *those* words in order to achieve a certain end. Grice points out that in these cases we are more like listeners than like speakers. Indeed, it happens *to* me that those words feature in my mental life in some way.

(e) Similar cases in which (i) is not satisfied are those in which someone retrieves from the memory a sentence or a formula with the purpose of decoding the content it expresses. Suppose I wonder what exactly the Pythagorean Theorem says; for that purpose, I may retrieve its formula from my memory, say it to myself, or write it down, and then think it through. This may help me entertain the theorem, so (iii) seems to be fulfilled, and so does (ii). However, it fails to satisfy (i), because in writing down on paper out of memory '$a^2 + b^2 = c^2$' I do not *mean that* $a^2 + b^2 = c^2$ (where 'c' stands for the length of the hypotenuse of a right triangle, and 'a' and 'b' for the lengths of the two other sides). Uttering the formula or writing it down is not yet meaning anything, but merely retrieving the words from memory, which is similar in the relevant respect to copying the formula out of a math book. I do intend to reproduce the exact formula, but I do not mean the content of the theorem by my utterance, because I do not yet entertain that content. The process of (re)producing a sentence out of memory and *then* interpreting it may be aimed at (re)discovering what the sentence *literally* expresses (as in the above case), or what the speaker meant by a certain utterance of that sentence. Suppose I doubt whether my friend was happy or not about the birthday present I gave her: I first think what were her exact words, and I remember that she said 'I also sometimes give the books that I like as birthday presents.' I may then go on to think whether she meant that it was not nice of me to buy her the books that *I* like (instead of considering her own taste), or whether she meant it was nice of me to do that (instead of buying her some book I don't like or I haven't read).

(f) The use of 'Every bottle is empty' that Speaks discusses is distinct from all the above cases, and not reducible to them. Cases such as this one are of the kind that Grice calls 'silent thinking', although the silent aspect is not essential. Cases of thinking out loud, in which the speech is overt, belong to the same kind of episodes of thinking in which phenomenologically language figures explicitly. I will use in what follows 'thinking out loud' as interchangeable with 'use of language in thought', to refer to all cases in which language is used in thought in the sense defined above and described here, both cases in which the utterance of the sentence is loud and cases in which 'an aural mental image of a sentence' (García-Carpintero 2009: 2) is somehow produced.

All these uses are, according to Grice, such that 'the utterer neither thinks it possible that there be an actual audience nor imagines himself as addressing an audience' (Grice 1989: 113). That is to say, they are different from above cases of type (a), (b) and (c).[9] They are also different from cases (d) or (e) because intuitively it cannot be denied that I mean something by the sentence I utter. To consider an example along the same line with the ones Speaks gives, suppose I suddenly notice that it is 16:10 and that I am late for the meeting, and I utter spontaneously 'It's already 16:10!' Such cases intuitively fulfill (i) to (iii). That in some such cases condition (i) is fulfilled is shown by the fact that, if asked 'why did you say "already"?' I can easily explain what I meant by that, namely, that is too late to arrive in time for the meeting. But not only such spontaneous isolated utterances fulfil the three conditions. An utterance may be part of a more complex process that involves various steps, such as calculating, making inferences

---

[9] I cannot agree with Grice's further characterization of these cases as being such that the speaker 'nevertheless intends his utterance to be such that it would induce a certain sort of response in a certain perhaps indefinite kind of audience were it the case that such an audience was present.' (Grice 1989: 113) If having this intention is part of the prima facie description of the kind of cases that constitute silent thinking, then I doubt we can easily identify such cases. Grice attempts here to show that silent thinking, which he classifies as different than type (c) cases, can be reconstructed in a way that would avoid that it be a counterexample to his analysis of speaker meaning. But the reconstruction is hard to accept for the following reason: if Grice admits that the speaker does not think it to be possible that there be an actual audience, it is not clear that it is rational for her to have the intention to produce a certain effect, where there is no such audience. It may be true that speakers have the belief that if a certain kind of audience were present, the utterance would have a certain effect on it. It is also plausible that we have (usually, non-occurent) beliefs with similar conditional contents that accompany most of our acts, e.g., when I open the door I have the belief that if there is someone on the other side, I may hit her with the door. But it is less plausible that one can act on an intention with that conditional content when one also has the belief that the antecedent is false.

in a chain, making a plan for a holiday trip, imagining a story etc. In some of these cases the utterance is less spontaneous and more predictable, compared to the cases discussed above in which just one isolated thought pops up in one's mind. Where there is such a chain of thoughts organized according to some rules, taking the next step in the calculation (respectively, drawing the next inference, deciding the next destination along the way, deciding what happens next in the story) is constrained by the previous steps and by the rules of the activity undergone. However, these utterances are still spontaneous in a sense that I will discuss later. What is important for our purposes here is that these cases are good candidates for use of language in thought. The language is used to make judgments, and, when one is not addressing any audience, they seem to fulfil the three conditions.

One last thing to mention is that the endorsement of the proposition entertained is not essential for a mental episode to be of the kind of using language in thought. Even if in many cases of thinking out loud the subject indeed makes a *judgment* (i.e., she endorses the thoughts she forms), thinking out loud needs not lead to endorsing the thought. I may simply come up with an hypothesis, or ask myself a question. Or I may make a formal derivation from what I take to be false premises, or make a calculation applying rules that I know will not get me to a true result. In all these cases I am not endorsing the thought, but I do entertain the outcome. Condition (iii) is fulfilled in these cases as well, because it requires that I make a judgment *or* entertain a thought. Actually, it is not relevant for the purposes of our discussion whether the subject endorses the thought she has made or simply entertains it.

4 An argument against alleged uses of language in thought

Here is a simple argument against the claim that cases of type (f), which seem to get closest to being the kind of use of language in thought that Speaks's test relies on, are actually instances of this use of language. The argument purports to show that no use of language can fulfil conditions (i) and (iii) simultaneously. The argument is the following: if a use of language fulfils condition (i), then the speaker *means* something by the words she uses. But meaning that p is an intentional action, and so the speaker has an intention about the content p. If I mean that p, then the thought that p will help me choose my words to utter. Which means that I cannot arrive at the thought that p via the utterance of s. Here is a detailed version of the argument.

1. According to (i), the speaker utters s *meaning* that, say, p;

2. If the speaker means that p in uttering s, then the utterance is the realization of an intention to Φ that p.

3. If an action is the realization of an intention, then the intention guides the action (in particular, the choice of the sentence to utter).

4. If an intention guides an action, then the content of the intention is available to the subject performing the action.

5. Therefore the subject entertains p independently of uttering the sentence (and just by intending to do so).

6. Therefore, uttering s cannot play a causal role in getting the subject to entertain p.

7. According to (iii), uttering s plays a causal role in getting the subject to entertain p.

8. Therefore, condition (i) and (iii) cannot be fulfilled simultaneously.[10]

---

[10] Galen Strawson suggests a similar argument when he writes that in the cases of thinking, 'which particular content it is [that we are thinking] is not intentionally controlled; it is not a matter of action. It cannot be a matter of action unless the content is already there, available for consideration and adoption for intentional production. But if it is already there to be considered and adopted it must already have "just come" at some previous time in order to be so available...' (Strawson 2003: 235)

Some observations are needed before I go on to consider a number of possible objections. Meaning something by uttering a sentence is not something that happens *to* someone, but it is something that the subject does. It is an intentional action, as it is within the subject's rational control both what sentence to utter and what proposition to mean by uttering it. That is why speaker-meaning must be accounted for in personal-level terms, in terms of propositional attitudes and inferences, and not in terms of causal processes. Moreover, the account must include a rational reconstruction of the speaker's intentions. This point is independent of whether a Gricean-style analysis of speaker-meaning in terms of the speaker's intentions is correct or not. However, the argument does rest on the claim that speaker-meaning that p in uttering s entails having intentions about p. It is not relevant what exactly is the content of the intention, and so, the intention is not specified with respect to the value of 'Φ'. *If* Grice's analysis of speaker-meaning is correct, then the intention to Φ that p is the intention to get the audience (whatever counts as audience in these cases) to believe p when s is a declarative sentence; in Neale's (1992: 550) version it is the intention to get the audience to actively entertain the thought that p. These analyses introduce further intentions that speakers have when they mean that p in uttering s, but it is sufficient for accepting (2) that all these analyses introduce one intention of this form. Premise (2) does not commit one to a particular analysis of speaker-meaning, and it also does not commit one to there being any successful analysis of speaker-meaning at all. It only says that whenever a speaker utters a sentence s meaning that p she has an intention with a content of the form 'to Φ that p', even if there is no unique value of 'Φ' for all cases of speaker-meaning that p in uttering s. On the other hand, if one rejects premise (2) one also has to give up the project of looking for an analysis of speaker-meaning in terms of speaker's intentions. This is prima facie a point in favour of (2), at least among those who defend such analyses. Moreover, intuitively cases of thinking out loud take place in conversation as well. So, if one wants to deny that they are the realization of an intention, then one has to admit that many cases of solitary use of language, as well as many cases of use of language in conversation, are not intentional uses of language.[11] Another point in favour of (2) is that it is compatible with the claim that speaker-meaning may be a result of habit,[12] and with holding that the intention that involves *p* is not always conscious. García-Carpintero (2001: 120) argues that rational reconstruction needs not postulate conscious, explicit and occurent beliefs.

I will focus now on some possible objections to the argument, and how they can be dealt with. Premises (1) and (7) entail that whatever the speaker means by uttering *s*, that is the thought that she gets to entertain as a result of that utterance. It can be objected that conditions (i) to (iii) of the definition of the use of language in thought do not entail that the utterance of a sentence in thought leads to entertaining the same proposition *p* that the speaker means by that utterance. (iii) only requires that an outcome of uttering *s* has to be the thinking of a thought. However, a reason to think that the speaker means by the utterance of *s* precisely the thought that she entertains or the judgments that she makes in that particular episode of thinking out loud is that we do expect to get the same answer when we ask a speaker 'What do you mean by *s*?' and when we ask 'What were you thinking when you said *s*?', with respect to the same episode of thinking out loud (assuming that the last question inquires for the judgment made, i.e. for what is required for the utterance to fulfil

---

11 Kent Bach suggested to me in conversation that one could give a simple reply to Speaks's argument, namely, that there are no uses of language in thought, in the intended sense, because the subject cannot mean anything when there is no audience whatsoever, as she cannot have the required intentions. But this is not obviously so. On the contrary, many authors admit that some of these cases are at least prima facie counterexamples to Grice's analysis of meaning precisely because they seem to be cases in which the subject means something by her utterance. See Grice (1989: 112-3), Schiffer (1972: 76-80), Harman (1977: 422), Vlach (1981: 384-6), Speaks (2003: 29-31) and Speaks (2008: 109, fn. 3).

12 As David Lewis famously pointed out, 'An action may be rational, and may be explained by the agent's beliefs and desires, even though that action was done by habit, and the agent gave no thought to the beliefs or desires which were his reason for acting. A habit may be under the agent's rational control in this sense: if that habit ever ceased to serve the agent's desires according to his beliefs, it would at once be overridden and corrected by conscious reasoning.' (Lewis 1975: 148)

(iii)). On the other hand, it cannot be denied that there are cases in which someone utters *s* meaning that *p*, which leads her to think that *q*. I may be wondering whether anybody ever long-jumped over 28 feet, and say to myself 'Bob Beamon long-jumped over 29 feet way back in 1968.'[13] By saying this I may get to think that *somebody* jumped over 28 feet. Or I can say to myself 'It's very hot today', which may lead me to realize that I forgot to pick up my sunglasses this morning when I left home. If these are episodes of thinking out loud of which (1) and (7) are not simultaneously true, then they are cases to which the conclusion of the argument does not apply. However, I think the argument applies to these cases as well. The former case is one of drawing an inference, in particular, an existential generalization. In the latter case, a psychological association has taken place, which led from one thought to another. In both cases I entertain two thoughts, the thinking of the former leading to the thinking of the latter. The judgment made in uttering *s*, as mentioned in (iii), is the first, and not the second, in both cases. The entertaining of the second thought is due to a posterior mental episode of drawing an inference, and making a psychological association, respectively. One reason for this diagnosis is that there are two separate mental events, not just one, the second being caused by the first. If not one, but a chain of inferences or psychological associations is made, we are not tempted to say that only one episode has taken place, an episode of uttering *s* meaning that *p* and judging that *q*, *r*, *t*, etc. The episode of thinking out loud is that of uttering *s* meaning that *p* and entertaining *p*. Actually, Speaks explicitly rules out cases in which a speaker entertains *p* as a result of uttering *s*, and infers that *q* from *p* and some other proposition entertained in the context (Speaks 2008: 119, fn. 10).

Another reason why we should not want to treat the above cases as instances of uttering *s* meaning that *p* and judging that *q* is that if an utterance of 'It's very hot today' could be used in thought to think that I forgot to pick up my sunglasses, then there is no limit to what thoughts one can think by uttering any sentence whatsoever.

---

[13] This example is a modification of the one given in Bach (2005: 5).

If any sentence can be used to entertain virtually any thought, then there are no asymmetric phenomena of the kind that are present with uses of language in conversation but not in thought, and for which, according to Speaks's test, a Gricean conversational account fits best. In particular, if this is so then there are no conversational implicatures. Of course, Speaks does not want his argument to generate this conclusion, and so the use of language in thought that Speaks has in mind is such that the proposition meant by uttering *s* is the proposition entertained, and not some other proposition in some way related to it.

I turn now to an objection that targets premise (7). Matthew Soteriou argues that there is *a kind of* thinking out loud that is not to be analyzed as having two components, the thinking of *p* and the uttering of *s*:

> In the case of thinking out loud, say, calculating whether *p* out loud, it seems wrong to think of the out-loud utterances as overt actions that merely accompany, and that are separable from, the real mental activity of calculating whether *p*... In the case of thinking out loud, I suggest we should regard the overt bodily action of speaking out loud as a *vehicle* of the mental action, and not as a separable action that merely accompanies the mental action. (Soteriou 2009: 241)

Soteriou admits that there are cases of calculating without saying anything out loud, and also cases in which one says out loud something that one thought of previously. But his proposal is that there is a third type of action which instantiates 'a basic, non-reducible type, that we might call *mental action with an overt-bodily-action vehicle* (in this case, calculating whether *p out loud*)... So an event of one's verbal utterance can instantiate two types of act – one's saying that *p* out loud, and one's judging that *p*, *because* it instantiates a third basic, non-reducible type of act, namely one's judging that *p* out loud.' (Soteriou 2009: 241) If Soteriou is right, then premise (7) is false: thinking out loud is not to be analyzed as a combination of an episode of uttering *s*, which then leads to a different mental event of entertaining *p*. Instead, there is just one mental episode of thinking out loud that *p*. This amounts to denying that (iii) is a condition for using language in thought, because according to (iii) the utterance of the expression causes the event of judging or thinking a proposition. Moreover, a similar line of thought may lead to denying premise (2): it may be held that, although meaning that *p* by uttering *s* is an intentional action, there is no separate mental episode of intending to Φ that *p* by uttering *s*, which then causes or guides the uttering of *s*. This point is in line with the view that the intention with which an action is performed is part of the description of the action, and not a separate mental state. According to G.E.M. Anscombe, the intention is a constitutive element of the action, conceptually inseparable from it. She writes that it is a 'mistake [...] to think that the relation *being done in execution of a certain intention*, or *being done intentionally*, is a causal relation between act and intention [...] [I]ntention does not have to be a distinct psychological state which exists either prior to or contemporaneously with the intentional action whose intention it is.' (Anscombe 1983: 179–80)

Soteriou's argument for his proposal is that if we conceive of thinking out loud in some other way, 'we would not seem to have a genuine case of calculating whether *p out loud*, but rather a case of the agent saying out loud what he or she had just done.' (Soteriou 2009: 241) However, I am not sure that the consequence is unacceptable. Maybe thinking out loud is indeed a case of saying what one has just thought. Soteriou's claim is plausible for phenomenological reasons: it does not seem that with an utterance of type (f) discussed above, such as calculating out loud, or noticing that *p* follows from *q* out loud, there are two mental events: one of having a certain intention (to Φ that *p* by uttering *s*), and a separate mental and physical event of actually uttering *s*. Uses of language in thought are *spontaneous* mental episodes. They are not planned for in advance, and are not the realization of a prospective intention (or intention for the future, that is, an intention that clearly precedes the act). Moreover, spontaneity is not a contingent feature of the examples gathered under type (f), but a necessary characteristic of uses of language in thought. If there is a prospective intention that precedes the utterance of *s*, then the utterance can play no role in getting the subject to entertain *p*.

Therefore, all plausible candidates for a use of language in thought, from a phenomenological point of view, are those in which there are no such prospective intentions to utter *s* meaning that *p*, and so the utterance is spontaneous. However, this phenomenological evidence does not suffice to conclude that there is no intention to Φ that *p* in uttering *s*. The spontaneous character of cases (f) is compatible with there being two mental events that take place simultaneously. And in some cases there is phenomenological support for the claim that there are two distinct mental events: imagine a case of calculating or thinking out loud similar to those discussed under category (f), with the only difference that some deficiency in the production of the utterance gets in the way so as to impede the successful performance of the utterance (e.g. the speaker swallows a fly, or starts to cough, exactly in the moment when she opens her mouth to utter *s*).[14] It seems that in such cases we are capable of entertaining the proposition we intended to voice, independently of the failure to voice it. This means that it is not one, but two mental events that were taking place simultaneously.[15] The lesson to be drawn is that the character of spontaneity of cases (f) is not a reason for rejecting that they are realizations of intentions. The thought experiment presented shows that the existence of the intention to Φ that *p* (or of some other mental state with *p* as content) is not conceptually dependent on the successful accomplishment of the utterance.

The above thought experiment also provides phenomenological evidence in favour of the conclusion of the argument I proposed, that is, that when thinking out loud the utterance of the sentence does not lead to thinking the content one meant by that utterance. The thinking of the content is independent of uttering the sentence. Other phenomenological data that support the same point may be drawn from cases of mispronunciation. As in communication, one may also

---

14 Manuel García-Carpintero brought to my attention these kind of cases in personal communication.
15 These episodes are failed attempts to use language in thought, and not instances of such uses. They fail on condition (i), i.e. the speaker did not mean a full proposition by the fragment of sentence that she managed to utter; she has not managed to utter the sentence by which she means that *p*.

mispronounce a word when using language in thought. Consider a mental experiment, similar to the one Speaks proposes, in which I say to myself 'All the bottles are full' meaning that all the bottles in the room are *empty*. I do not intentionally use 'full' to mean *empty*, rather this is a result of a mistake at the level of producing the correct word. But it would not be possible for me to think *empty* and say 'full' if the utterance of the word played a role in my forming the thought, as condition (iii) requires for speakers when they use language in thought. It must be the other way around. So, the utterance of the words in cases of type (f) is not the cause of my entertaining the thought. Such cases suggest that the thought is formed independently of the production of the utterance. This would not be possible if thinking out loud consisted in a single irreducible mental event of *thinking out loud that p*.

Finally, let me propose an explanation for why cases of type (f) *seem* to fulfil condition (iii), that is, why an utterance by which the subject meant that *p* seems to have played a causal role in getting the subject to form the thought that *p*. In complex processes of thinking that are made up of various steps (such as making plans step by step, evaluating arguments, making calculations or formal derivations etc.) it is important to keep track of the outcome of the previous steps. The success of the whole enterprise depends on the correctness of each step. Therefore, such complex processes may benefit from the use of devices that may help the memory. Writing down the result of the previous step, or saying it out loud, facilitates memorizing it. These episodes of verbalizing what one has just thought are useful during such mental processes that have various steps organized in a chain. The use of language in (f) seems to be nothing more than a way of taking notes, that is, a device that helps fix into the memory the content that was already judged. To pursue further the comparison with taking notes, the suggestion is that the interaction between *reading* these notes and *deciding* the next step to be made gives the impression that words help entertain a thought. Indeed they do, but the sentence that I use to memorize *p* for further use in the chain of reasoning does not help me entertain *p*, but facilitates the next steps in the process, such as an inference from *p* to *q*. This error theory does not apply equally well to cases of isolated thinking our loud, which do not form part of chains of reasoning. Thus, in the case of noticing out loud that it is already 16:10 the explanation does not work, because there is no next step in a chain of reasoning that the voicing of the thought helps get at. But it is also true that in these cases the intuition that language plays a role in forming the thought is less strong.

To sum up, I have argued that the use of language that Speaks's test requires for it to function is intuitively most closely related to cases of type (f). I have proposed a definition of the uses of language in thought relevant for Speaks's test, and I have argued that there are no cases of language in thought, as defined. Therefore, the question of the title should receive a negative answer: there are solitary uses of language, but these are not *uses of language in thought,* if the latter concept is understood according to the characterization I have offered, suggested by Speaks in his article. Thinking out loud should be analysed as a complex act in which the thought is voiced out loud, although the voicing does not play any causal role in bringing about the thought.*

References

Anscombe, G.E.M. (1957). *Intention.* Oxford: Blackwell.
Bach, K. (2005). On referring and not referring. In Lepore, E. & Smith, B. (Eds.). *The Oxford handbook of philosophy of language.* Oxford; New York: Oxford University Press.
García-Carpintero, M. (2009). Singular thought and the contingent a priori. *Revue Internationale de Philosophie.* Special issue 'Contemporary Analytic Philosophy of Mind' edited by Joëlle Proust, *62,* 79–98.
——— (2001). Gricean rational reconstructions and the semantics/pragmatics distinction. *Synthese, 128,* 93–131.

---

* A previous version of this article was presented at the conference Context and Levels of Locutionary Content, Lisbon 3-4 December 2009. I am thankful to the comments received from those present in the audience, especially François Recanati, Kent Bach, Manuel García-Carpintero, Isidora Stojanovic, Gunnar Björnsson, and others.

Grice, H. P. (1989). *Studies in the way of words.* Cambridge, MA: Harvard University Press.

Harman, G. (1977). Review of Jonathan Bennett's *Linguistic behavior. Language, 53,* 417–424.

Hornsby, J. (2005). Semantic knowledge and practical knowledge. *Proceedings of the Aristotelian Society, Supplementary Volume 79*(1), 107–130.

Lewis, D. (1975). Languages and language. In Gunderson, K. (Ed.). *Language, Mind and Knowledge.* Minneapolis, Minn.: University of Minnesota Press. Reprinted in Geirsson, H. & Losonsky, M. (Eds.) (1996). *Readings in Language and Mind,* (pp. 134–155). Cambridge; Oxford: Blackwell Publishers.

Neale, S. (1992). Paul Grice and the philosophy of language. *Linguistics and Philosophy, 15,* 509–559.

Saul, J. (2002). What is said and psychological reality: Grice's project and relevance theorists' criticisms. *Linguistics and Philosophy, 25,* 347–372. Schiffer, S. (1972). *Meaning.* Oxford; New York: Oxford University Press.

Sellars, W. (1967). Some reflections on thoughts and things. *Noûs, 1*(2) (May 1967), 97–121.

Soteriou, M. (2009). Mental agency, conscious thinking and phenomenal character. In O'Brien, L. & Soteriou, M. (Eds.). *Mental actions.* Oxford; New York: Oxford University Press.

Speaks, J. (2003). *Three views of language & the mind.* PhD dissertation. Princeton University.

——— (2008). Conversational implicature, thought, and communication. *Mind & Language, 23*(1), 107–122

Stanley, J. (2005). Hornsby on the phenomenology of speech. *Proceedings of the Aristotelian Society, Supplementary Volume 79*(1), 131–145.

Strawson, G. (2003). Mental ballistics or the involuntariness of spontaniety. *Proceedings of the Aristotelian Society, 103*(3), 227–257.

Vlach, F. (1981). Speaker's meaning. *Linguistics & Philosophy, 4,* 359–392.

Author Index

Abbott, 30, 38
Abusch, 36
Alston, 42
Alwood, 246
Anscombe, 301
Ariel, 85
Arnold, 87, 95
Asher, 81
Atlas, 38, 246
Atran, 129
Au, 87, 90, 91
Auden, 223
Austin, 20, 41, 161, 194, 195

Bach, 6, 18, 20, 115, 118, 120, 153, 187, 188, 193, 195, 202–205, 286, 298, 299
Ball, 11, 187, 208
Barwise, 171
Beall, 237–240
Beaver, 23, 27, 38
Benz, 269
Berkovski, 213
Berkovsky, 12
Berkum, 87, 91, 95

Bezuidenhout, 10, 79, 80, 85, 98, 102
Bierwisch, 111, 113, 128, 129
Birner, 87
Blakemore, 102
Bloom, 129
Borg, 5, 9, 13, 51, 54–59, 66, 69, 74, 79, 105, 116, 187, 189, 201, 206, 256
Brandom, 66
Brown, 87, 89, 90
Burge, 251
Burks, 1
Böer, 24

Cappelen, 5, 13, 51, 54, 57, 58, 79, 80, 116, 187, 189, 208, 220, 255
Caramazza, 87, 91
Carnap, 68
Carston, 97, 102, 113, 115, 116, 120, 121, 128, 151
Chierchia, 23, 43, 272
Chierchie, 37
Chomsky, 52, 55, 66

Clark, 171
Clinton, 161
Cohen, 113
Collins, 69
Comrie, 1
Crawley, 94
Crinean, 91, 92
Cruse, 111, 114
Culicover, 121

Dalrymple, 201
Dancy, 52
Davidson, 17, 199
Dole, 161
Donnellan, 44, 151, 163
Dretske, 171
Dummett, 20, 238

Erteschik-Shir, 87

Falcato, 13, 255
Ferretti, 91
Fintel, 23–25, 27, 32, 37, 45, 275
Fish, 87, 89, 90
Fodor, 9, 67, 68, 71, 111, 112, 115, 131, 132
Fox, 275, 279
Frege, 1, 41, 140, 153, 163, 243, 258–259, 287
Frisson, 97

García-Carpintero, 2, 7, 8, 17, 26, 28, 47, 284, 294, 298, 302
Garnham, 87, 91, 92
Garrett, 67

Garvey, 87, 91
Gazdar, 246, 274
Gernsbacher, 86
Geurts, 23, 27, 42, 153
Goodman, 161
Gordon, 86, 87
Green, 42
Grice, 11, 13, 14, 25, 35, 42, 161, 170, 171, 269, 273, 284, 285, 287, 290–292, 294, 297, 298
Grosz, 85
Guerry, 91
Gundel, 85

Hale, 65
Hargreaves, 86
Harman, 66, 200, 298
Harnish, 18, 20
Hawthorne, 208
Heim, 27, 275
Herzberger, 244
Hindriks, 19, 41
Hobbs, 81
Horisk, 99–101, 103, 104
Horn, 13, 241, 244, 246, 247, 273
Horwich, 66

Iacona, 8
Israel, 171

Jackendoff, 66, 97, 102, 111, 113, 114, 121, 129, 130, 133
Johnson, 65, 133
Jäger, 269, 276

Järvikivi, 96

Kadmon, 23, 32
Kaplan, 1–3, 5, 12, 54, 139, 140, 151, 163, 164, 199, 213, 216, 217, 225, 227, 233, 255
Karttunen, 45
Katz, 111, 120, 148, 153
Katzir, 279
Kehler, 81, 87, 95
Kempson, 246
Kennedy, 127
Keyser, 65
Kleene, 244
Klein, 131
Kleinman, 94
Koornneef, 87, 91, 95
Korta, 11, 161, 162
Kripke, 13, 140, 151, 153, 164, 242, 246
Kölbel, 187, 189, 208
Künne, 240, 241, 244

Lackey, 19
Lambrecht, 87
Lascarides, 81
Lasersohn, 7
Lepore, 5, 13, 51, 54, 57, 58, 67, 80, 112, 115, 116, 131, 132, 187, 189, 208, 220, 255
Levin, 61, 62, 69, 88, 133
Levinson, 24, 38, 113, 128
Lewis, 25, 31, 151, 199, 208, 269

Lycan, 24

MacFarlane, 7, 8, 187, 189, 208
Mann, 81
Marques, 12, 235
Martínez Manrique, 128
Martínez-Manrique, 9
Matsumoto, 279
May, 200
McConnell-Ginet, 23, 37, 43
McElree, 97
McKoon, 87, 91
McNally, 127
Mill, 156
Moldovan, 14, 283
Moravcsik, 111
Murphy, 114, 131

Neale, 243, 297
Nunberg, 102

Osborne, 271

Pagin, 68
Parikh, 269
Parsons, 252
Pelletier, 68, 240
Perry, 1, 11, 161, 162, 171, 187, 188, 191–194
Pickering, 97
Pietroski, 11, 52, 61, 66, 187–189, 205
Pinker, 61, 62, 64, 66, 68, 133
Pistoia-Reda, 13, 269
Pitt, 111, 133
Poser, 278
Potts, 23

Predelli, 7, 151, 196, 197, 199, 204, 209
Pustejovsky, 64, 66, 97, 102, 111, 131, 133
Pyykkönen, 96

Quine, 1, 120

Rabin, 270
Rappaport Hovav, 69, 133
Rast, 2, 153
Rawls, 20
Recanati, 4, 5, 7, 54, 59, 102, 115, 120, 153, 187, 188, 191, 194, 195, 197, 202, 220, 222, 260, 261, 263–264, 284
Reichenbach, 1
Reimer, 227
Richard, 252
Roberts, 84
Rotschild, 127
Rubinstein, 271
Russell, 1, 140, 153, 163, 242

Saddock, 31, 40
Sadock, 132, 246
Sainsbury, 243
Salmon, 151
Scearce, 87
Schiffer, 283, 290, 292, 298
Schlenker, 32
Schreuder, 111, 113, 128, 129
Searle, 18, 20, 35
Segal, 127
Simmons, 69
Simons, 25, 32, 36, 38

Smiley, 244, 252
Soames, 57, 199
Soteriou, 300, 301
Speaks, 283–288, 290, 291, 293, 298, 304
Spelke, 129
Sperber, 115, 123
Stainton, 240
Stalnaker, 8, 12, 21, 25–30, 33, 34, 36–40, 45, 213–215, 233
Stanley, 6, 52, 153, 187, 189, 197, 203, 220, 221, 290
Stern, 12, 213, 218–222, 224, 229, 233
Stevenson, 87, 92–96
Stewart, 91
Stojanovic, 7, 8, 10, 139, 144, 147
Strawson, 243
Szabó, 6

Tappenden, 238, 244–246, 252
Tarski, 199
Taylor, 131
Thompson, 81
Travis, 7, 13, 52, 54, 66, 112, 116, 121, 125, 131, 264–265, 267

Vicente, 9, 112, 128
Vlach, 42, 298

Ward, 87
Weiner, 19
Wettstein, 120, 163, 169
Wierzbicka, 111

Williamson, 8, 18, 20, 40, 43, 46
Wilson, 115, 123, 124

Yablo, 22
Yeats, 223

Zwicky, 132, 246

LISBON PHILOSOPHICAL STUDIES
uses of language in interdisciplinary fields

A Publication from the Institute of Philosophy of Language at the New University of Lisbon

Lisbon Philosophical Studies – Uses of Language in Interdisciplinary Fields is the book series of the Institute of Philosophy of Language at the New University of Lisbon. Its aim is the publication of high-quality monographs, edited collections and conference proceedings in areas related to the philosophy of language, such as aesthetics, argumentation theory, epistemology, ethics, logic, philosophy of mind and political philosophy. The purpose of the series is to reflect the activities of the Institute as well as contemporary research in these areas, encouraging the interchange of arguments and ideas between philosophy and other disciplines.

Address for Correspondence:

Instituto de Filosofia da Linguagem
Faculdade de Ciências Sociais e Humanas
Universidade Nova de Lisboa
Av. de Berna, 26-C
1069-061 Lisboa
Portugal

www.ifl.pt

Vol. 1 António Marques & Nuno Venturinha (eds)
Wittgenstein on Forms of Life and the Nature of Experience.
2010. ISBN 978-3-0343-0491-7.

Vol. 2 Luca Baptista & Erich Rast (eds)
Meaning and Context.
2010. ISBN 978-3-0343-0574-7.